The Handicapped Child

Educational and Psychological Guidance for the
Organically Handicapped

The Authors

AGATHA H. BOWLEY
Ph.D., F.B.Psy.S.

Consultant Psychologist, Cheyne Centre for Spastic
Children; and Horsham and Crawley Child Guidance
Clinics

LESLIE GARDNER
B.Sc., Dip.Ed., Dip.Psych.

Principal Psychologist, The Spastics Society, London;
and Audiology Unit, The Hospital for Sick Children,
Great Ormond Street, London

The Handicapped Child

Educational and Psychological Guidance for the
Organically Handicapped

AGATHA H. BOWLEY
LESLIE GARDNER

Third Edition

The Williams & Wilkins Company
Baltimore

© E. & S. Livingstone Limited 1957, 1969

© LONGMAN GROUP LIMITED, 1972

ISBN 0 443 00906 6

First edition   .   . 1957
Second edition .   . 1969
Third edition   .   . 1972

*Printed in Great Britain by
Northumberland Press Ltd, Gateshead*

PREFACE TO THIRD EDITION

A LTHOUGH the second edition of this book was published as recently as 1969, in response to the constant demand a new issue has become necessary, and we decided to produce a third edition to include new material and to be more comprehensive. As a result of the requests and comments of our readers and reviewers we have included among the handicaps studied in this book chapters on children with Spina Bifida, minimal Brain Damage (including dyslexic, aphasic and epileptic children) and multi-handicapped children.

We have considerably enlarged the chapter on the Spastic and Deaf and added new references to the chapter on the Autistic as well as a note on new research studies and methods of teaching. The main part of the text as before deals with Cerebral Palsy, because this is so complex a subject, and because during the past two years new methods in treatment and education have been developed.

We have tried to fill some of the gaps in our knowledge concerning these various physical disabilities. We write as psychologists concerned with clinical assessment, family guidance and educational advice primarily. We work in close association with medical and teaching personnel, with therapists and social workers. We have every opportunity to follow through many of the children we have seen at a tender age to adolescence and beyond, and are naturally well aware of the physical and social problems involved in adjustment, in learning and in employment as well as the psychological ones. The very fact that this book is published under a joint authorship indicates the need for a team approach even between psychologists whose background, training and experience are by no means identical. The pooling of knowledge thus gained should be an enrichment.

We hope this may provide a standard textbook on educational, psychological and social aspects of organic handicaps in children, which is at present unavailable. Our aim has been to cover all numerically and educationally important physical and sensory handicaps in children. The readership should include a wide variety of students and young professionals i.e. teachers, psychologists, doctors, social workers, child care workers, educational welfare officers, health visitors and the various therapists. It should serve as an authentic reference book for these, and be of interest to some parents.

We wish to acknowledge our gratitude to the late Dr. Cyril Potter, to Mr. Michael Colborne Brown, to Miss Eire Clarke and to the Heads of Sunshine Home Nursery Schools for valuable advice concerning the chapter on blind children; to Dr. Ursula Shelley, Dr. John Foley, and to the staff of the Centre for Spastic Children, Cheyne Walk for help with the chapter on cerebral palsied children; to Mr. James Loring, Director of the Spastics Society, for advice and guidance: to Dr. Louis Minski, Dr. Henry Rees and to Miss Joan Taylor for their contributions and constructive criticism of the chapter on autistic children. We also wish to record our gratitude to Miss Nancy Anderson of the Spastics Society for generous secretarial help.

The authors are alone responsible for the views expressed in this book.

AGATHA H. BOWLEY
LESLIE GARDNER

London, 1972

INTRODUCTION

THE purpose of this book is to set down in terms intelligible to the non-specialist reader, certain facts and findings concerning six types of handicapped children, based on first-hand experience and from a study of the literature. It is our sincere hope that it will provide factual information which will help to allay anxiety and to build up an informed, constructive and sympathetic approach towards children who are handicapped.

The handicapped child is even more dependent than the ordinary child on the understanding and skill of those adults responsible for his care. His development will be affected if he is handled by uninformed, embarrassed or excessively sentimental adults. It takes courage, wisdom and faith on the parents' part to face the fact that a handicapped child has been entrusted to their care.

Our approach to caring for handicapped children depends on our attitude to the whole problem of suffering and adversity in human life. The various techniques and practical methods are of little avail unless their use is founded on the attitude of compassion.

Our philosophy may be summed up in the following terms; 'to love—to understand—and to help.' In common with all children the handicapped have the right to opportunities of developing their abilities to the optimum levels that are possible. We hope this book will help to enhance these opportunities.

CONTENTS

CHAPTER I

THE CHILD WITH CEREBRAL PALSY

Introduction

CEREBRAL palsy (C.P.) is a complex condition. The one thing that all cerebral palsied children have in common is a difficulty in controlling certain of their muscles. They differ from other children who lack control of their limbs in that these difficulties are not due to any damage or paralysis to the limbs themselves, as in the case of polio or dislocated hips, but to faulty development in part of the brain that would normally control movements of the body. Apart from this common feature of poor control of limbs, which may vary from a degree that is hardly detectable to an almost complete lack of voluntary motor control, cerebral palsied children have little else in common. Indeed it is difficult to find two C.P. children who are alike, for the impairments in their brain development can take so many different forms, sometimes affecting, in addition to motor control, their intelligence, vision, hearing, speech, and their emotional state. In a few children we find all these capacities affected greatly. In others some capacities are affected greatly and others only slightly. In yet another child we may find none of these areas affected significantly.

One can formally define C.P. as a 'disorder of movement and posture resulting from a permanent non-progressive defect or lesion in the immature brain', but we must be careful not to obscure the fact that persons with C.P. differ very widely from one another. Much needless argument could be avoided if the *diversity* of C.P. conditions was properly understood: for example when two groups of spastic children are being compared in respect of say, rates of progress, we must be sure that the two groups are comparable at the outset: they may all be spastic, but the spastics in one group could be very different to the spastics in the other group. Formal definitions and classifications have their uses, particularly for research and administrative purposes, but they tend to concentrate on the *obvious* feature of the child's condition, such as his physical condition, whereas the less obvious features, such as the intellectual

1

and emotional features, may be the most important ones in reaching an understanding of his needs and ways in which he may be helped.

It is this complexity and diversity of cerebral palsy that has contributed to the delay, until recent decades, in setting up proper facilities compared to, for example, the blind and the deaf child, for whom facilities such as special schooling have been in existence for centuries. Although cerebral palsy was described in medical terms as early as 1843 by a certain Dr. Little, and Sigmund Freud showed an early interest writing on C.P. in 1891, the condition was regarded largely as a medical and surgical matter, and its implications for training, therapy, education, social and vocational work, remained unexplored. It was commonly assumed that the condition was associated with severe mental retardation and it was not until the 1930s that more accurate assessments showed that at least half of these children had an intelligence that was more or less within normal limits and that the great majority were capable of benefiting by training, therapy, and education.

In this country, the interest in cerebral palsy has grown enormously in the past twenty years, with the help of voluntary organizations such as the Spastics Society, which was founded by a group of parents in 1952. Their efforts helped to ensure that cerebral palsied children were no longer a neglected group. Our knowledge of the nature of cerebral palsy, its causes, prevalence, and the various forms of treatment and education has steadily grown in the past few decades. In view of the complexity of the condition, we certainly cannot relax our efforts to reach a deeper understanding of how it affects children, their families and its impact on the wider community, and how various services, working in partnership with the parents, can contribute most effectively to alleviating some of the worst effects of the handicap. We are still a long way from achieving our ultimate aim for all handicapped persons—the aim of gaining the maximum possible degree of independence and self-sufficiency so that they can share more and more in the wider life of the ordinary community. Let us first consider the size of the problem.

The Incidence of Cerebral Palsy

It has been estimated that there are around 100,000 persons with cerebral palsy in the U.K., of which about 40,000 are under the age of 15 (Evans 1968). Estimates of the incidence of C.P. births have varied from 1 to 5·9 per thousand live births in various studies, the difference being due in part to differing techniques of case finding and differing definitions of cerebral palsy which is not always easily detected at very young ages. The very high figure of 5·9 per thousand emerged from the Schenectady County Study (Levin *et al.*, 1949) which was based on very intensive case finding techniques, including not only the usual techniques of searching school rolls and clinic lists, etc., but an actual house to house survey of 16 per cent of the County. Although thoroughly carried out, the incidence is twice as high as most other large scale surveys have indicated: the most recent of these is by Rutter *et al.* (1970) and probably offers the most reliable incidence figures: 2·9 per thousand based on studies of 11,869 children aged 5–15 living in the Isle of Wight, including post-natal cases such as those children who had become cerebral palsied because of encephalitis. Thus in any large city one would expect to find approximately 290 C.P. children per 100,000 children of school age. As for persons with C.P. over the age of 15, the numbers might be slightly less, due to the higher mortality rates amongst cerebral palsied compared to ordinary persons. These mortality rates are over ten times higher, and this probably accounts for the slightly lower incidence of C.P. persons aged 15 and over. In Ingram's study (1964), the incidence for the age group 15–39 was 2 per thousand, giving a total of about 37,000 persons in the U.K. in this age group. Mortality rates amongst older spastics are not yet reliably known but Crothers and Paine's (1959) study suggests that although these mortality rates are higher than normal, the majority of these occur under the age of 20 and they conclude that the majority of spastics who survive to the age of 20 have a considerable life expectation—perhaps normal in many cases. Until further studies have been completed, a prevalence rate of about 1 per thousand seems a reasonable assumption for C.P.s aged over 40—giving an estimated total of 24,000 in the U.K. for this age group. These estimates of the size of the problem can be summarized as follows:

Ages	Prevalence rate per thousand	Estimated approximate total
0–14	2·9	39,000
15–39	2·0	37,000
40 plus	1·0	24,000
		100,000

Has the incidence of C.P. changed in recent decades? Not as far as we can tell. Past records are rarely accurate enough for comparison with recent surveys, but there is little definite evidence to suggest any major changes in the incidence over recent decades. A study in Bristol (Woods, 1963) offered suggestions of a decline in the number of spastics born in the period 1953–58, attributing this to improved ante-natal and obstetric care; but this has not been substantiated by other studies. Indeed, there are some factors that may be leading to a slightly higher incidence. Although ante-natal and neo-natal care and treatment facilities are improving, there is the paradox that better medical services of this kind can lead to an *increased* incidence of spastics in the community, because more babies can then survive who formerly did not do so. The situation is more clear cut in the case of spina bifida. It would be unwise to assume that the incidence of cerebral palsy will change dramatically in the next decade or so.

Does the incidence vary in different regions of the U.K. or in different countries? There is no clear evidence that it does: rates for different parts of the U.K. are in close agreement, on the whole, and so are rates for other industrialized countries. Studies from non-industrialized countries are rare, but an interesting survey of the prevalence of C.P. amongst various cultural groups in Israel (Margulec, 1966) again showed considerable similarities, comparing cases from immigrants born in Afro-Asian countries with Israel born cases. The Afro-Asian rates were rather lower and this could be explained by difficulties in case finding and by high mortality rates amongst the poorer immigrants, rather than any major difference in the actual incidence at birth. These interesting studies, however, need further elaboration.

The Causes of Cerebral Palsy

The *causes* of C.P. have not yet been established with certainty, but there is considerable evidence to show that a variety of conditions contribute to the onset of C.P. Certain cells of the baby's brain may be damaged either before, during, or after birth, and the commonest cause of damage is lack of oxygen (anoxia) to the baby's brain, for even a short period of time. Various things can cause this lack of oxygen, such as infectious diseases or extreme birth difficulties. About a third of C.P. children are born prematurely and have a low birth weight, the incidence of an abnormal labour history is four times as common as in the ordinary population. Fortunately, the majority of premature babies and those having a difficult birth, turn out to be quite normal, but these conditions can occasionally cause complications such as lack of oxygen and so give rise to cerebral palsy.

We do not know why some premature babies are cerebral palsied, whilst the majority are not. Forceps delivery is four times more common than amongst the normal population. This is not to suggest that forceps necessarily *caused* any injuries: their use is merely an aftermath of other difficulties that precluded a normal birth. In view of the frequency of difficult births amongst first born children, it used to be assumed that more cases of C.P. occurred in the first born. Subsequent research has not confirmed this, *e.g.* in Hopkins' (1954) study of 654 birth histories of C.P. children, no particular birth order showed a higher correlation with C.P. Twins, however, are more common amongst C.P. children: around 5–10 per cent in several surveys, including Henderson's (1961) study of 240 cases, and there is a slight tendency amongst twins for the first born to be more often affected than the second born twin.

Excessive jaundice after birth, such as that due to blood group incompatibility, occasionally causes athetosis, but in recent years great strides have been made in preventing this type of brain damage by means of prompt blood transfusions very soon after birth. Although the great majority of cases of cerebral palsy are caused by factors which are operating during pregnancy or at the time of birth, about 10 per cent become affected during the early years of life, due for example to severe infections, such as meningitis or encephalitis, or obvious damage to the brain, such as through a serious road accident.

Hereditary causes are rare, and only in a small percentage of families do we find more than one child affected, or any marked history of any relatives being affected. Extremely young or old mothers are slightly more 'at risk' than others. All social classes are equally at risk as far as C.P. is concerned. Males are more common than females (61 per cent of Ingram's sample were males).

A great deal of research is being carried out into the many causes of cerebral palsy, with the ultimate aim of preventing its occurrence in future generations. At present the best available preventive measure is to ensure a high standard of ante-natal and obstetric care. If it were feasible to put into practice all the recently gained knowledge about more effective care, such as in the prompt treatment of jaundice in new-born babies, a significant percentage of cases could be prevented.

Types of Cerebral Palsy

Children affected by cerebral palsy are frequently all referred to as 'spastic' but there are, in fact, four main types:

1. *Spastic.*—This is the largest group; about 75 per cent of C.P. children show spasticity, that is marked rigidity of movement and an inability to relax their muscles, due to damage to the cortex affecting the motor centres. The extent of the handicap varies. In monoplegia, only one arm or leg is affected; in hemiplegia one side only is affected, the right arm and leg or the left arm and leg; in paraplegia the legs only are affected; while in quadriplegia (sometimes called diplegia when the legs are more affected than the arms) all four limbs are spastic.

2. *Athetoid.*—In this condition the child shows frequent involuntary movements which mask and interfere with the normal movements of the body. Writhing movements of the limbs, the face and the tongue, grimacing, dribbling, and slurred speech commonly occur. Hearing defects are fairly common (over 40 per cent) in this group, which interfere with the development of language. Damage to the basal ganglia of the brain appears to be the cause of this condition. Less than 10 per cent of C.P. children show athetosis.

3. *Ataxic.*—In this condition the child shows poor body balance, an unsteady gait, and difficulties in hand and eye co-ordination and control. Injury to the cerebellum is the cause of this type of cerebral palsy, and it is comparatively rare.

4. *Mixed and Others.*—Nearly 10 per cent show mixed types of C.P. and a small percentage show special kinds of muscular tension, such as dystonia, hypertonia, hypotonia, rigidity, and tremor.

The type of cerebral palsy that a child has tells us little about how handicapped he actually is. It is important, therefore, to know, in addition to the type and the number of limbs affected, the *degree* to which his motor control is impaired. Most observers would describe a child who can walk and talk, and whose physical movements are just a little clumsy, as mildly physically handicapped. A child whose speech is indistinct, who has some difficulty in controlling his hands, and who can walk, although unsteadily, is usually described as moderately physically handicapped. A severely handicapped child is one whose independence is very limited because of very limited control of his arms and hands and legs. The muscles controlling speech are also likely to be affected.

Most studies of large representative groups of C.P.s have indicated that almost one-third of C.P.s are mildly, one-third moderately, and one-third severely handicapped—the variations between different studies being due to differing methods of rating the degree of handicap. Objective measures of degrees of physical functioning are available (Holt, 1965; Holt & Reynell, 1967; Lindon, 1963) and these are very useful for detailed studies of progress over time. Having classified a child in respect of the type of cerebral palsy, the number of limbs involved and the degree of physical handicap, we have made a beginning, but only a beginning, in understanding his condition and working out the best ways of helping him. As we have mentioned, the majority of cerebral palsied children have other handicaps in addition to their motor difficulties.

Additional Handicaps

It is often found that the brain damage has not only affected the development of movement, but also, in varying degrees, the development of intelligence, vision, hearing, speech and other factors important to the child's progress.

It is imperative that parents, teachers and therapists be aware of these factors, since in some cases they affect the behaviour of the child. In other cases, however, the mere fact that the child has a particular medical label attached to him is of very little importance in the child's life. We must distinguish between important and unimportant labels. For example, the label 'athetoid with a high tone hearing loss, epilepsy and some degree of optic atrophy' may sound formidable, but in fact this description could apply to a child who merely shows very mild clumsiness, has virtually normal hearing for speech and who has had perhaps two fits in his whole life and perfectly reasonable vision for ordinary purposes—in short a nearly normal child as far as education and social functioning are concerned. It is this *functioning* that we must measure and understand, and the labels or diagnostic categories are only useful if the degree to which they affect the child's life can be specified. Otherwise they can be misleading—and sometimes very worrying to parents and teachers.

The major additional handicaps associated with C.P. are as follows:

1. *Epilepsy.*—Epilepsy has been found to occur in between 25 and 35 per cent of cerebral palsied children. Illingworth (1958) reports an incidence of 32 per cent in 250 cases, Woods (1956) reports 38 per cent out of 301 cases, and Henderson (1961) found 25 per cent in 240 cases and regarded this as an under-estimation. In a survey of 104 educable children at the Cheyne Centre, London, one of the authors (A.H.B.) found an incidence of 36·5 per cent. The definition of epilepsy mostly used in these researches was the occurrence of more than one fit after the first two weeks of life— and in fact the majority of spastics have very few fits. Less than 10 per cent of Henderson's sample of 240 C.P. children and

adolescents were having regular fits (more than one per month). Approximately 15 per cent of the sample were on anticonvulsant drugs, which are very efficient in controlling fits. Oversedation can of course lead to drowsiness. In a few children it is difficult to strike the balance between eliminating the risk of fits on the one hand, and maintaining the child's normal state of alertness on the other. Epilepsy is more common among quadriplegics and hemiplegics than other types of cerebral palsy and in Rutter's (1970) study it was noted that amongst children excluded from school on account of severe physical and intellectual handicaps, epilepsy was found in as many as 70 per cent, compared to 28 per cent amongst the children with C.P. who were attending school. In severe cases, epilepsy interferes seriously with learning and frequent fits may result in some intellectual dysfunctioning, but this may be only temporary, and such cases are very rare.

2. *Visual Defects.*—A high proportion of cerebral palsied children suffer from *visual defects*; poor visual acuity, nystagmus, strabismus, refractive errors, and other oculo-motor defects. The educational implications of these are not always fully understood. Asher and Schonell (1950) noted 25 per cent in their series of 400 children, especially among the quadriplegics. Dunsdon (1952) found 29 per cent in 545 cases, while Douglas, in 1960, reported squint in 37 per cent of 160 C.P. persons under 20 years of age. In the Cheyne Clinic survey of 104 cases 35 per cent showed ocular defects. Many of these defects are comparatively minor and many can be successfully treated in early childhood.

3. *Hearing Losses.*—A partial degree of *hearing loss* is frequently found in these children, more especially with athetoids where the loss is often one of high-tone deafness. Dunsdon reports 18 per cent in her series, Woods only 20 cases in 301 children, while Fisch's (1957) detailed study of 427 cases found 25 per cent, and in 16 per cent the defect was serious. A figure of approximately 15 per cent is probably the most reliable estimate of the number of C.P.s having an educationally significant hearing loss requiring the use of a hearing aid, and the regular help of a visiting Teacher of the Partially Hearing, and in some cases, the facilities of a Partially Hearing Unit. Without such help their language development would be seriously impaired.

4. *Speech Defects.*—Speech defects occur if the control of the facial and respiratory muscles, the tongue, or lips is poor. These defects range from very minor articulation defects to a complete absence of speech. Approximately 50 per cent of Henderson's (1961) sample had some degree of speech defect, and almost 20

per cent had no intelligible speech—the majority of the latter being also of impaired intelligence and their lack of speech being due to a combination of factors. Feeding is difficult in many such children but early physiotherapy and speech therapy may do a great deal to improve the situation.

5. *Intellectual Impairment.*—There have been a number of surveys showing the *distribution of intelligence* among cerebral palsied children. It has been found that, usually, children with the greatest physical handicap have the poorest intelligence, which in view of the extent of the brain damage is understandable. Usually

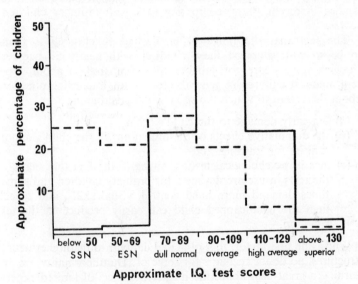

FIG. 1.—The distribution of intelligence test scores comparing C.P. and normal children (continuous line, ordinary children; dashed line, C.P. children).

spastic quadriplegics are less intelligent as a group than the hemiplegic group, although of course there are startling individual exceptions to this general group finding. Some severely motor handicapped children have an extremely high intelligence and some mildly motor handicapped children have very limited intelligence, or many specific learning difficulties. It is unwise to infer mental status from the degree of motor disability. The difference between the athetoid and the spastic group is negligible. Most surveys report a figure of between 40 and 50 per cent of cerebral palsied children to be of subnormal intelligence (approximately 25 per cent severely subnormal, I.Q.s 0–49, approximately 21 per cent E.S.N., I.Q.s 50–69). In a survey at the Cheyne Centre of 255 children, 41 per cent were found to be educationally or severely subnormal.

As for those with higher intelligence, approximately 47 per cent score within normal limits (dull, average and high average), leaving about 6 per cent in the upper intellectual ranges, most of whom can and do pursue academic education, sometimes with considerable success in spite of severe physical handicaps. The distribution of intelligence test scores is summarized in Fig. 1, based on many studies in recent years, comparing C.P. with ordinary children's scores.

The fact that the range of intellectual functioning is found to be so wide amongst these children, with nearly 50 per cent showing some degree of subnormality compared to about 3 per cent amongst children in general, raises some interesting questions about the extent to which the subnormality is due to:

(a) the early damage to the child's brain
(b) the cumulative effects of the limitations in the child's opportunities for learning, and
(c) bias in psychological testing, owing to the fact that many of the tests in use are designed for ordinary children and sometimes demand more hand control, visual skills, and speech than the handicapped child can easily produce in the test situation.

Whilst the first factor, that of actual damage to the higher neural structures, no doubt accounts for some of the subnormality, we are learning a great deal about the long-term effects of limited experience and opportunities for learning.

Special Learning Difficulties

Some children with cerebral palsy have no difficulty in keeping up with ordinary children in the long process of learning to become mature, independent, and responsible adults. Indeed their handicap sometimes becomes a spur to greater learning than they might otherwise have achieved in their social, emotional, and educational development. Many children, however, do learn slowly. Amongst obvious reasons for this are the effects of their physical and sensory and speech impairments that limit the degree to which the child can explore his surroundings and gain experience and understanding of his world. The effects of limited experience, if allowed to continue over many years, can be profound and the task of parents and teachers and therapists is the urgent one, as far as the very handicapped young child is concerned, of providing maximum stimulation at the right level, of bringing stimulation to the child in situations where he cannot reach out for it, as early as possible.

Other limitations are gradually becoming clearer. A considerable number of children whose physical and sensory handicaps are really quite mild have special learning difficulties which are quite distinct from general intellectual retardation. For example, many spastics have disorders in *visual perception*; exemplified by difficulties such as in matching shapes, distinguishing shapes which appear alike, distinguishing the outline of a drawing from its surrounding background, in recognizing the different directions of certain shapes such as the letters 'b' and 'd'. Other spastics appear to perceive shapes satisfactorily for their age, but have enormous difficulties in constructing patterns out of bricks, completing jig-saws, and writing and drawing. These are known as *visual-motor disorders*; and appear to be more common amongst spastics than athetoids (Wedell, 1960, 1968). An excellent survey of visual-perceptual and visual-motor disorders is to be found in a monograph by Abercrombie (1964).

The fact that these disorders can be seen in some children whose hand control and vision are quite near to normal, and whose verbal and social reasoning may be at a very high level, suggests that these are special learning difficulties, possibly due to unevenness in the development of certain parts of the brain and the higher central nervous system.

Another kind of special learning difficulty encountered in some children is that of *distractibility*. Such children have great difficulty in controlling or focussing their attention. For example they are easily distracted by slight sounds or movements in a classroom that ordinary children would have little or no difficulty in ignoring, and this results in a short span of attention which frequently interferes with their learning at school so that their attainments are eventually very patchy. Distractibility does not only occur in cerebral palsied children. Indeed it is often seen in children without external signs of physical handicap, such as those who have suffered from meningitis and whose general behaviour is overactive and restless. Various terms have been used to describe such a condition, *e.g.* minimal cerebral dysfunctioning, brain injury, the hyperactive/distractible syndrome, but our knowledge so far is too limited for any general agreement on terms. Psychologists and educationalists, whose work in the field of special learning difficulties is being increasingly used, include Marianne Frostig (1968) and William Cruickshank (1961) in the United States, and Francis-Williams (1970) and Tansley (1967) in the United Kingdom, who are concerned not only to produce more accurate techniques for measuring such features as visual perceptual disorders and distractibility, but to suggest actual training techniques that may help to overcome some of the difficulties. Scientific studies of the long-term results of such training programmes are not yet available and this is partly because of the tremendous complexity of these learning difficulties. These points are discussed in more detail in a later chapter of this book.

Multiple Learning Difficulties

A child rarely has only one kind of difficulty, such as in confusing left and right directions or in co-ordinating his motor and his visual responses. He is more likely to have a *combination* of several of the difficulties we have mentioned, which may be quite mild when looked at singly but which *multiply* into a formidable learning handicap when combined in one child and affect him right from birth. Effective learning depends on the gradual building up of the ability to combine various motor and sensory and perceptual impressions. For example a baby of 12 months exploring a box of bricks is engaging in a wide variety of learning experiences. He is learning that bricks have shape, colour, texture, that they can move in various directions, can be put together to make a shape, and will fall if pushed from an upright position but not if they are already lying flat. Bricks can disappear into a box and be made to reappear again. Large bricks will not go into a small box, and so on.

To a baby these are new discoveries. To pursue them he must be able to combine what he sees and feels and hears and what he perceives and remembers. His later learning, for example of reading and writing, depends on much the same processes at a more advanced level, and without these earlier experiences he will run into difficulties. Piaget's work describes the development of these skills as a continuous interaction between the child, his past experience and his immediate situation. All children, according to Piaget's theory (1956), pass through four stages of learning ability, from the early sensory motor phase to the mature adolescent phase of abstract formal and logical thought, the child 'graduating' through these four stages in sequence, the later stages being dependent on the successful mastery of the earlier ones. It is therefore not surprising that many spastic children do run into difficulties which become very apparent when they reach school.

All children, perhaps with the exception of some extremely subnormal or autistic ones, have a strong drive to explore their environment, an inbuilt curiosity. What happens to this curiosity, these exploratory drives, depends on what kind of environment surrounds the baby, such as whether opportunities for movement, manipulation and mastery of objects, are available, and in the case of spastics, what actual help can be given with the physical difficulties that impede expression of his exploratory drives. This is one of the major tasks of parents, teachers and therapists in providing for the handicapped child.

Lastly we must mention the *emotional barriers* to learning. Children who show the special learning difficulties we have described are sometimes quick to realize that their efforts do not match up to what their parents expect or to what other children accomplish, hence their self-confidence and morale are likely to suffer; they become over-anxious about failure, and give up so quickly that their learning advances only at a very slow pace.

It is therefore important to detect these learning difficulties as early as possible so that we can avoid aggravating the child by pressing him too much with tasks that he finds very difficult, and taking steps to introduce very gradual training, much of which can be carried out by parents at home, with the help of occupational therapists and teachers.

Psychological Assessment

The purpose of psychological assessment is to measure how far the handicapped child has reached in his learning, so that advice can be given about the type of training most likely to be helpful during the next few years. We have described the very wide range of different levels of intelligence and different kinds of special learning difficulties that are found amongst cerebral palsied children. How does the psychologist measure these? Let us first consider the *measurement of general intelligence.*

For the majority of C.P. children, the standard individual psychological tests are of considerable value, such as the Stanford-Binet, Wechsler and Merrill-Palmer Scales. In the Stanford-Binet Scale, the child is presented with a wide variety of problems, to do with the meaning of words, sentences, and pictures, the matching of shapes, copying of shapes, remembering a series of numbers, and patterns on a card, etc. The Merrill-Palmer, consisting primarily of practical rather than verbal problems, is of special interest to children under 5. The method by which the child solves the practical problem is often a valuable indication of his intellectual functioning. As with all psychological tests, the child is given standard instructions about the problems and his responses are scored in accordance with given standards. The standard procedures allow us to compare the performance of a particular child with that of a large group of typical children of his age, on whom the test was originally constructed. Can such tests, based on the responses of ordinary children, be considered fair for handicapped children? We have mentioned the many ways in which handicapped children are deprived of ordinary experience and in any case they are sometimes unable to express their thoughts, because of limited speech and hand control. In a sense then, ordinary intelligence tests are unfair, but in the hands of an experienced psychologist, accustomed to communicating with very handicapped children and able to interpret the results carefully in the light of the child's background, the results are of considerable value in classifying children into certain learning groups, such as those who are above average, the average and slightly below, the slow learning subnormal group, and the very slow learning severely subnormal group. This gives parents, teachers, and therapists an approximate idea of the intellectual level so that training can be provided that is appropriate. For example, a 6-year-old who scores on the tests at about a 3½-year level and falls within the slow learning educationally subnormal group will need to continue with play material that will help him to build up his basic ideas of size and shape, with simple jig-saws, nests of cubes, and brick building, rather than attempt more complex and abstract material, such as letters and numbers, that the average 6-year-old can manage. The results of general tests of intelligence, such as the Stanford-Binet and the Wechsler Intelligence Scales for Pre-School or School-age Children, provided the child's handicaps are not severe, are also of use in helping to decide what kind of school or training group will be most helpful for the next stage in his learning, such as a Training Centre, School for Educationally Subnormal Children, or an ordinary school. Most psychologists would agree that there is nothing sacrosanct about general test results and their interpretation of them, especially with young handicapped children. On the whole, the intellectual ratings of children remain fairly constant over the years, e.g. in Nielsen's (1966) review about 70 per cent of the children's scores remained more or less constant when they were retested. In Gardner's (1970) study, about 80 per cent of 203 C.P. children studied over a 5-year period, remained in roughly the same intellectual level of schooling.

A small percentage changed, such as from a S.S.N. to E.S.N. level, some unaccountably, some because of being essentially borderline in the first place, and some because of therapeutic and educational help, and increased emotional maturity due to improved family circumstances. In a few cases the changes were artificial, due to errors in assessment procedures. This emphasizes the need for frequent reassessment and a flexible approach to training, education and therapy, starting early in the child's life.

Special Tests for the Severely Handicapped

So far we have mentioned tests of general intelligence of the type constructed originally for ordinary children. These are useful to the majority of cerebral palsied children, but clearly inappropriate to the severely handicapped, such as those who have no speech, no

FIG. 2.—Example of a multiple choice test card: the severely handicapped child watches the examiner pointing at each picture in turn; then gives any kind of signal when the 'odd one out' is reached.

useful hand control, and whose posture and head control may be so poor as to need constant support. Is it possible to assess their general intelligence? Not with any great accuracy, not only on account of the child's enormous difficulties in communication, but because one cannot be sure of the extent to which his sheer lack of experience in so many spheres of life has held up the development of his intelligence. What we can do is to try to establish a base line—an estimate of the minimum level of learning ability, usually expressed as a 'mental age' below which the child is unlikely to fall—above which he may rise, given plenty of experience of the right kind to make up for what he has missed.

To assess this base line for the very handicapped child, the psychologist uses tests of a 'multiple choice' type, to which a simple sign for 'yes' or 'no' can be given by the child. For example the

Columbia Scale of Mental Maturity (Burgemeister, 1954) has several pictures on a large card, one of which differs from the others by virtue of its colour, shape, size, class of objects, etc. The psychologist points to each picture in turn and the child has to give any kind of sign when the correct picture is being pointed to. The sign can consist of any kind of response, a murmur, a lifting of the head, or even a generalized body movement. The test contains 100 large cards, covering an age range of approximately 3–11 years. There are not enough items at each age to make it a very accurate test so it usually forms part of a larger battery.

Another test which can be administered in a similar way is the Raven's Progressive Matrices Scale, from age 6 onwards, although a poor performance may indicate visual perceptual disorders rather than low general intelligence, so again one has to rely on a battery of tests and never on a single one.

A test which is less dependent on visual perceptual skills is the Peabody Picture Vocabulary Test in which the child has to indicate which of four pictures on each card corresponds to the word given by the psychologist, e.g. 'Which is table?', 'Which is horse?' at age 2, graduating to quite complex pictures and words, such as ones depicting 'astonishment', 'communication', for older children. The 150 cards cover an age range from 2 to 10 years and can be administered to children who lack speech and hand control but of course demands adequate hearing. An English version of the test, for children over age 5, has been produced by Brimer (1963)— and one for pre-school children (1970).

A more comprehensive scale of language development on both the receptive and expressive sides of language, has been produced by Joan Reynell (1969) for ages 1–5 years. It uses familiar everyday objects and toys which are usually of greater interest to children than pictures, and has the great merit of not only measuring a child's expressive speech, from his early vocalizations to quite complicated sentences, but his *inner* language—his understanding of speech, and these measurements are particularly important in our assessments of children who have no speech or are too shy to use it. Since the tests have been specially developed for handicapped as well as for ordinary children, their administration has been arranged so that children can show their understanding of language by means of whatever minimal motor responses they can make, such as by simple pointing to objects in response to instructions, or by 'eye glance' if they cannot use their hands. The toys are large and well spaced enough to allow such responses, in such a way that the examiner can, in nearly all cases, determine exactly what the child means. For the partially hearing, the Columbia and Raven's Scales are useful, and the Nebraska Scale has been specially designed with the deaf children in mind but demands rather too much hand control for many cerebral palsied children.

For the partially sighted, the Williams Scale for Blind and Partially Sighted Children is of considerable value, provided the child's speech and hearing are adequate.

So far we have dealt with tests of *general* learning abilities, of the verbal and non-verbal types. There are also tests of *specific* abilities and disabilities which analyse in great detail a child's particular strengths and weaknesses. Often in the process of testing general intelligence, such as on the Stanford-Binet or Wechsler Verbal and Performance Scales, the psychologist notes an unevenness in the child's test scores that suggests special learning difficulties. We have mentioned the special learning difficulties in respect of the visual perceptual and visual motor areas; a large discrepancy between a child's verbal and performance scores of over 20 points on the Wechsler Scale may suggest these. Special tests such as the Marianne Frostig (1964) Developmental Test of Visual Perception can be used to throw some light on the difficulty. If the child's verbal scores are markedly below his scores on visual perceptual tests, a more detailed analysis of his understanding and expression of language, his abilities to communicate without words, and other aspects of communication can be explored by the Illinois Test of Psycholinguistic Abilities (Kirk and McCarthy, 1961). Both these tests can be used for children approximately aged 3–10. They are still in experimental form, particularly as far as cerebral palsied children are concerned, but show promise in respect not only of highlighting particular difficulties, but in promoting remedial techniques.

Psychologists have also constructed measures of the social development of handicapped children, and this aspect is just as important as the child's intellectual and educational development. Rating scales such as the Vineland (1947) and Gunzburg's Progress Assessment Charts (1966) give useful pictures of the C.P. child's daily living skills, such as his capacities for self help, play, and social activities. For very handicapped and retarded children a very detailed and useful scale which analyses the development of 'self help' (dressing, feeding) has been developed by Burland (1970). The ideal tests and rating scales are not those that merely measure abilities and disabilities but those which point to some areas in which extra help should be given to the child, setting reasonable short term targets for the child and the staff concerned with him, and providing a series of accurate measurements of progress over the years.

The Need for Continuous and Comprehensive Assessment '

In assessing the learning abilities amongst C.P. children, with their wide range of assets and handicaps, of differing backgrounds of experience, the psychologist can never rely on a single test and he must have at his command a wide range of tests, some of which we have mentioned, and must be constantly on the alert in discovering the reasons why a child has failed a particular test item. He must constantly ask whether the failure was due to poor vision or poor hand control, attention or visual perceptual difficulties—or did the child perceive the problem correctly but fail to express the answer correctly? Has fatigue set in or has the child become negative or uncommunicative? It is essential to consider all such questions before coming to an opinion about whether the child's intelligence is seriously impaired. We cannot rely on assumptions such as that heavily handicapped children are likely to have serious impairments in their intelligence (on the whole they have, but there are exceptions) or that lightly handicapped children necessarily have only minor learning difficulties (some lightly handicapped children, with high aspirations, develop major emotional problems which affect their learning) or that athetoids are more intelligent than spastics (the difference is very slight). The complexities of cerebral palsy are too great for any simple assumptions and reliable assessments are best based on repeated observations over long periods. The ideal setting for assessments is one in which the response of a child to various types of training and teaching can be closely observed over many months. This is not always practicable at present but examples can be seen such as at the Cheyne Centre (Bowley, 1967; Blencowe, 1969) and at the Spastics Society's long-term Assessment Centre at Hawksworth Hall (Gardner and Johnson, 1964).

Since the incidence of spasticity is not high enough to warrant long term day Assessment Units in areas other than large cities, there is an advantage in establishing Assessment Units that can provide for many types of handicapped children. A good example of a Unit providing early assessment and education on a long term basis for almost every type of handicapped child is the Katharine Elliot School in Shrewsbury (see Rabinowitz, 1966; Loring, 1968). Many Local Authorities are now providing Assessment Classes, sometimes attached to normal schools, sometimes to special schools, chiefly for young retarded children: the Department of

Education and Science (1970) surveyed 33 of these in 1967 and 1968. The standard of assessment work in some Units was reported to be low, chiefly because of lack of expert staff, such as visiting psychologists, doctors and social workers, but the survey illustrates the valuable trend in helping to ensure proper multi-disciplinary services in the future, within an educational setting where long term observations and experimental trials of various educational methods can be carried out. Every County should have community based Assessment Classes wherein parent participation with teachers, therapists and social workers can be encouraged. Parents rightly object to the kind of assessment that attempts to label a child once and for all on the basis of a single brief interview, and to the kind of assessment that is not followed by practical guidance, treatment and good early educational opportunities.

The Problems of Parents

The parents of very handicapped children have very real practical and psychological problems in the upbringing and care of their children. The arrival of such a child is usually a shock, and many mothers find it very difficult indeed to accept the facts, and to plan care and training constructively. Often they feel in some measure to blame, and feelings of guilt are very natural and fairly common in such cases, though usually quite unfounded. It seems something of a slur on the family name, a stigma and an embarrassment to all concerned. Sometimes, though this is rare, the parents find it hard to love their disabled child fully and feel resentful and hostile towards the world and everyone who tries to help. But usually a very close tie grows up between the mother and child. In a few parents this tie becomes so extremely close that they refuse to consider outside help, such as residential care, in cases where the child's physical and intellectual handicaps are so severe as to dominate the entire family's life. Obviously the mother is emotionally involved in an extreme degree, and to fail to recognize this is to court disaster. Once a mother has accepted the cruel fact that her child is severely and permanently handicapped, a second stage of adjustment has to follow, that of coming to terms with the long term implications, in respect of family life, feeding, playing, social activities, education, health, job prospects and marriage; in short all aspects of the life of the whole family for many decades. The very phrases 'acceptance of' and 'coming to terms with' severe handicap only superficially describe the tremendously complex and subtle adjustments that parents of a very handicapped child are expected to make. The balance of all these, with pessimism and hopelessness on the one hand, and over-optimism and denial of reality on the other, must be very difficult to maintain, and professional workers are sometimes presumptuous in the advice that they give parents. For example glib advice to 'treat him as normal' is clearly out of the question in the case of a very handicapped child. The reality of handicap is that there are some things the child cannot and never will do, for example walking or writing. This is not to deny that there are many things he *can* do: and that there are many substitutes and alternative skills that he can develop, given expert help, that will make a great difference to his life, such as using a wheelchair, or typing efficiently. Some parents need almost as much help as the child, to come to terms with the facts, to accept the limitations imposed by the handicap realistically, and at the same time to appreciate the amount of ability and independence that the child can achieve. Long term support from a social worker can be very valuable to such families: intensive case work is necessary when the parents' denial of reality is strong.

Some studies of the impact of handicap on family life have helped to throw light on some of these problems. Sheila Hewett's (1970) study was based on a representative sample of 180 families with cerebral palsy in the Midlands. Although on the whole many of the families were coping well (better than many professional workers might have expected, the point being that the latter's experience is usually confined to those families who cannot cope), some were showing extreme tensions. These tensions were exacerbated by factors such as a lack of information about cerebral palsy (40 per cent did not know their child was spastic till past the age of 2 and 17 per cent had never been told), difficulties in obtaining suitable equipment and gadgets, particularly wheelchairs, poor assessment and nursery facilities (62 per cent of the under 5s had no nursery day care of any kind), lack of schooling or training for the retarded child (37 per cent of the over 5s had no education or day care of any kind provided by the Local Authority), extra financial burdens and a lack of any single agency to whom parents felt they could easily turn to when they needed advice. This last point is also emphasized in the National Children's Bureau's study *Living with Handicap* (Younghusband *et al.*, 1970). Parents in many areas are confronted by bewildering, complex, differing but overlapping services, such as hospitals, clinics, Local Authorities, voluntary societies, schools and so on, so that even for relatively simple needs such as for a special wheelchair, many different agencies may have to be contacted. These need co-ordination at both national and local levels. The newly organized Local Authority social services will help in these respects, as outlined in the Seebohm Report (Report of the Committee of Local Authority and Allied Personal Services, July 1968) which advocates combining the fragmented and piecemeal services that exist in some areas into a more unified and comprehensive organization, focussing on the child and his family within the community. One of the aims of the new social services departments of the Local Authorities will be to ensure continuity of care throughout the child's life, into school leaving age and beyond where necessary. It is important as social workers have emphasized to consider the family as a unit, that the needs of the rest of the family, the husband and brothers and sisters are not neglected, and that the spastic child is not allowed to become the centre of attention in the home. The other children should be taught not to give in every time to the disabled child, and the more rough and tumble he can take the better. Sometimes it is wise for the family to go on a short holiday without the handicapped child, who may spend the period in a children's hospital or Family Help Unit, and often enjoy the experience. It is most important to keep things in the right perspective.

Sometimes, as a severely handicapped child becomes older and heavier, the problem of his day-to-day care may become too great a burden for his family, especially if a suitable day school is not available. Then it is best for all concerned for the spastic child to attend a boarding school, where all aids and appliances will be available and where he will be well taught and cared for by a specialist staff. Frequent visiting is encouraged and holiday times and half-term holidays will, of course, be spent at home. Sometimes the severely handicapped child really benefits from being away for a period from the anxious and close concern of his devoted parents; the family, on the other hand, may find relief from his constant care and be more able to live a full and normal life. But the child under 7 should not, in our opinion, go to boarding school unless a family emergency arises. Many families have built up a very satisfying life while keeping a severely handicapped child at home and sharing his care and letting him join into family activities as much as possible. In some cases it is found that the presence of a handicapped child in the family has proved enriching and most rewarding but, of course, it is important not to allow the older children to feel too responsible for him to the detriment of their other interests. The care of such a child can be a shared responsibility between the parents, the brothers and sisters, the relatives and the teachers, therapists and doctors attached to the school and hospital which the child attends, the voluntary agencies, and the social services of the Local Authority. The growth of these services in recent years has increased the possibilities for children to remain within the normal community and share ordinary family life.

Early Care and Training

The Spastics Society publishes a number of excellent pamphlets which give practical guidance and scientific information to parents of spastic children. The names of several are listed at the end of this chapter. In recent years a great deal has been done to educate public opinion, to give them factual knowledge about cerebral palsy and the ways by which these children can be treated and educated. A tremendous interest and concern for the problems presented by these children has been shown in recent years, and it is rare to find a case of cerebral palsy undetected at school age.

It is generally agreed that early diagnosis and treatment is of the utmost importance. If the spastic condition is not evident at birth it usually becomes clear in the first few months, when instead of beginning to lift his head or move his limbs freely the baby remains passive. By six months, if the baby is making no attempt to sit up, the doctor should be consulted. If severe mental retardation is excluded, a diagnosis of cerebral palsy may be made. Early treatment, training and advice is important, enlisting the help of several disciplines, such as physiotherapists, speech and occupational therapists. The trend in recent years is to encourage parents to carry out treatment in the natural setting of the home, rather than putting a child through a series of formal exercises in a clinic —although these may have their place when the child is older in conjunction with treatment at home and within the school. Mothers feel relieved when they find they have a vital part to play in treatment.

(a) *Physiotherapy.*—Ideally physiotherapy should start during the child's first year, as soon as the mother is ready to accept advice on training.

In cerebral palsy, the part of the brain which controls the movements of the muscles has been damaged and the physiotherapist's aim is to provide systematic training that will help the child to make correct and useful movements. Left to himself the child would choose the easiest way, using the strongest muscles and letting the weaker ones atrophy. Contractions and tensions thus develop and these constitute a 'secondary handicap' which must be prevented wherever possible. The whole process of training is very slow and the child has to pass very gradually through the normal developmental sequence of physical growth and locomotion—to lift and hold his head erect, to sit supported in a suitable chair fitted with a tray for his toys, to roll and gradually to crawl, supported by a crawler perhaps, and he will need space on the floor to practise these activities. We know of a 3-year-old in a nursery school who is allowed to take messages to the kitchen by rolling, which he does with great pride. As the return journey usually takes some 20 minutes, urgent messages are sent by speedier routes!

Some children will never be able to walk, but they may learn to ride a tricycle with skill and safety. A triplegic boy at 7 was accepted in a normal primary school, and used to ride his tricycle alone along the avenues to school with his calipers strapped on behind. His mother had great faith and great courage and knew when to let go and let him prove his independence. Many spastic children will be able to use braces and crutches and we often witness the child's great delight when after much coaching he finds he can move about alone, and will convey his calipers home with great pride and delight, demanding almost that they should go to bed with him. Sometimes rapid skill in their use is expected and much disappointment experienced when immediate success is not forthcoming. It is most important to teach him that he can only hurry slowly. Many parents find great difficulty in allowing their handicapped child to meet normal hazards and to do much for themselves. An important part of the educational work of a centre is to teach parents what are reasonable expectations and what are necessary limitations for their particular child. The staff at a centre also need to review, from time to time, the strengths and limitations of the treatment they are offering. A most valuable practical guide to parents *Handling the Young Cerebral Palsied Child at Home* has been written by Nancie Finnie (1968) based on the methods of the Bobaths at the Western Cerebral Palsy Centre. A more technical description of the latter's pioneering work is to be found in their monograph (1966). *Principles of Treatment in Cerebral Palsy* by S. Levitt (1970) is also helpful.

(b) *Speech therapy* proves necessary for many of these children. Once again an important aim is to educate the muscles—this time of the lips, the tongue, and the throat, which if left alone may not learn the correct movements. First, the child must learn correct voicing and breathing; next sucking, swallowing, and blowing; then babbling and the gradual introduction of syllables and words with meaning; finally simple phrases and sentences. The therapist's approach is one of constant encouragement for the young child to communicate in ways that have meaning to him, and, of course, the parents' encouragement at home, where countless opportunities arise for the child to use speech with understanding, is very important. If there is any degree of hearing loss all this will be a great deal more difficult, but a hearing aid can be fitted in many such cases and auditory training commenced with the assistance of a qualified teacher of the deaf. The co-operation of the parents at this early stage is absolutely essential, for the baby has to learn to watch the mother's lips and expression and should receive a great deal of encouragement and praise for his own efforts to imitate sounds. Feeding is often difficult for spastic children, but speech therapy can help in teaching the child to swallow and to suck and to chew. We know of one speech therapist who usually commences her sessions with iced lollies as a sucking and swallowing exercise, which is deservedly popular! This will also help control the dribbling which is so common with many athetoids.

The full co-operation of parents in all this programme is of great value. Asher Cashdan (1966), who has been carrying out some research on child-rearing practices in Manchester, writes as follows: 'Handicapped children need language stimulation more than normal ones, and they need it for longer periods; they often need experiences brought to them because they cannot go out and seek them. If they are not talked to, not taken shopping, do not play with local children or even their own brothers and sisters, and do not take a full part in activities within the home, the effects of their handicaps will be increased rather than lessened.'

A great deal of help can be obtained from the cerebral palsy centre with adapting furniture, potty chairs, and equipment to suit the child's particular needs. He may need a wheel chair which he can learn to propel himself. He may need a play chair with wooden beading fixed round the edge of the tray so that his toys will not constantly roll on to the floor. His play table may need to be raised on wooden blocks to the right height and he will need toys which he can control and handle. Discreet choice of radio and television programmes can also help a busy mother with normal household care to attend to. Home care is nearly always best for the handicapped child and if parents feel they have plenty of support and expert guidance at each stage of growth they will be able to tackle this tremendous task of caring for a spastic child intelligently and courageously. Some will need constant reminders that the cerebral palsied child is first and foremost a *child* and needs, therefore, to be treated as such, and not as a poor disabled invalid or a tender greenhouse plant!

(c) *Occupational Therapy.*—Occupational therapy is a method of treatment which is closely allied to teaching in the pre-school period especially. Its purpose is to improve fine motor skills, develop self-help and daily living activities such as feeding or dressing, and to undertake, together with teachers and psychologists, training in many aspects of learning, such as improving visual perceptual skills and specialized methods of communication.

Many cerebral palsied children have special difficulties in understanding spatial relationships, in discriminating shape or direction. He may be confused about the position of his body in space. Hand dominance may not be fully established and confusion in reading and writing correctly, e.g. by reversing letters such as b, d, p, q, n, u, may occur and impede later school work. Skilled occupational therapy in these early years coupled with good nursery school experience may do a great deal to prevent some of the learning difficulties commonly reported of older brain-damaged children.

The occupational therapist works with one child alone or with small groups. Matching of shapes and colours, sorting similar patterns, fitting puzzles or form boards, tracing shapes and letters, drawing in sand, copying bead or matchstick patterns, learning parts of the body by simple games, learning to button or tie shoes, and learning to persist in a simple task are invaluable aids to improving perceptual ability and prepare the way for more formal learning later. Looking, listening, touching, and naming reinforce learning and help to compensate for the restrictions of learning imposed by the physical handicap and a sheltered environment.

The use of appliances and supports are another important part of occupational therapy—wrist supports, head support, the right type of chair, the proper utensils to aid independence, and the use of a typewriter when indicated.

Experience has shown that quite young cerebral palsied children can use typewriters at the age of 5 or 6, when they would normally want to begin to write letters or copy words. Occupational therapists select the most suitable type, an electric typewriter, or one with a specially enlarged keyboard. They find out from experiment which is the easiest position and the easiest hand or even foot or mouth movement for the particular child and give the child short practise periods several times a week. In general we have found this most rewarding with the more intelligent children and judge that a mental age of about 6 years is the most appropriate time to begin work of this kind. Intelligent athetoid children with limited speech gain a very great deal from the use of typewriters and a very marked improvement in behaviour, in responsiveness, and increased happiness often results. Most occupational therapists and teachers would agree that it is a waste of time persisting with frustrating efforts to teach a heavily handicapped child to write with a pencil when it is clear that he will never have sufficient hand control to write legibly or with ease or speed. He should, of course, be urged to use his hands for every expressive activity or for large movements of which they are capable.

(d) *New Systems of Treatment and Early Education.*—We have described the traditional methods of treatment by physiotherapists, occupational and speech therapists, developed over the past 50 years. In recent years some new, radical and comprehensive methods have been developed: these break away from traditional treatment carried out by several separate therapists and teachers, and advocate instead a *unified* approach that aims to deal with all aspects of the handicapped child's development, not only his motor development, but his perception, attention, language and early educational skills, etc., in accordance with the carefully devised strict programme of step by step sequential training. Two large scale systems of treatment are currently being practised in several countries, the Peto method and the Doman-Delacato method.

The Peto method is of particular relevance to the treatment and education of severely handicapped cerebral palsied children. It has been developed in Budapest at the State Institute for Conductive Education of the Motor Disabled under the direction of Professor Peto who died in September 1967. The Institute continues to admit children for one to two years intensive treatment on a residential basis and trains 'conductors' who act as physiotherapist, speech therapist, occupational therapist, teacher and nurse. The Spastics Society has encouraged trials of these new techniques in this country. The children are educated in groups of from 10 to 20 children under one conductor and her assistant. All the daily activities are carried out in the group which obviates handling by many different specialists in different places and reduces the 'fragmentation' that most very handicapped are subjected to, such as when, in the course of one day their speech, motor activities, daily living skills, and formal education are dealt with by different personnel of different disciplines, in different settings, often with little real link up between all these various activities. The room has the minimum of distracting material, but visual aids, occupational therapy materials, charts and pictures are produced at the appropriate time. The room is furnished with slatted wooden plinths used for eating and sleeping on, and for the required exercises. Special chairs without arms are used for sitting and as walking aids.

The training programme is a highly structured one and the day is carefully programmed. General training to promote general body control, *e.g.* lying still, turning over, sitting with feet on the ground and hands on the table etc. comes first. As the child attempts to perform the exercise he repeats loudly and slowly his intention *e.g.* 'I join my hands together' and counts rhythmically to five, all the children in the group performing the same action and saying the same words. This is known as 'rhythmical intention'. Continuous verbalization in simple language accompanied by the appropriate movement no doubt aids concentration and helps him to exclude other activities thus possibly enabling the cortex to form new neuro-physiological pathways. Rhythmical speech and counting reinforce the action necessary to move a limb and a new movement pattern is developed. This theory has some basis in the work of Pavlov and has been described by Luria (1961).

This general training in body movement is followed by specific programmes of exercises devised to develop particular skills, *e.g.* pre-writing exercises, perceptual training, body image training, independence in eating, drinking, dressing and undressing and using the pot. The exercises are carefully worked out to perform the sequences leading to the performance of a functional task.

It is too early yet to assess accurately the value of this new method known as 'conductive education', but preliminary trials with heavily handicapped children, especially athetoids, do suggest some progress towards independence of movement, speech and everyday skills. Increase in confidence, and enthusiasm in participation are very evident in the groups. As a result of a short period of intensive treatment at a very young age it is hoped that many of these children, hitherto regarded as ineducable non-participators in the classroom, may be able to benefit from special school education, or according to the claims made in Budapest, from normal education. A detailed description of conductive education and tentative conclusions can be found in an article by Esther Cotton and Margaret Parnwell (1967). A number of special schools and centres have been using the Peto method in modified forms and in many ways it has revolutionalized their educational approach. Cerebral palsied children need a more structured, more repetitive programme than ordinary non-brain-damaged children. They need more reinforcement by verbalization and bodily activity, by seeing and hearing and touching and linking their sensations to form percepts and later concepts. In this way they may gain greater control of their movements and actions and organize their thought processes more effectively.

The important features of the Peto method can be summarized as: (a) its emphasis on group treatment which produces high motivation amongst some children; (b) a well thought out programme, largely of motor training for the severely handicapped; (c) it is applied intensively at an early age (often starting at age 3 full-time, all day and every day for a couple of years); (d) by one expert conductor trained in several disciplines, so that she can act as an important focal point in the child's life. Such radical and intensive methods certainly deserve close study, since conventional methods of helping the motor development of very handicapped young children are by no means always successful.

Another radical and intensive system of motor treatment is that propounded by Glen Doman and Carl Delacato in the Philadelphia Rehabilitation Centre, established in 1955. In 1963 this became part of the Institutes for the Achievement of Human Potential, and the Doman-Delacato methods of treating cerebral palsied and other types of brain injured children have the aim of producing movement patterns by means of an intensive programme of repetitive movements to be carried out largely by parents (in contrast to the Peto method). The movements are patterned in accordance with the sequences of movement that normal children go through, in for example the various stages of locomotion (rolling, crawling, creeping, standing erect with support and so on until normal walking is achieved). The theory is that the damaged child's central neurological organization can be enhanced by such procedures, and substantial improvements are claimed, provided the parents can carry out the very intensive and continuous training. Careful records of neurological development are kept, and the use of these for evaluative studies are described by Doman and his colleagues in Wolf's (1969) study of the results of treatment in C.P. Large scale studies of the effectiveness of such methods are still awaited.

The difficulties of mounting such studies are enormous. Comparable groups of untreated children, for the purposes of contrasting their spontaneous progress over the years with the treated groups, are hard to find. It is also difficult to find large enough groups of treated children to allow statistical comparisons.

The advantage of the more systematic intensive programmes of treatment, such as the Peto and Doman-Delacato, is that they do have definite aims and methods, which can be subjected to precise measurement, preferably by independent researchers. They are also important in turning our attention to the possibility that very early and very intensive motor treatment may lead to greater progress

Learning positions for crawling and standing.

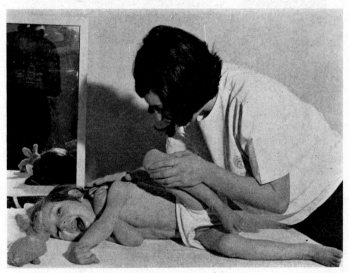

Physiotherapy exercises.

[*To face page* 28

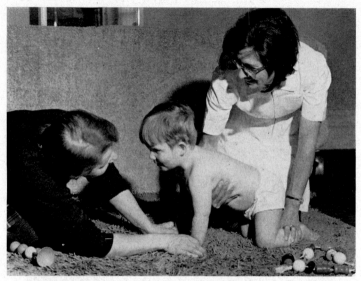

Mother being shown the correct position for crawling.

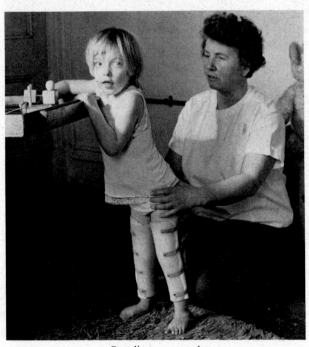

Standing supported.

Standing with slight support.

Riding a tricycle with back support and double pedals.

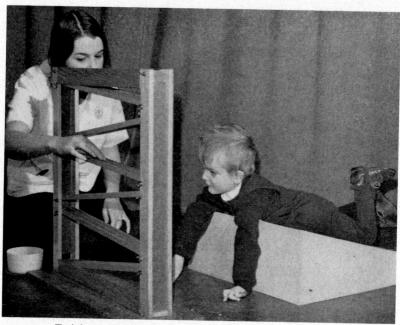

Training correct eye movements and weight bearing on hands.

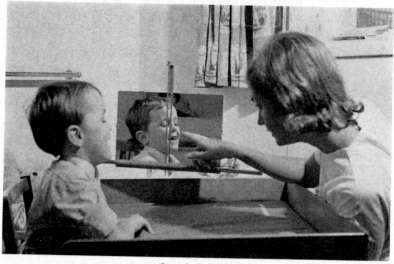

Speech therapy.

A hearing test

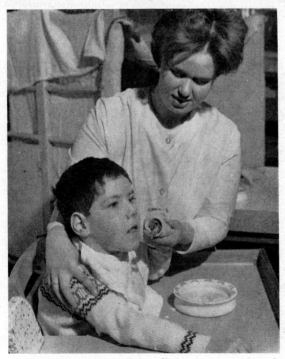

Learning to feed.

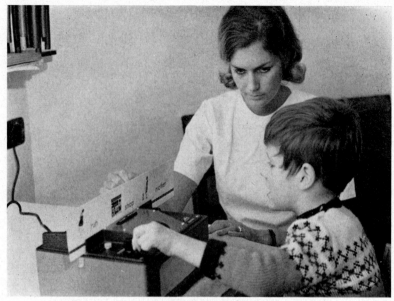

Using the Language Master.

'Typing with enlarged letters on an electric typewriter.'

Playing cricket.

Learning to read.

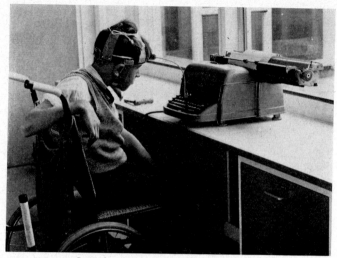
Learning to type with head pointer.

Enjoying a swim.

than we have hitherto thought possible. Part of this progress might
be due to the enthusiasm that is generated amongst the staff by
having a systematic method, rather than the intrinsic merits of the
system. This remains to be seen. We can only find out the answers
to such questions by continued research.

Emotional Development

Children with cerebral palsy are often described as emotionally
labile which means that their feelings are strong, easily aroused,
difficult to control, and very fluctuating. They may show quite
violent anger at frustration which they have to experience so often.
They may show acute fear in a new situation or when unsteady
and afraid of falling. They may show depression and tearfulness.
In her study of fear and frustration of such children in a residential
hospital school, Maureen Oswin (1967) gives some vivid examples
of behaviour problems encountered in school due to the frustration
of the physical handicap. Depression, withdrawal from people,
refusal to work or co-operate may occur and the reasons for this
must be fully understood. It seems likely that some C.P. children
may have an extended period of the natural emotional instability
that is found in ordinary young children, due to their impaired
neurological condition. For example their capacity to inhibit strong
feelings may be delayed in its development by several years, after
which they will show greater stability and less fluctuation of mood.
In Rutter's (1970) sample, nearly 40 per cent of the C.P. children
were rated by teachers as psychiatrically disturbed and the authors
conclude that this very high rate, over five times that of the general
population, must in part be due to brain dysfunction and could
not be wholly attributed to environmental influences, such as
faulty reactions by parents and the community to the handicapped
child. Capacity to learn will be affected by moodiness, fear of
failure and of social incompetence. Later, during adolescence, a
return of moodiness and difficult behaviour may be expected as
the young person has to begin to face up to the demands of
community life and contend with normal physical changes and
increased frustrations, including a feeling of rejection by non-
handicapped peers. A very stable, consistent, and regular routine
with the minimum of excitement or stress will increase stability
and reduce emotional disturbance and distractibility.

It is not surprising that these children, sometimes well past
babyhood, give way to tantrums when one remembers how
dependent the child is on the whim of the adults around him and
how frequently he will have to face frustration. His toys roll out

of reach, his bricks constantly fall over because he cannot control his movements sufficiently; his pencil will not move in the direction he wishes. He has to wait for an adult to fetch what he wants, to give him his food, or take him to the toilet. It is remarkable that so many spastic children show such cheerfulness, patience, and dogged determination in the face of so many obstacles. It is a healthy sign when a spastic child can show occasional defiance and rebellion. Sometimes he is resistant to physiotherapy; sometimes he tries to deny the existence of a spastic arm or leg and resents treatment which forces the disabled limb on his notice. It is wise to suspend treatment for a period in such cases. Sometimes he will draw a bizarre type of man with one arm much smaller than the other or one leg left out altogether. This seems an attempt to express strong feelings about his disability.

Obviously the more independent the child can become, the more skills he can acquire, the greater his sense of achievement and feeling of self confidence will be. Depression and anxiety may occur in adolescence, but in childhood, given good therapy, good teaching, and an accepting, supporting home behind him, the cerebral palsied child can enjoy life at school and at home.

Early Education

The education and training of a young handicapped child cannot begin too early. He has to be taught skills that an ordinary child picks up more or less spontaneously or incidentally during his early years, such as speech and locomotion. Children start to learn, right from birth, to organize the mass of impressions they receive from the outside world, to make sense out of the sight and sounds and the feel of things around them, exploring, manipulating, vocalizing and generally gaining an increasing measure of understanding and control of their surroundings. Now the handicapped child tends to miss out on much of this early experience, and to become bored and frustrated if he continually fails to reach a satisfying degree of control.

The early stimulation and experience that parents, and only parents, can normally provide is, of course, tremendously important, for they are the child's first teachers. It is clear, however, that many parents need help in providing proper stimulation, and there is an urgent need for more special nursery school provision.

In some areas, particularly larger towns, such provision is available, sometimes for children as young as 2 or 3 years such as in one of the Spastics Society's local group centres. At this age priority is usually given to daily physiotherapy, occupational therapy, and speech therapy, if needed, but the child also enjoys play activities and simple nursery occupations with a small group of similarly handicapped children in a stimulating environment, and cared for by adults specially trained and with adequate knowledge of his needs. The advice that they can give to parents is invaluable.

One of the great advantages of this type of early education is that the child can spend part of the day in an atmosphere where his severe disability is accepted as a matter of course, and away from the anxious concern of his devoted family. While his difficulties are fully understood, he is expected to measure up to certain standards of independence and skill often not demanded of him at home. It is a great deal easier for the trained staff of such a centre to treat the young severely handicapped spastic child with reasonable, kindly, firm, and even detached care than the mother who is so intimately and emotionally involved with the child. Indeed when parents and teachers were asked to record their observations of social maturity and self-reliance on the Vineland Scale (Doll, 1947) on the same child at the same time independently, we found that in each case the social age found from the teachers' ratings was considerably higher than that obtained from the parents' ratings. The child strives to live up to his teacher's expectations while the parents do not demand so high a level of achievement.

The gradual learning of independence in simple routine matters is of great importance for the spastic child, both for his self respect and his self confidence in community life. Sometimes it is well nigh impossible for him to help to feed himself, to dress himself, or wash his hands or fetch his toys. All the comparatively simple skills that an ordinary 4-year-old can achieve quite easily, such as undoing coat buttons, turning on taps, threading beads, using a crayon or paint brush, or moulding clay or plasticine into shapes are virtually impossible to many children with cerebral palsy until they have been able to learn by constant training and therapy, some degree of control of their hands. Washing, toilet, and feeding processes are not hurried at school; the child will have special equipment provided which will make feeding and toilet training easier, and both speech therapists and occupational therapists may help with this. He may have a hole cut for his plate and mug, and spoons and forks with large handles easy to grasp. Drinking through a straw may help to develop correct swallowing movements and indirectly control drooling which is such an impediment to some of these children.

Manipulation of material, which will increase motor skill, is made more possible by fitting a tray with a raised edge to the child's chair if he cannot sit in an ordinary chair at a table. He can then use many of the usual nursery school educational apparatus, sorting and matching games, puzzles, bricks, beads, dough, clay, and manage sit-down painting or drawing at an easel. He can enjoy a sand tray and a water trough if adequately supported in either a sitting or a standing position.

Locomotion, which provides little difficulty for the ordinary 2-year-old, is often something which the cerebral palsied child has slowly to acquire. In the nursery school he is given opportunity to hitch or roll or crawl, whichever is possible and most beneficial for him. Close co-operation is necessary between the teacher and the physiotherapist so that the right type of movements can be encouraged in a free environment. He can be encouraged to clamber on the climbing frame, to push wheel toys around, to climb up steps and slide down the chute if he is able. He gains confidence and courage, and learns to disregard the occasional tumble. This type of free activity in nursery schoolroom and garden can make up for cramped living conditions at home, particularly for those living in 'high rise' flats.

Creative Activity is of immense importance to a child who has to be frustrated in so many ways on account of his motor disability. Sand and water, clay, dough, or other modelling materials provide good opportunities. Finger painting may be possible when the control of paint brush or crayon is beyond his powers. Brick building and constructional toys can be a great delight unless manual control is too limited or uncertain and then such activities become merely irritating and unrewarding. Athetoid children experience special difficulties because involuntary movements constantly interfere with such activities and cause his bricks to be scattered all over the floor. Many valuable special toys for the handicapped have been designed at the Nottingham Child Development Research Unit, under the direction of John and Elizabeth Newson.

Imaginative Play is part of the young child's means of communication, of expression, and his method of relieving feelings of fear, of hostility and frustration. In pretending games, family games, bus driver, engine driver, cowboy, policeman, and hospital play especially the child reflects and interprets his experiences in his environment. By this type of play he learns to express, re-direct, and modify his feelings. The play, with other children in the group, helps in this process which is so valuable for emotional development. By this means too he learns to make a more satisfactory relationship to other children near his age. At home he may be competing always with active and able brothers and sisters and feel always a little inferior. Or he may be always sheltered and protected from showing initiative and independence. In the nursery school for cerebral palsied children, his companions have similar handicaps, similar problems, and similar frustrations. He can compete on more equal terms and can even assist a child more handicapped than himself. A great deal of healthy social growth goes on in the group. He learns to combine efforts for a definite purpose such as playing at shops, to accept leadership, to make a good partner, sometimes engage in healthy mischief, and to enjoy all the fun and enrichment of personality from playing and quarrelling together. Active play out of doors has been encouraged amongst the C.P. children at Cheyne Centre by the use of the special Adventure Playground for Handicapped Children in Chelsea.

Group Activities.—Some time is also given for simple organized activities. The children listen to stories and rhymes. They enjoy action songs and just listening to music. A percussion band is a popular feature of the programme, and some suitable instrument can be found for most of the children however disabled they may be. Such social activity is immensely stimulating to a young cerebral palsied child who may previously have remained much of the day in his cot or pram while his mother busied herself with the housework and the rest of the family were at school or at work. As a result he is more contented, less irritable, sleeps and eats better, and is generally more happy at home as well as at school.

As we have mentioned, there is an urgent need for much more special nursery provision, where teachers and therapists can work not only closely together, but in close co-operation with the parents. The Plowden Report (H.M.S.O., 1967) emphasized the need to establish nurseries in Education Priority Areas to combat the social and cultural deprivation that exists for some children in many of our urban areas. The deprivation that most handicapped children suffer, by virtue of restricted motor, language and social activities, can be equally formidable and considerable priority needs to be given to them in providing special nursery facilities. In Sheila Hewett's study (1970) less than 40 per cent of the C.P. children had full or part-time nursery day care and much of this was available through the Spastics Society's centres in the region. Only 10 per cent had Local Authority provision, and the latter's contribution to nursery schooling for the handicapped leaves much to be desired. The National Children's Bureau's survey (Younghusband, 1970) in ten Local Authority areas showed that very little pre-school provision was available for the handicapped: only in two areas could facilities be described as fairly satisfactory. In these, special efforts had been made to provide not only a purpose built Unit attached to a physically handicapped school but to admit small numbers of handicapped children to ordinary day nurseries and to encourage the formation of play groups, etc. In most areas such facilities are uncommon. In future all new schools for the physically handicapped will include nursery Units but this will not immediately alter the situation in most areas. With greater facilities, an early start can be made in overcoming some of the special learning difficulties that we have previously mentioned, such as the difficulties in visual perception, attention span, and the emotional barriers that spring from repeated early failures, before these difficulties have become ingrained. It is to be expected that, with early nursery school help, a greater proportion of cerebral palsied children will be able, at ages 5 or 6, to pass on to the type of school that almost every parent hopes for—the ordinary school within their community.

Education After Age 5

At 5, as with the ordinary child, a decision usually has to be made about the type of schooling that will be most helpful for the handicapped child. This decision has to be taken with great care. Between 25 and 50 per cent of cerebral palsied children attend normal schools in many areas, according to surveys by Hewett (1970) and Henderson (1961), although there will be great variations in this figure, depending on local circumstances. In most areas, children with mild physical handicaps and average intelligence can usually attend the ordinary school, but it must be clearly established that they are free from the subtle kinds of special learning difficulties that we have mentioned.

The decision to place a more handicapped child in an ordinary school must rest on many factors, such as the presence or absence of special learning difficulties, the degree to which his speech is affected, the personality of the child, notably whether he is oversensitive and overanxious about failure, or resilient and well able to stand up to emotional as well as physical knocks. Another important consideration is the attitude of the staff at the ordinary school, and as Norah Gibbs (1965) has pointed out, staff vary in their abilities to cope with the presence of a handicapped child. Further thought needs to be given to how ordinary schools can be assisted in making better provision, such as by employing a part-time remedial teacher, and some alterations of the buildings, such as provision of a wooden ramp alongside stairs that might be too difficult for spastics to negotiate.

In a follow-up study of 104 C.P. children who had left Cheyne Centre 17 per cent were attending normal schools (Bowley, 1967 b). It was found that a fair proportion, notably those with good intelligence, good verbal ability and mild physical and special learning difficulties were showing good adjustment and progress, but three pupils were causing concern, in spite of good intelligence, two of these having subtle visual and hearing difficulties. Further studies of the integration of physically handicapped children into normal schools are being made, such as by the Department of Education and Science, and this will help to clarify the situation. Another difficulty for some children is the need for therapy and this can sometimes be made by sessional visits to a clinic.

A halfway house between the normal school and the special school is a very useful provision for many handicapped children, for example the provision of small special units for the physically handicapped, attached to the normal school, along the lines of the partially hearing units, which in the main have been successfully attached to normal schools. Very few such Units exist for the physically handicapped (they are more common in Scandinavian countries where particular efforts have been made to avoid segregated handicapped schools) and clearly the physical difficulties involved, such as getting children to various classrooms and playgrounds when hundreds of physically active ordinary children are around, can be great, but further experiments along these lines would be worthwhile. They allow opportunities for at least a partial integration of ordinary and handicapped children, the experience of which can be as fruitful to the ordinary child as it is to the handicapped, for we can hardly expect ordinary children to develop sound and realistic attitudes towards the handicapped if they never have opportunities for meeting them. The disadvantages of such integration is that the competition can become too great. There are dangers in asking a handicapped child to attempt too much, to struggle all the time to keep up with ordinary children.

For the more handicapped children, a more sheltered school career is often necessary, at least for a period. Day schools for the physically handicapped are available in most large towns and the majority have a large proportion of cerebral palsied children in their classrooms, together with children having other, usually milder, handicaps, such as mild cases of polio, and congenital defects such as a dislocated hip. In a follow-up study of the progress of fourteen children attending day P.H. schools, one of the authors (A.H.B.) found that on the whole their social and educational progress was satisfactory, but four pupils needed more specialized teaching and six were showing some signs of stress resulting from tensions at home. The following case notes on follow-up interviews illustrate the way these children were adjusting as they grew older and nearer adolescence.

E.O. admitted to Cheyne at *c.* 2 years. (Attended 5 years.)
Diagnosis:

> Diplegia, epilepsy, dysarthria.
> Average intelligence (I.Q. 97/104)
> *Reviewed at 10 years 9 months.*
> Average intelligence (Wisc. Verbal I.Q. 103).
> Average verbal comprehension (37 percentile on English Picture Vocabulary Test)
> Reading age—8·3 years (Holborn Scale)
> Arithmetic age—10½ years (Wisc.)
> Block Design Test—8·6 years.
> Bender-Gestalt Designs—a good attempt on early designs but great difficulty owing to limited hand control
> Handwriting—a great problem to her

There is no doubt that E. is of good average intelligence and it is characteristic of her that she uses her potential to its fullest capacity in many respects. Speech disability handicaps reading and physical disability impedes writing, but her dogged persistence and her determination, her excellent sense of humour and her interest and alertness in respect of everything going on around her are very marked. She had a very insecure early life, but since her father's re-marriage she has had a more settled family life and enjoys her baby brother and sister. She still feels apprehensive in new situations; she went on the school holiday journey to Holland but does not want to go on another. She attended the Cheyne Holiday Club once, but was unwilling to come again. She is always worried about hospital visits. She shows firm attachment to her stepmother. Her definition of brave was 'you do something you don't like which is frightening' and this probably sums up her own feelings.

Educationally E. is making excellent progress, though learning to type would help her to express her ideas. Physically her progress is very limited and she finds wearing her calipers something of a problem. On the whole her general adjustment is good though moodiness and tearful scenes do occur.

K.P. is, at 14½ years with an I.Q. of 74, a very immature, distractible, slow learning child who will need prolonged education and vocational training if she is to prove employable. She is a hemiplegic who underwent a hemispherectomy when quite young. She has good use of one hand and is very active and mobile. On the Bristol Social Adjustment

Guide she gained a score of 17 suggesting considerable instability. She is described as erratic, restless, often losing and forgetting things, with poor concentration and variable moods. She is over-friendly with adults, tries to monopolize the teacher, sidling up to or hanging round the teacher and talking excessively about her doings. She is distressed by any correction, but quickly forgets. She is usually on bad terms with other children, is disliked, shunned, jealous and cannot share friends or form other than shallow, fleeting relationships. She shows occasional temper if provoked, but is 'generally kind and helpful'. She 'would like a boy friend', but is not popular and is described as 'socially unacceptable'. K. has a great deal of growing up to do, but her physical condition is against her.

E.P. at 14½ years is extremely happy at her day P.H. school. She is quadriplegic and had mild epilepsy. She is of average intelligence (I.Q. 108). Though slow in speaking and writing, she has learnt to type and hopes to obtain a post as a typist when she leaves school. She is a Girl Guide, belongs to two youth clubs and has won a cup for swimming. She made the Christmas cake for the family! She is a member of a lively East End family of four and has a twin brother. She has had good support and very sensible handling by her mother. She seemed mature, fairly competent at managing her own affairs, very content and was weathering adolescence well.

The mixing of children having minor and major degrees and types of handicap has some advantages compared to the specialized C.P. schools, but provision of therapy, specialized teaching, and equipment for the severely handicapped is not always adequate. For these children a specialized school for the cerebral palsied is necessary. Some of these are day schools and others, such as those provided by the Spastics Society, are residential. The advantages and problems of the latter have been fully analysed in an article by Loring (1965). In a typical C.P. school, the staff to pupil ratio is high, usually one teacher to eight children, and in order to deal with the multiplicity of handicaps, much of the teaching is individual or in very small groups. Small units are also valuable for those children with major additional handicaps such as the partially sighted and partially hearing. The Spastics Society's schools provide especially for these and for other exceptional groups such as the subnormal, and the Grammar school pupils.

The teaching staff are able to specialize in developing ways of minimizing the many barriers to learning that we have mentioned, such as the difficulties in hand control, in speech, in eye movements, in co-ordinating hand and eye, in visual perception, and in problems of distractibility and emotional instability. Full use is made of special equipment such as adjustable desks and chairs to allow a proper sitting position, mechanical aids to communication such as electric typewriters and tape recorders, and experiments are carried out with more advanced equipment such as the P.O.S.S.U.M. and other equipment that can be operated by children having only a minimum of motor control. The P.O.S.S.U.M., for example, allows even grossly handicapped children to manage an electric typewriter at a reasonable rate, and the uses of this kind of electronic aid, for young children, have been well described in an article by Jenkin (1967). Another example of very specialized equipment is the Touch-Tutor (Thompson and Johnson, 1971), an electronic device that enables programmes of perceptual learning (such as matching and discriminating shapes, as a prelude to reading) to be given to children whose only means of response is to touch one of three display panels—this is enough for the Touch-Tutor to register the correctness or otherwise of the response and to reinforce the correct response by means of a tape recorded voice.

The development of these means of communication is usually sufficient to allow most children to follow an ordinary curriculum, although at a slower pace than in an ordinary school, since many of the ordinary experiences and informal opportunities for learning that ordinary children enjoy and which form a basis for later school learning have to be carefully provided for the very handicapped child, within a school time-table that is already interrupted by the needs for the various therapies. Experiments in new techniques of teaching are usually more easily carried out in specialized C.P. schools, since many of the staff have accumulated a great deal of experience, on the basis of which they can evaluate some of the latest advances in educational techniques, such as the Frostig method of visual perceptual training and the Peto method of conductive education.

Education is, of course, much more than a matter of learning a curriculum. Social and emotional development of children in special schools, especially learning to co-operate, to give and take, and consider the needs of others, is a prime consideration.

Day versus Residential Schooling

The decision to send the child away from home is often a very painful one to parents. Residential schools are necessary because in a sparsely populated area there are simply not enough very handicapped children to warrant setting up a special school. When the child is young, home tuition can sometimes fill a gap but is usually no substitute for a full school life. Residential schooling may also be necessary if a child's home is very unsettled. Most head teachers would agree that the age at which a child should enter residential schooling should be over 7 years, unless family circumstances are exceptional or the child is greatly frustrated through lack of expert teaching and therapy. Close contact must be maintained between the home and the child. Letters, telephone calls, frequent visits, including overnight stays by parents and the long holidays at home, all help to preserve the vital link between the child at boarding school and his family life. Frequent contact between home and school also helps the staff and parents to arrive at a united plan for helping the child, such as continuing treatment during the school holidays.

A handicap as complicated as cerebral palsy calls for a wide variety of day and residential schools and through the joint efforts in recent years of voluntary, local authority, and state agencies there appears to be a sufficient number of school places available in this country, except, as we have mentioned, at the nursery stage and for some multiple handicapped school children, such as the deaf, cerebral palsied children and those who are subnormal. This is not to say, however, that we can relax our efforts to improve the *effectiveness* of the education provided for certain groups, through research and experiment, for example into the best ways of teaching reading and arithmetic to children with perceptual disabilities, the best ways of teaching speechless children, of helping those who are overactive and distractible. At the lower end of the intellectual scale, there is an enormous job to be done. The services for the severely subnormal C.P. child (who represents nearly 25 per cent of the C.P. group) are far from adequate.

The Severely Subnormal C.P.

This large group has been relatively neglected in the early days of building up facilities. Priority was given to the more intelligent 'educable' spastics who appeared more likely to profit than the very retarded ones, and more likely to produce results that would help to break down public indifference. Facilities for the so-called 'ineducable' spastics (*i.e.* those whose mental levels tend to be below half of normal, and who are unable to learn reading, writing, and arithmetic and other basic academic skills sufficiently to use them effectively as tools) have therefore lagged seriously. This is indeed unfortunate since it meant that parents who were faced with caring for a child who has two major handicaps (subnormality and C.P.) received less help than those whose children had only one major handicap. The strain of caring for and training a child with two major disabilities at home is enormous. An extreme and very moving example of the family disruption that such a strain can provoke has been portrayed in Peter Nichol's play *A Day in the Death of Joe Egg*. A delicate balance has to be struck between the needs of the child, and those of his brothers and sisters, his mother and father: the relationships between all members are affected.

Clearly, care and training for such unfortunate children must be shared between the family and the wider community. Day facilities such as special care units, junior training schools, and local spastic group day centres are available in some areas. Here they learn the rudiments of self help in eating, dressing, toilet, and in mobility so far as they are able. They gain stimulation from play activities, from simple group activities, and from direct training in perception using the nursery school type of occupations. The social experience is of tremendous value to them and they can receive daily physiotherapy if they will respond. The parents at the same time gain a much needed respite from their daily care. Even three attendances a week is a very great help to the families concerned. In some cases the child responds so well that he can be upgraded to a formal school, and some of the older children may learn the rudiments of numbers and reading.

One quadriplegic lad of 20, known since 10 years of age, was attending a Day Training Centre regularly. His capacity was about the level of a 4½ years old. He could match colours and pictures, grade sizes, count in an automatic way, copy a circle, a cross but not a square or a star. He made an attempt to write his name. He echoed everything said to him, whatever was asked him. He named pictures and could carry on a simple conversation, using phrases, simple sentences and single words. His verbal comprehension was assessed at about a 5-year level. He was cheerful, co-operative, contented and most amenable. His father said he was most helpful at home in the house, enjoyed the Training Centre and spent a good deal of time living with his aunt in the country during holiday periods. He was learning basket work, swimming and football. He was able to feed, wash and dress himself (with the exception of tying his tie) as his quadriplegic condition was comparatively mild. He was said to be well liked in the Centre and the neighbourhood and would accompany his father on many trips and drink orange juice in the pub on a Saturday night with him. He was the only child and appeared to be well accepted by his kind understanding parents. His father was in a skilled job as an electrician. The general adjustment of this severely subnormal spastic lad was very good.

There is still a shortage of properly staffed Units for these children: in Sheila Hewett's (1970) sample, nearly one-third of the subnormal spastics over age 5 had no unit whatsoever to attend. It is expected that the new section of the Education Act (1970) will improve the quality and quantity of such services, since it places all subnormal children, including the severely subnormal, within the framework of the local Education Authorities, clearly recognizing that their prime need is for special educational, not health, facilities. The new Act should promote increasing numbers of properly trained teachers and assistants.

Residential care is needed for children whose handicaps are particularly severe and when home conditions are very difficult, and this can be provided in some hospitals for the severely subnormal. A few of these provide excellent training, but many are unfortunately understaffed, badly housed, and poorly equipped, and able to provide little more than custodial care, which many parents find unacceptable. Parents are rarely given any part to play in the upbringing of their child.

A model residential unit for 120 trainable severely subnormal children, excluding those who are so grossly retarded and physically handicapped as to need full time nursing care, was opened by the Spastics Society in 1966, where the staffing and facilities are first rate. The aims of this unit (Meldreth) are described by James Loring (1966) and the primary aim is that of promoting the child's social development. Towards this end children are placed in small family-type units, within which their capacities of self-help and some degree of independence, such as in dressing, are developed, together with their capacities to contribute towards the running of their community, by helping other children, coping with messages, feeding pets etc. Trained therapists and teachers are provided who have a particular interest in helping what must surely be the most challenging group of handicapped children. Much needed research into the best means of promoting progress such as by new training methods and scientific ways of measuring progress is being carried out (Burland, 1969; Burland and Petitt, 1970; Levett, 1970).

Meldreth then is a model project. Its cost is high but the ultimate benefit to hundreds of severely handicapped children and their families will undoubtedly be very great. Residential provision for the majority of severely subnormal spastics must be a local community responsibility. The alternative to large hospital institution is the small home or hostel, built to house about 26 severely subnormal children—a few of whom would also have severe cerebral palsy, the point being that the less physically handicapped majority could help the more heavily handicapped, and that all the children whether attending full-time (if the family is unable to manage) or as weekly boarders, and the staff, can retain links with the ordinary life of their families and the community, instead of being in effect segregated in large impersonal hospitals. These concepts of community care have been developed by Tizard (1964) and Kushlick (1965) and large scale studies are being completed in the Wessex region. Some authorities are providing hostel care of this kind with considerable success and at reasonable cost. Community based homes and hostels are unlikely to provide for all very severely physically and mentally handicapped children, some of whom need very intensive care and treatment that is better provided in a larger Unit, subdivided as far as possible, with medical and nursing help. But the majority of S.S.N. spastics do not need the latter, and every effort should be made to provide family and community type facilities, which will allow at least some measure of integration with the non-handicapped. It is to be hoped that this work marks the beginning of an era in which our generation faces up to some of the tremendous problems that previous generations have shamefully neglected.

The Intellectually Gifted C.P. and the Aims of Education

What of the children at the other end of the intellectual scale, those of sufficiently high intelligence to profit by academic schooling, examinations and higher education? As we have noted in a previous section, something like 5 per cent of C.P.s are of high average to superior intelligence (I.Q.s above 110) and just under 1 per cent are exceptionally bright (I.Q.s above 130). When the accompanying physical, sensory or speech handicaps are mild, no particular problems may arise, provided the spastic's aspirations are realistic; for example it must be appreciated that even a slight speech defect could be very troublesome to a would-be linguist. Particular stresses arise when high intelligence is accompanied by severe spasticity or athetosis, affecting many avenues of expression and communication. Then we have the special challenge of 'a mind imprisoned in a defective body'.

For example we can consider the case of David: he was a rhesus baby, jaundiced. Described as floppy: athetosis suspected at age 6 months, not feeding, sitting properly. Good attention and drive noted in his pre-school days but no speech developed. Hearing proved normal. Condition on entering special school for cerebral palsied children at age 7 described as 'very severe athetosis: no speech, very little control of hands and legs: virtually helpless'. Yet he was determined to communicate and could nod and shake his head in response to questions and showed good comprehension. By age 12 he was reading well, and could indicate the correct answers to complicated questions about what he had read. Psychologist estimated his intelligence as at least I.Q. 125, and noted good mathematical skills. Beginning to use electric typewriter well, using a headband with a pointer attached: could also 'converse' by pointing to letters on a board. Gained entry into specialized grammar school: grasp of English, Maths and History reported excellent but means of communication too slow for 'O' and 'A' level exams. Wide interests including travel and classical music. Transferred to higher education centre: worked extremely hard for examinations. Some emotional difficulties: unco-operative and irritable at times, especially with houseparent staff on whom he was completely dependent for washing, feeding, toileting, etc. Psychologist commented: the gap between his superior intelligence and his negligible motor and speech skills is so vast that he has, in a sense, rejected his body as worse than useless—merely a source of frustration. Experiments with P.O.S.S.U.M. equipment attempted, but his headband method of typing developed sufficiently for him to sit 'A' levels in several subjects. He passed and is considering university entrance: the practical daily care and social life problems will be tremendous. Hopes eventually to become a journalist, in spite of almost complete physical and speech handicaps, and has already published articles.

Fortunately, such cruel combinations of extremely high intelligence and extremely limited physical, speech and general communication abilities are rare, yet we can learn a great deal from extreme cases in understanding and planning facilities for the less extremely handicapped concerning, as we have seen, their need for careful assessment and extra help in at least partially overcoming some of the communication difficulties such as by the use of special equipment. As electronic engineering and computers become more highly developed in the next few years, it is likely that more special equipment to supplement impaired speech and hand control, will become available. For example the development of a 'talking machine' based on a tape recorder that could respond to easily and rapidly given instructions should be a possibility for some speechless children.

Extreme cases also give us clearer insight into the emotional conflicts that are more likely to arise in a sensitive, highly intelligent spastic than in a duller one. In David's case the discrepancy between his adult intellectual status on the one hand and his almost infant-like dependence on other people for daily care on the other, often led to conflicts, not only within David but within the persons relating to him. His behaviour at one moment was that of a very mature adult, the next as a dependent helpless child. The transitional period from the role of the dependent child to an independent adult through which most children slowly pass seems never ending for David.

Similar problems affect less extremely handicapped persons though fortunately to a much lesser degree in most cases. In a follow-up study of 20 C.P. children with I.Q.s ranging from approximately 115 to 140, one of the authors (A.H.B.) found that the majority were making satisfactory progress socially and educationally over the 5–10 year period that they were under review, in various schools, both normal and special.

Follow-up notes on three of these children were as follows:

J.P., a very intelligent little girl (I.Q. 127, paraplegic), with excellent verbal ability, attended a normal school and was very advanced in Reading and outstanding in Arithmetic. She wrote an expressive poem at the age of 9. She can use her left hand effectively. But writing remains a problem because at 10 years of age she cannot keep up with the rest of her class. It has been arranged for her to use a silent typewriter to help her. Speed of movement is also a difficulty, and the school is taking the view that undue allowance must not be made for her if she is to remain in a normal school. She has good sticking power and I think will win through. She has a lively sense of humour and seems well adjusted to her disability. She remarked when the class were preparing a Nativity Play, 'Funny if you made *me* an Angel. Fancy an Angel on crutches!' Her school commented, 'A charming and intelligent child, who, by her unfailing cheerfulness in face of her disability and by the amount of enjoyment she extracts from everything, is an inspiration to grownups and children alike.'

T.H. (I.Q. 129, triplegic) worked his way to the senior class of the normal junior school with some stress and much determination. Tears were shed when at first he could not play football. Now he takes part, lurching about with an unsteady gait, but with tremendous enthusiasm. He is very skilled in practical pursuits and an excellent reader, with a remarkably adult vocabulary. But he is a severely handicapped child and shortly the difficult decision will have to be made as to whether he will do best in a Spastic Grammar School or can compete in the normal one. One feels, to reach his best level he needs the aids and special facilities provided by such a school as the Thomas de la Rue Residential Spastic School. He is a sensitive and an adopted child who is liable to drive himself too hard, and he needs protection from too keen competition.

J.C. (I.Q. 119, athetoid) was a most interesting boy. He made good progress in a P.H. school, using his high intelligence effectively, learning to type and doing especially well in Mathematics. He achieved a

place at the Thomas de la Rue Spastic School and made good, working
for 'O' and eventually 'A' levels. He also is a boy of great determination,
battling against all odds and determined not to let his twin normal sister
outshine him. He is very eager to prove his capacity and shows almost
a dare-devil attitude. He insisted on going on a pony trek, on riding
in a chair unstrapped up Glen Shee in Scotland and is now determined to learn to drive a car, and this despite quite severe athetosis
and high tone deafness! He is rather strained and at $17\frac{1}{2}$ one felt he
was setting himself rather impossible standards. He is now beginning
to think of a job and determined to find one for himself when he has
completed his examinations. He recently wrote to the G.L.C. to
enquire prospects and is interested in the possibilities of working for
London Transport, planning new trunk roads and traffic improvements. One feels sure this boy will make good and find some satisfactory use for his good intelligence, and good practical ability. He is
quite determined to help himself, and shows impatience at maternal
solicitude.

The important factors that promote satisfactory adjustment
appear to be: (a) good drive and persistence and resilience on the
part of the child; (b) the support of concerned parents; (c) special
advice and attention regarding communication difficulties, such as
in writing and speech in their early school years, followed up by
considerable ingenuity on the part of the teachers in later years,
such as by encouraging the use of typewriters and dictation to
class-mates in cases where writing was impaired, and (d) that all
concerned with the pupil were striking a reasonable balance between
overprotection on the one hand and underprotection on the other,
i.e. neither showing too much concern over his handicap so that
he is more or less carried along as a passenger in the school, nor
at the other extreme of making impossible demands such as subjects demanding quick and accurate motor control (P.E., craft-
work, etc.). Some of the difficulties that intelligent C.P.s have in
adjusting to normal grammar school are outlined in an article by
Gardner (1968) discussing the case of an athetoid girl whose difficulties were more in social-emotional adjustment than educational
progress: the girl was eventually transferred to a grammar stream
in a secondary school for C.P. pupils and settled well to the less
demanding atmosphere there. Specialized grammar schooling is
available through the Spastics Society for very handicapped bright
pupils and the success rate in academic examinations is high, partly
through the skill of experienced teachers who not only know their
subjects but who have grasped the more difficult art of communicating with very handicapped pupils.

For the not too severely handicapped the aims of education can

be very similar to those that are advocated for ordinary children—
a blend of aims, of self-fulfilment, of the development of potentialities, intellectual, physical, emotional, the aims of working
towards a career and of service to the community. These various
aims are not always completely compatible for ordinary children:
for the handicapped pupils even greater difficulties are apt to
arise. The presence of a considerable handicap means that achievements are bound to be low in certain areas. Self-fulfilment aims
(such as an interest in art or poetry) may conflict with vocational
and economic aims. Ordinary children can usually compromise,
pursuing both aims and managing tolerably well in both. But the
handicapped spastic has less scope: his range of alternatives is
limited, such as by the simple time factor for example (the fact
that he may need five times longer to type an essay than it takes
an ordinary child to write one). Should he therefore abandon the
self-fulfilment aims such as his interest in art, and concentrate
solidly on academic work such as English and maths that may lead
to 'O' and 'A' level exam successes and a professional career later?
But there is a further problem: academic examinations are often
the key to a professional career for ordinary pupils; they are not
necessarily so for very handicapped pupils. So the very handicapped
pupil may have to aim at a less demanding career, such as a semi-
skilled or technical one rather than a professional post. Should the
curriculum therefore be altered accordingly, such as spending less
time on English and more on technical drawing and workshop
experience? Does this also mean that he should spend more time
on improving his motor skills such as through some of the intensive
methods of training that we have mentioned, like the Peto method?
Follow-up studies of school children in various types of special
schools suggest that their motor skills do not improve significantly
as they go through the school and perhaps more intensive motor
training would pay better dividends than certain academic subjects.
But if the pupil is very severely handicapped we might in any case
expect very little motor improvement, even through very intensive
training. Should we in these cases abandon the idea of working
towards employment for gain—and concentrate on self-fulfilment
aims?

Many of these questions were debated at a multidisciplinary
Spastics Society seminar, including groups of psychologists, social
workers, teachers, medical officers, Y.E.O.s and others (Gardner,
1969): no simple answers emerged and there is still some uncer-
tainty about the aims of education for the severely handicapped

pupil and what 'style of life' we might envisage following certain aims.

However, a small number of severely handicapped C.P.s have followed academic careers at university level with some success. Some universities have been extremely helpful in providing the necessary extra facilities: York, for example, has been built with a view to providing easy access for physically handicapped students. Fellow students on the whole have been helpful with matters such as transport, accommodation, providing copies of lecture notes for spastics whose writing is too slow, and so on. In a U.S. study (Muthard, 1968) it was noted that the attainments of a sample of eighty handicapped students were on the whole somewhat lower than ordinary students and that subsequent careers were quite satisfactory but some problems remained in that although most of the handicapped graduates obtained jobs, these were seldom at the level or salary to which they felt entitled. As Mary Greaves (1969) who has first-hand experience of problems herself points out, better counselling services are needed (as indeed they are for ordinary students) including the pooling of experience by appointments officers so that further lessons can be learned about providing the best opportunities for handicapped graduates.

Further Education, Training and Employment Prospects

We have touched on the difficulties of transition from school to work that beset very handicapped adolescents, as they leave the relatively planned and ordered atmosphere of school and are often suddenly thrust into the wider world. For many C.P.s, whether they be mildly, moderately or severely handicapped intellectually or physically, additional help is usually needed over the transition period, particularly in respect of their need to develop some degree of social and emotional independence. A period of further education and training is often useful such as those provided by the Spastics Society which runs residential centres of various kinds, some providing scope for further academic studies, some for general education and social training, some for vocational training, either technical or commercial, and there are, of course, schemes available through other agencies that provide for a variety of handicaps. The Department of Employment also provides training centre places though these are usually only suitable for the mildly handicapped.

Surveys of representative groups of spastics, *i.e.* including those who are mildly as well as those who are moderately and severely handicapped, by Ingram (1964) and Hellings (1964), have shown that about 40–50 per cent obtained open or sheltered (earnings near to normal) employment. Many are helped by an early assessment of their employment potentialities such as by attending a Spastics Society assessment course (Morgan, 1966). Those spastics too handicapped for employment or special vocational training can attend Work Centres. The Spastics Society has over 25 such Centres, where a variety of simple work opportunities are available even for the very handicapped, who can at least earn considerable pocket-money. Some Work Centres have hostels attached for those spastics whose homes are in relatively isolated areas, or whose families can no longer provide for their care.

Clearly great efforts have to be made to ensure reasonable employment prospects for handicapped persons, by the many agencies involved, state, Local Authority and voluntary agencies. Mary Greaves (1969) in her very useful study of the employment of the disabled, emphasized the need for some degree of integration of these services. Much also depends on the attitudes of employers and fellow workers. These are influenced by a variety of factors ranging from the general state of employment in the economy, to the deeper attitudes of the community towards handicapped persons in their midst. Some of the older ideas of segregation of the handicapped still persist and in a sense handicapped persons form a 'minority group'. Being demonstratively different in some respects from the ordinary population they are apt to become victims of some of the prejudices and discrimination that confront most minority groups—based on ignorance, stereotyped thinking and fear. It is our job to dispel these prejudices.

Organizations and Literature

The parents' first consultations are likely to be with their family doctor, but since cerebral palsy is not a common condition, he is likely to refer to specialists, hospital services, and to Local Authority services which are usually available through the Medical Officer of Health and the Social Service department for the area.

As the child becomes older his needs become less medically, and more socially and educationally orientated. In addition to Local Authority services, the Spastics Society provides a variety of services. The Society is a voluntary organization, well described by Richard Dimbleby (1964), which has over 170 local groups, and provides assessment and training and educational services, some in conjunction with Local Authorities and Hospital Boards. The Spastics Society advisory services are open to all, and information about its various services, such as assessments, schools, careers, help with holidays and family emergencies, clubs for teenage spastics, aids and appliances, etc. is given in the pamphlets *The Spastics Society Year Book, Schools and Centres*, obtainable from the Services Department of the Spastics Society, 12 Park Crescent, London, W1. The Society publishes *Spastics News* monthly, and contributes to more technical journals, such as *Special Education* and *Developmental Medicine and Child Neurology*. Parents pamphlets such as the following are also published occasionally: *The Early Years* (1967); *Facts about Cerebral Palsy* (1967); *The Hemiplegic Child* (1964); *Spastic Cerebral Palsy* (1970). Several films suitable for professional and parent groups, such as 'Three for Society' and 'Stress', are also available through the Spastics Society.

References

ABERCROMBIE, M. J. L. (1964). Perceptual and visuo-motor disorders in cerebral palsy. *Little Club Clin. Dev. Med.*, No. 11. London: Spastics Society/Heinemann.
ASHER, F. and SCHONELL, F. E. (1950). A survey of 400 cases of cerebral palsy in childhood. *Archs. Dis. Child.*, **25**, 124, 360.
BLENCOWE, S. N., editor (1969). *Cerebral Palsy and the Young Child*. Edinburgh and London: Livingstone.
BOBATH, K. (1966). The motor deficit in patients with cerebral palsy. *Little Club Clin. Dev. Med.*, No. 23. London: Spastics Society/Heinemann.
BOWLEY, A. H. (1967a). Studying children from Cheyne. *Spec. Educ. incorp. Spast. Quarterly* **56**, No. 1.
BOWLEY, A. H. (1967b). A Follow-Up Study of 64 Children with Cerebral Palsy. *Dev. Med. Child Neurol.*, **9**, No. 2.
BRIMER, M. A. and DUNN, L. M. (1963). *English Picture Vocabulary Tests*. Bristol: Educational Evaluation Enterprises.
BURGEMEISTER, B. *et al.* (1954). *Columbia Mental Maturity Scale*. Revised Edition. New York: World Book Co.
BURLAND, R. (1969). The development of the verbal regulation of behaviour in cerebrally palsied (multiply handicapped) children. *J. Ment. Subnormality*, **XV**, Part 2.
BURLAND, R. and PETITT, P. F. (1970). *Meldreth Assessment and Training Chart 1. Personal Independence*. The Spastics Society/Meldreth Training School.
CASHDAN, A. (1966). Child rearing practices and the development of the handicapped child. In *The Spastic School Child and the Outside World*, edited by J. Loring and A. Mason. Spastics Society/Heinemann.
COTTON, E. and PARNELL, M. (1967). From Hungary: the Peto Method. *Special Education*, **56**, No. 4.
CROTHERS, B. and PAINE, R. S. (1959). *The Natural History of Cerebral Palsy*. Cambridge: Harvard University Press.
CRUICKSHANK, W. M. (1961). *A Teaching Method for Brain injured and Hyperactive children*. New York: Syracuse University Press.
CRUICKSHANK, W. M. (1966). *Cerebral Palsy: its Implications and Community Problems*. New York: Syracuse University Press.

50   THE HANDICAPPED CHILD

6

* DEPARTMENT OF EDUCATION AND SCIENCE (1970). *Diagnostic and Assessment Units for Young Handicapped Children. Education Survey 9.* London: H.M.S.O.

DOLL, E. A. (1947). *Vineland Social Maturity Scale.* Nashville: American Guidance Service Inc.

DOUGLAS, A. A. (1960). The eyes and vision in infantile cerebral palsy. *Trans. Ophthal. Sec. U.K.*, **80**, 311.

* DUNSDON, M. I. (1952). *The Educability of Cerebral Palsied Children.* London: National Foundation for Educational Research.

EVANS, C. M. (1968). *Survey of the Spastics Society's Services.* London: The Spastics Society.

FINNIE, N. R. (1968). *Handling the Young Cerebral Palsied Child at Home.* London: Heinemann.

FISCH, L. (1957). Hearing impairment and cerebral palsy. *Speech*, **21**, 43.

FRANCIS-WILLIAMS, J. (1970). *Children with Specific Learning Difficulties.* Oxford: Pergamon Press.

FROSTIG, M. (1968). Testing as a basis for educational therapy. *Assessment of the Cerebral Palsied Child for Education*, edited by James Loring. London: The Spastics Society/Heinemann.

FROSTIG, M. *et al.* (1964). *The Marianne Frostig Developmental Test of Visual Perception.* Palo Alto, California: Consulting Psychologists Press.

GARDNER, L. (1969). Planning for planned dependence *Special Education*, **58**, No. 1.

GARDNER, L. (1970a). Handicapped children in ordinary schools. *Teacher's World*, No. 3141.

GARDNER, L. (1970b). Assessment and outcome. *Special Education*, **59**, No. 4.

GARDNER, L. and JOHNSON, J. (1964). The long-term assessment and experimental education of retarded cerebral palsied children. *Dev. Med. Child Neurol.*, **6**, 250.

° GIBBS, N. (1965). Some educational problems of children with cerebral palsy. *Spastics News*, August.

GREAVES, MARY (1969). *Work and Disability.* London: British Council for Rehabilitation of the Disabled.

GUNZBURG, H. C. (1966). *Progress Assessment Charts.* London: National Association for Mental Health.

HELLINGS, D. A. (1964). *Spastic School Leavers.* London: The Spastics Society.

HENDERSON, J. L. (1961). *Cerebral Palsy in Childhood and Adolescence.* Edinburgh: Livingstone.

HEWETT, S. with J. and E. NEWSON (1970). *The Family and the Handicapped Child.* George Allen & Unwin.

H.M.S.O. (1967). *Children and their Primary School.* London.

HOLT, K. S. (1965). *Assessment of Cerebral Palsy*, Vol. I. London: Lloyd-Luke.

HOLT, K. S. and REYNELL, J. K. (1967). *Assessment of Cerebral Palsy*, Vol. II. London: Lloyd-Luke.

* HOPKINS, T., BICE, H. V. and COLTON, K. (1954). *Evaluation and Education of the Cerebral Palsied Child.* Washington, D.C.: International Council for Exceptional Children.

ILLINGWORTH, R. S. (1958). *Recent Advances in Cerebral Palsy.* London: Churchill.

INGRAM, T. T. S. *et al.* (1964). Living with cerebral palsy. *Little Club Clin. Dev. Med.*, No. 14. London: The Spastics Society M.E.I.U./W. Heinemann.

JENKIN, R. (1967). Possum: a new communication aid. *Special Education*, **56**, No. 1.

KIRK, S. A. and McCARTHY, J. J. (1961). *Illinois Test of Psycholinguistic Abilities.* Urbana, Illinois: Institute for Research on Exceptional Children.

KUSHLICK, A. (1965). Community services for the mentally subnormal: a plan for experimental evaluation. *Proc. Roy. Soc. Med.*, **58**, 374.

KUSHLICK, A. (1966). A community service for the mentally subnormal. *Social Psychiatry*, 1, 2 and 73.

LEVETT, L. M. (1970). *A Method of Communication for Non-Speaking Severely Subnormal Children.* London: The Spastics Society.

LEVITT, S. (1970). Principles of treatment in C.P. *Norw. J. Physiotherapy*, No. 10.

LEVIN, M. L., BRIGHTMAN, I. J. and BURTT, E. J. (1949). The Problem of Cerebral Palsy. *New York J. Med.*, **49**, 2793.

LINDON, R. L. (1963). The Pultibec system for the medical assessment of handicapped children. *Devl. Med. Child Neurol.*, **5**, No. 2.

LORING, J. A. (1965). The contribution of a voluntary society to special education. In *Teaching the Cerebral Palsied Child.* Spastics Society/Heinemann.

LORING, J. A. (1966). Meldreth: a pioneer unit. *Special Education*, **55**, No. 1.

LORING, J. A., editor (1968). *The Assessment of the Cerebral Palsied Child for Education.* London: Spastics Society/Heinemann.

LURIA, A. R. (1961). *The Role of Speech in the Regulation of Normal and Abnormal Behaviour*, edited by J. Tizard. Oxford: Pergamon Press.

MARGULEC, I., editor (1966). *Cerebral Palsy in Adolescence and Adulthood: a Rehabilitation Study.* Jerusalem: Academic Press.

MORGAN, MARGARET R. (1966). Predictions, Provision and Progress. In *The Spastic School Child and the Outside World*, edited by J. Loring and A. Mason. Spastics Society/Heinemann.

MUTHARD, J. E. and HUTCHISON, J. (1968). *Cerebral Palsied College Students: their Education and Employment.* Gainesville: University of Florida.

NIELSEN, H. H. (1966). *A Psychological Study of Cerebral Palsied Children.* Copenhagen: Munksgaard.

OSWIN, MAUREEN (1967). *Behaviour Problems amongst Children with Cerebral Palsy.* Bristol: Wright.

PIAGET, J. and INHELDER, B. (1956). *The Child's Conception of Space.* London: Routledge & Kegan Paul.

RABINOWITZ, A. I. (1966). A Nursery School in Shropshire. *Special Education*, **55**, No. 4.

REYNELL, J. (1969). *Infant and Young Children's Language Scales, Manual and Test Material.* Slough, Bucks.: National Foundation for Educational Research.

RUTTER, M., GRAHAM, P. and YULE, W. (1970). A Neuropsychiatric Study in Childhood. *Little Club Clin. Devl. Med.* Nos. 35 and 36. London: Spastics International Medical Publications/Heinemann.

TANSLEY, A. E. (1967). *Reading and Remedial Reading.* London: Routledge & Kegan Paul.

THOMPSON, D. A., and JOHNSON, J. (1971). The Touch-Tutor at Hawksworth Hall. *Special Education,* **60,** No. 1.

TIZARD, J. (1964). *Community Services for the Mentally Handicapped.* London: Oxford University Press.

WEDELL, K. (1963). The Visual Perception of Cerebral Palsied Children. *Child Psychol. Psychiat.,* **1,** 215.

WEDELL, K. (1968). Perceptual motor difficulties. *Special Education,* **57,** No. 4.

WOLF, J. M., editor (1969). *The Results of Treatment in Cerebral Palsy.* Springfield, Illinois: Thomas.

WOODS, G. E. (1957). *Cerebral Palsy in Childhood.* Bristol: Wright.

WOODS, G. E. (1963). A Lowered Incidence of Infantile Cerebral Palsy. *Dev. Med. Child Neurol.,* **5,** 449.

YOUNGHUSBAND, E. *et al.,* editors (1970). *Living with Handicap.* London: National Children's Bureau.

CHAPTER II

THE CHILD WITH BRAIN DAMAGE

Introduction

THE term 'brain damage' is unsatisfactory as it presumes more knowledge about certain children than we actually have, but the term has not quite outlived its usefulness in drawing our attention to a very intriguing and heterogeneous group of children, whose special learning and behaviour difficulties have become much better understood in recent years. What sort of learning and behaviour difficulties do we mean? Parents' and teachers' descriptions often include the following features: 'He is restless, fidgety, difficult to manage; has no self-control, is undisciplined and cannot stand frustration; she breaks things impulsively and has lots of accidents; she is bird-witted, inattentive, distractible, always on the move; he is clumsy and hopeless at school work in spite of high intelligence; she can talk the hind leg off a donkey, but cannot put anything down on paper.'

Now many of these features can be applied to almost every child at one time or another: normal children at certain ages and in certain situations are expected to show some of these features: emotionally disturbed children show many and so do some children brought up in socially and culturally deprived areas. But do particular, long standing combinations of some of these features, suggest a category of handicap—that of brain damage or minimal cerebral dysfunctioning? It is likely that they do, although there are many ambiguities in this field.

We have briefly discussed brain damaged children in other sections of this book, such as the spastic and hydrocephalic children whose brain damage has well recognized physical accompaniments, such as lack of motor control. Readers will be familiar with brain damage in adults, such as those due to head injuries, leading to a temporary loss of speech (aphasia) and strokes leading to some loss of control of one side of the body (hemiplegia). When it comes to new-born and young children, who may have no definite physical signs, the concept of brain damage is on a much less firm foundation. We are not yet clear exactly what it involves, concerning the neurological causes of their condition, the effects on the learning and behaviour of the child, and their remediation.

It was Strauss and Lehtinen (1947) who in the Forties crystallized many of the ideas about brain damage and their effects on behaviour, that were intriguing neurologists, psychologists and educators around that time. Looking at children whose learning was retarded, Strauss considered that most cases could be classified into two major groups (with some overlap): (1) the endogenous group: those whose retardation was caused by familial or genetic factors (such as mongol children whom we now know to have a chromosome defect). (2) the exogenous group, those whose retardation 'came from without' as it were, due to some damaging agent often during pregnancy or around the time of birth which had impaired an immature brain that would have otherwise developed normally. For example, a virus infection to the mother during the early months of pregnancy, such as rubella, is believed to be one cause of brain damage.

Strauss' major interest, however, was not so much in the causes, but in the behaviour and learning of these children. He believed that the brain damaged group showed certain patterns of behaviour and learning, notably involving hyperactivity and distractibility, and linking with perceptual and behaviour difficulties, that fall into a recognized pattern, and could not be explained or understood by reference to other explanatory concepts. In other words such children could not be regarded as generally mentally subnormal, or emotionally disturbed as a result of poor parental attitudes, or affected by social deprivation, or by physical and sensory handicaps such as visual and hearing difficulties. The explanations instead were along neurological lines, to the effect that the higher nervous system had suffered some kind of damage and that this resulted in odd, patchy, uneven behaviour and learning.

Subsequent research suggests that Strauss overstated his case: the evidence for any definite patterns of behaviour is tenuous: although some children show some characteristics, the link with neurological causes is even more tenuous. However, Strauss' ideas are a valuable starting point in this field. Let us briefly consider a case history.

GRAHAM: referred to the Schools Psychological Service for 'backwardness and emotional disturbance' at aged 7. Psychological interview showed normal general intelligence (Binet I.Q. approximately 100) but with many odd and uneven features. Graham was noted to be particularly poor at copying and creating drawings: on purely practical tests of his performance abilities, severe visual motor and visual perceptual difficulties were shown (Wechsler Performance I.Q. approximately 60 compared to a Verbal I.Q. of over 100).

His educational attainments were also uneven: his reading was almost normal whilst his writing and arithmetic were practically nil. He could count a little by rote but had no knowledge of number concepts.

His major problems were in his behaviour: his distractibility and restlessness were extreme. In the individual interview he showed considerable 'forced responsiveness', was easily distracted by slight visual and auditory cues, and quite unable to stick to the point in conversation. Linked with this was his excessive motor disinhibition—he seemed compelled to touch things and could rarely sit and contemplate anything. He also showed occasional perseveration, repeating questions, drawings, and odd movements, such as obsessionally patting his head. His speech was telegraphic.

His general behaviour was even worse. He was generally hyperactive, restless and unconforming in the classroom, wandering around, failing to join in group activities, lying on the floor when he felt inclined or under the teacher's desk, showing many odd movements, talking to himself. He was such an interference with the work and behaviour of other children that he was offered only part-time infant schooling after the age of $5\frac{1}{2}$ and excluded completely from school at the age of 7. The school noted his vivid imagination, but apart from his keenness on animals, they could find nothing positive to say about him and tended to regard him as subnormal.

The medical history was suggestive but not very definite. He had been diagnosed at the age of 3 as a case of mild hypotonia and clumsiness. His E.E.G. showed nothing strongly abnormal. His early history showed some difficulties at birth. His mother was unwell throughout the pregnancy with a threatened abortion, and he was jaundiced on the second day and seemed sleepy and did not suck very well for some time. Developmental milestones were rather slow; he walked at 17 months but fell easily. He was treated for 'knock knees'.

His family is of professional class and there are two younger normal siblings. His mother was a very sensible, warm person and was becoming very despondent about Graham's behaviour both at home and at school. The parents were at a loss to account for his behaviour and at odds with the school authorities.

This brief picture of Graham's history and behaviour is typical of many children who are designated as brain injured. His difficulties cannot be explained by reference to general subnormality or to parental handling—which had been excellent; he had no obvious physical or sensory handicaps, nor was he deprived of experience. Let us see what light other studies can throw on these sorts of problems, first dealing with the question of the incidence and causes of brain damage.

Incidence and Causes

The incidence of brain damaged children amongst those attending normal schools is estimated to be quite high, varying between 1 and 7 per cent of the general school population which means that most age groups in most schools might have one or two such children. Estimates of the numbers are bound to vary because of the vagueness of the definition, once we leave the relatively well defined groups of brain injured children, such as spastics who show definite neurological signs. In a large scale study of 810 children aged 8–9, attending normal schools in the Cambridge region, Brenner (1966) suggested that nearly 7 per cent show difficulties on visual perceptual and visual motor tests that are commonly used to assess brain damage. In a study which involved the screening of over 2000 junior school children, one of the present writers (Bowley, 1969) produced a more realistic figure of 1·5 per cent and we will consider this study in more detail later.

The medical background of such children usually shows some suggestive features such as a history of birth difficulties, including signs of asphyxia, jaundice, or either a too rapid or too prolonged delivery, but these are rarely conclusive, for many children for whom birth difficulties are reported show quite normal development later on. E.E.G. studies at any age are also apt to be inconclusive, for as Schulman (1965) points out, many normal children show abnormal E.E.G. recordings and some very abnormal children show no abnormal E.E.G. records. Objective techniques for detecting the presence of brain damage are still in their early stages.

The causes of brain damage are many and varied and can occur either during pregnancy or at birth or after birth and at any time in later life, such as due to encephalitis. During pregnancy, as we have mentioned, virus infections can occasionally cause damage and so might excessive drug taking or excessive exposure to radiation. During birth anything that might interfere with the foetal oxygen supply to the brain might be suspect. Rhesus incompatability can occasionally cause brain damage, but modern preventive measures in the case of this defect are nearly always effective. After birth, rare diseases, such as meningitis, can occasionally lead to brain damage: so of course can serious head injuries.

Our concern in this chapter is mainly with the behaviour and learning difficulties that often accompany brain damage. As Birch

(1964) has pointed out, our knowledge of the causes of brain damage is very sketchy: there are many kinds of brain damage ranging from minimal, hardly detectable states to severe and obvious conditions. We will not find a single cause and every individual case may show some unique features. The efforts of psychologists, therapists, educationalists and social workers should centre on the description and understanding of the behaviour, and the educational and social needs of these children—a difficult task when present knowledge of the neurological background is so sketchy, but a task which cannot be ignored. Children such as Graham simply cannot be ignored.

The Behaviour and Learning of Brain Damaged Children

The most frequently reported behaviour and learning difficulties in brain damaged children were listed by Clements (1962, 1966) in the following order:

(a) Hyperactivity and restlessness.
(b) Perceptual motor impairments, such as poor drawing and constructional skills.
(c) Emotional erraticness, such as sudden emotional outbursts without obvious causes.
(d) Clumsiness and poor motor co-ordination.
(e) Attention disorders, such as distractibility and perseveration.

Most clinicians working in this field would feel that a child showing several of these features over a lengthy period might be brain damaged and that such an explanation is more plausible than alternative explanations, such as mental deficiency, and environmentally caused emotional disturbance or physical or sensory handicaps—assuming of course that these other causes have been excluded. The term 'brain damage', as we have said, is unsatisfactory, but if it has been carefully considered and applied to a particular child then it implies that the other causes have been excluded. The important question is can we find out more about these difficulties and do something about them? Let us describe the difficulties in more detail and comment on some of the experimental treatment and remedial work that has been carried out.

(a) *Hyperactivity.*—Hyperactivity is often mentioned in reports on brain damaged children, partly because of its nuisance value, as is implied in terms often used: 'restless', 'disruptive', 'disorganized', etc. Cruickshank (1961, 1966) laid much emphasis on hyperactivity and its control, the theory being that in the normal brain, one of the functions of the cortex is to *inhibit* immediate motor reactions to a stimulus—partly to give us time to think about what we are doing. In the brain damaged child this inhibitory function of the cortex is presumed to be much reduced, and he seems almost compelled to make immediate physical response to what he sees and hears, and his parents complain: 'He grabs at anything at the table as soon as it appears' and teachers complain 'He leaves his desk and darts to the window whenever he hears a distant fire-engine'. With ordinary children there is usually a process of thought or feeling, however brief, that intervenes, between the perception of the stimulus on the one hand, and their motor response on the other (except of course in the case of reflex actions, such as blinking to a very loud sound). With the brain damaged child this intervening thought or feeling seems very reduced at times, and his behaviour is impulsive and overactive.

Research studies on hyperactivity have not been very clear cut. Indeed some research casts doubts on the very existence of hyper-activity. For example Schulman (1965) carried out some very objective measurements, using an actometer, in the form of a modified self-winding watch strapped to the child's wrist and ankle, the total day activity levels of 35 boys of roughly E.S.N. intelligence were recorded: no significant differences were found between those designated as brain damaged and those who were not. Other researchers, however, using different types of measurement, have shown different results, *e.g.* the Hutts (1963, 1964) used a special playroom to observe the child's movements: starting with the room quite bare, the child's movements were plotted on numbered squares on the floor space, and objective measurements of levels and directions of activities were recorded, in response to various controlled conditions in the room, for example the presence of a box of bricks, the presence of a passive adult, an active adult, etc. The use of this technique in measuring a reduction in a child's hyperactivity following certain drug treatments has been demon-strated. These studies show the importance of accurate measure-ments in helping us to reach an understanding of complex behaviour such as hyperactivity. The activity level of the child depends a great deal on what kind of situation he is placed in, and what adults are expecting him to do. It is perhaps the relative *aimlessness* of the brain damaged child's behaviour, in the eyes of the adult observer that is troublesome, rather than the actual amount of activity.

As for the treatment of hyperactivity, this work is still in its experimental stages: some alleviation through drug treatment has been reported, but medical opinion is divided on this matter, for though it may be possible to damp down the activity levels of some children, the side effects of massive sedation are not always acceptable.

Educationalists such as Cruickshank (1961) have tried to manage hyperactivity by arranging for a type of education that encourages plenty of motor response within a controlled setting, *e.g.* making great use of peg boards in simple number work, so that the child can enjoy plenty of 'motor expression', at least in the early stages. Parents' handling of the hyperactive child at home, must of course include a firm framework of discipline. For example, there must be times and places in which the child must be persuaded, gently but firmly, that he must show control, such as in his bedroom in the evening, with the knowledge that he will be able to 'let off steam' in some other time and place, such as in the garden. Excessive punishment or permissiveness is unlikely to help such a child to gradually gain more control of his impulsive movements— movements which of course may often appear to a parent to be a kind of deliberate disobedience, when in fact this is not the case with most of the behaviour of neurologically impaired children. Hyperactivity is related to another difficult feature of brain damaged children—that of attention disorders.

(b) *Attention disorders.*—These are more subtle than hyper-activity. Very active children are bound to be inattentive, such as certain youngsters who have had a serious attack of meningitis, and whose behaviour at least for some months after their illness can only be described as 'highly acrobatic': they rarely sit or stand still long enough to attend sufficiently to learn very much about a particular toy or object in the room. But attention disorders also occur in children who are not overactive: as we mentioned in our chapter on the cerebral palsied child, some children are highly distractible, showing great difficulty in controlling or focussing their attention. It would be wrong to call them inattentive: in a sense they are overattentive—but to too many stimuli. They seem to be unable to refrain from responding to stimuli that most children would regard as irrelevant, *e.g.* in the classroom, things that most children might find only slightly distracting, such as an ink blot on a page, the brain injured child is apt to find very distracting. Furthermore, his distractibility is not confined to the visual sphere: auditory and tactile stimulation can be equally distracting.

Objective measures of distractibility have not yet been satis-factorily carried out. Cruickshank and his co-workers attached great importance to distractibility, considering it to be a major factor, together with hyperactivity, in the behaviour and learning difficulties of brain damaged children: he used various means of measuring distractibility, including various figure/background tests, such as marble boards in which patterns had to be copied, and briefly exposed pictures of objects, all against a confusing background. In his very thorough 1957 study (revised 1965) on 325 brain damaged (cerebral palsied) children, great difficulties in these tests were revealed, compared to the performance of ordinary children, and these difficulties were largely thought to be due to distractibility—the theory being that the distractible child was unable to refrain from irrelevant 'background' stimuli, which diverted the child's attention from the main 'figure' to which he should be attending.

Educational implications of distractibility have been carefully studied by Cruickshank and he advocated, like Strauss, radical educational measures, such as setting up 'distraction free' classrooms, which were relatively bare, silent, small cubicles, providing a visually neutral background, against which the work material could be thrown into relief. The design of the work material itself followed the same reasoning, *e.g.* in a typical reading book the words are brightly coloured, against a perfectly plain background.

The effectiveness of this type of education has not yet been convincingly demonstrated and it has not gained wide-spread support in the U.K. This is partly because distractibility is not simply a matter of a distracting environment: it 'comes from within' and although a distractible child can probably be helped a little by having an environment that does not contain too many diversions, his difficulties cannot necessarily be solved in this way. In Roy Brown's studies, for example (1965, 1967) using formboard errors as a measure of distractibility amongst 28 severely subnormal children attending a Junior Training Centre, no differences were noted between the child's scores in their usual highly decorated, nursery type classroom, and their scores within a bare experimental room. Brown also differs from Cruickshank about the origin of some distractibility, pointing out that in some children it might be caused by poor environmental experience, such as prolonged hospitalization accompanied by a lack of stimulation, rather than brain damage. Brown's studies, however, are no more conclusive than Cruickshank's.

One cannot help feeling that some aspects of modern infant and junior schooling, with their emphasis on 'activity' methods, involving multi-sensory stimulation, and a great deal of practical activities, could aggravate the distractibility of some brain injured children—and the latter are likely to respond better to somewhat sheltered conditions, at least during the early educational years.

Distractibility not only occurs within one sensory system, such as the visual system: as Abercrombie (1965, 1968) points out, several sensory systems are involved in even simple activities, such as copying a diamond. The child's successful performance depends not only on visual information but on the sense of touch and movement as he guides the pencil: messages are fed back to the child through several senses about the correctness or otherwise about what he has done; since the child cannot attend to several at once, they compete for his attention, and the brain damaged child finds this particularly confusing.

Our educational measures must allow for these types of difficulties, and this calls for a careful consideration of what processes are actually involved in learning a particular task, and how these processes can be simplified. Our present understanding of distractibility is too patchy to point to any definite educational measures: in any case no single factor in the complex learning and behaviour problems of brain damaged children can be divorced from other difficulties that are present. Some educationalists have concentrated on motor inco-ordination as a very important factor of brain damaged children and suggest that measures to improve co-ordination may have a generalized effect on the whole learning of children with neurological impairments.

(c) *Clumsiness and Motor Inco-ordination.*—Clumsiness and motor inco-ordination are obvious in most cases of severe brain damage and the question arises whether slight clumsiness and inco-ordination might, by analogy, indicate the condition of minimal brain damage. According to many workers (Walton, 1962; Stott, 1966) this seems likely in the case of many children. Traditional neurological investigations have always included the study of both gross motor movements, such as balance and symmetry, and fine motor control, such as of hand and facial muscles, as possible indicators of dysfunctioning in certain parts of the brain. These clinical investigations, however, are rarely fine enough to detect minimal cases of motor inco-ordination and clumsiness, especially in younger children: therefore efforts have been made in recent years to develop finer standardized scales of 'motor proficiency' based on 'norms' that are applicable for children at various ages, including large numbers of children attending normal schools. For example several versions of Oseretzky's original scale are now available and these are proving useful: in a study of 9/10-year-old school children in the Isle of Wight, (Rutter, Graham and Yule, 1970) used a shortened twelve-item version of the Sloan scale of motor proficiency, and showed a high percentage (12 per cent) of 'severely clumsy' children amongst poor readers compared to ordinary readers. Another motor proficiency test developed by the same team is 'motor impersistence', which refers to the inability to sustain a voluntary act, such as closing eyes, protruding one's tongue, for a period of 20 seconds: failures on this test showed a considerable correlation with clumsiness.

Since minor impairments show some link with educational difficulties, the question arises, that if the motor impairments can be improved it is possible that there will be an accompanying improvement in educational and other skills. This approach under-lies several educational and therapeutic programmes, and we have already mentioned some in our chapter on cerebral palsied children, such as the Peto method of conductive education. Kephart in the United States, and Tansley in England, have developed educa-tional programmes designed to help 'clumsy' children. These pay great attention in the early stages, to improving motor responses, as a basis for more complex perceptual motor learning later. The carefully graduated programme of motor training, for example in Kephart's work starts with: (a) general posture and balance: these determine a child's 'point of reference' as far as his observations of objects in the external world and their position relative to him (left, right, up, down, diagonal, etc.) are concerned: (b) locomotion, including creeping, crawling, running, walking, hopping, skipping and jumping, by which a child explores the space around him: (c) contact, including the manipulation of objects with the hand, reaching, grasping, releasing; an impairment in any of these processes could reduce the information a child gains through manipulation: (d) receipt and propulsion: these include the child's relationship to moving objects, such as catching a ball and similar activities which involve a complex sequence of perceptual and motor actions.

Kephart has described his basic motor training programme in detail (1961, 1968) and Tansley (1967) working mostly with E.S.N. children in Birmingham, many of whom were considered to show minimal brain damage, has done valuable work in suggesting how such basic motor training can be linked later with perceptual training, that in turn may help to improve reading skills.

Valuable work in many aspects of motor skills and their train-ing has also been carried out by Connolly (1968) at the Spastics Society's Motor Development Research Unit at Sheffield; this work includes experiments in the use of operant conditioning techniques which will further our understanding of the complexities involved in motor skills and their essential link with perceptual skills. It is through a combination of perceptual and motor skills, as Piaget (1956) has shown, that so much of the foundations of learning, in the child's early life, are laid down and the results of the work we have described in training and conditioning some aspects of motor skills, particularly at an early age, are awaited with great interest.

(d) *Perceptual Motor Impairments.*—Perceptual motor impairments can best be illustrated by a brief case study:

Sally, now age 15, has minimal brain damage, with an accompanying mild degree of spasticity largely affecting her legs so that she walks unsteadily, whilst her hand control is almost normal, *e.g.* she can trace a complex pattern very well: her speech development is excellent, and she scores a Verbal I.Q. of 125 on the Wechsler Verbal Scale: yet in certain other respects her performance is almost unbelievably poor: in maths the simplest division sum will confuse her: in art her drawings are reported to be like those 'of a rather odd 7-year-old', whilst her domestic science teacher comments 'she can rarely get a pie in the oven'. It is understandable that this 'unevenness' in her performance in different spheres, causes tension—within Sally, her parents and her teachers and therapists. We normally expect a more even and consistent level of performance, unless of course the person concerned has an obvious physical or emotional or cultural handicap. Sally's real handicaps are quite subtle, and her difficulty is one of perceptual motor disorders.

Even a simple act, such as putting a pie in an oven, involves many components and we usually take their intactness for granted, including the following:

(1) The use of sensory information, vision, hearing and smell.
(2) The use of motor control such as in touching objects (with care in the case of a hot oven).
(3) The process of organizing sensory impressions to form a perception—such as of the completeness or otherwise of the object that we call a pie.
(4) The organization of movements—up, down, left, right, backwards, forwards, their speed and duration and what to do about obstacles (such as other objects that might be in the oven).
(5) The feedback of information about the effectiveness or otherwise of the movements that we make, and our response to this feedback in altering our performance.

(6) Our attention, memory and motivation, any of which will affect our performance.

(7) Most important, the process of intersensory integration—all these components must to some extent be *integrated* and somehow ordered into a coherent *sequence*. For example vision and touch may have to work together and in our simple example, Sally should first use vision to judge whether there is enough space in the oven, and if she considers there is, she should then confirm this by her action. Sally would usually act first, tending to use force when things did not seem to work out: her visual perception and the process of linking it with her movements, are so poor that she rarely tried to judge space and form in a normal way. She is undoubtedly impaired in several of the components we have mentioned and in the links between them, and her practical skills both in everyday life and in classroom activities were very weak: yet she is highly competent in many other directions, especially in her language and social skills and her general knowledge, and she is very likely to be successful in several academic examinations.

Psychological studies of groups of children showing similar impairments have been carried out by Wedell (1960, 1968), Abercrombie (1964a, 1964b) and Francis-Williams (1970) and these brought out the essential unevenness in the intellectual and educational performance of brain damaged children. For example Wedell's 1960 study, using very carefully devised tests on 73 brain damaged (cerebral palsied) children and 40 controls without brain damage, showed the difficulty the former had in tests involving the matching of figures, copying patterns of bricks, assembling jig-saws, etc., on which low scores were recorded on 25 per cent of the brain damaged children compared to less than 3 per cent of the controls. The tests were specially designed so that the child's motor control was not an important consideration. Abercrombie (1964b) confirmed that there was a high incidence of perceptual motor disorders amongst cerebral palsied children in her extensive study of thirty-nine cases and eleven controls, using the Wechsler Scales, the Frostig Developmental Test of Visual Perception and various matching tasks, both through visual and tactile means. The degree to which the children had sensory or motor handicaps was carefully assessed so that the influence of these could be allowed for. Seventy-five per cent of the cases showed specific perceptual motor difficulties on one or more of the tests, which could not be attributed to motor or sensory handicaps: children with equal degrees of motor handicap, but who were not brain damaged (*e.g.* cases of poliomyelitis) did not show such difficulties. Birch, in the U.S. (1964, 1965) and his co-workers have made considerable contributions to understanding the many puzzling features: he has shown that some brain damaged children have quite good visual perceptual skills (*e.g.* they can match picture to picture and shape to shape fairly normally), but they cannot *construct* patterns, either through making patterns with coloured bricks, or attempting to draw them: their difficulties were not due to perceptual disorders themselves but lay somewhere in the process of translating a perception into action. Birch's work also shows the enormous difficulties that brain injured children have in intersensory integration: in his 1964 study he showed that some brain damaged children could match geometric shapes visually, as well as ordinary children, but when visual information was reduced, for example one of the geometrical shapes in a pair being screened from view, and the children were asked to use their sense of touch and movement (tracking the outline with a stylus) to compare this with the visually presented geometrical pattern, large errors were recorded amongst the brain damaged children. They were unable to link the information they obtained visually, with the information they obtained through their sense of touch and movement. Although these results are tentative, they suggest at least considerable delay in the development of intersensory integration in brain damaged children, which could seriously limit the use they make of information from various channels, and so lead to confusion and educational retardation. Reading, for example, involves information from several senses.

A great deal has been learned from such studies of perceptual motor disorders in cerebral palsied children. Work with non-cerebral palsied children, although subject to the difficulties of diagnosis that we have already mentioned, is important in that it offers some explanation of learning difficulties that may be applicable to very large groups of children, including those attending normal schools.

In 1966 Brenner reported on the application of a battery of visual motor tests (including parts of the Bender Gestalt, Goodenough Draw a Man, Benton), and rated nearly 7 per cent of 810 normal school children aged 8–9 as showing visual perceptual and visual motor difficulties. Bowley (1969) using a large battery of similar tests, including the Frostig, reported an incidence of 1·5 per cent, designated as showing 'minimal cerebral dysfunctioning', out of a total sample that had been roughly screened, of over 2000 children. Cruickshank (1967) mentions incidence figures of between

1 and 7 per cent of the general population showing learning difficulties of a comparable kind.

Several workers in this field, following the lead in studies of brain damaged adults, have attempted to use Wechsler's Intelligence Scale as an indication of brain damage, notably studying discrepancies between the person's Verbal I.Q. and his Performance I.Q. on this scale. This has led to some exaggerated claims about incidence of brain damage amongst the general population. For example Clements and Peters (1962) considered that a discrepancy of 10–15 points between the verbal and the performance scores might indicate brain damage but according to Field's (1960) studies of the Wechsler Scale and its norms, this amount of discrepancy would be found in about 25 per cent of the general population—clearly a vast over-estimate. A useful discussion of these points is to be found in Rutter, Graham and Yule (1970) which concludes that large discrepancies, of the order of 25 points did appear to show some association with the presence of brain damage, as measured by other criteria.

Many workers have stressed the importance of the early detection of special learning difficulties in order that remedial work might be planned at a very early stage and so prevent a child from going from bad to worse, and to help reduce parental anxiety and confusion, which would otherwise affect the child's learning. Studies of perceptual motor difficulties in under fives are difficult to make, since the performance of young children is variable and erratic at the best of times, and this calls for very careful assessment of what types of behaviour in young children might be considered abnormal and might, in turn, be indicative of brain damage. Francis-Williams (1970) is one of the few workers in this country to have attempted such studies. She selected 44 cases out of a total of 3000, who had been noted to show 'minor neurological dysfunctioning' at birth, but who had no major birth difficulties and no major neurological signs in very early years—in other words there were no frank cases of spasticity, blindness or deafness or similar well recognized conditions. Over half the 44 children turned out to be of normal intelligence, and two-thirds of these showed impairments on certain tests, which were largely based on Frances Graham's work (1963) on the perceptual motor development of young children, and Joan Reynell's (1969) language tests. Her book also contains a useful general description of psychological assessment and educational techniques, including those for older children, and the work of Albetreccia, Strauss, Cruickshank and Frostig is well documented. Valuable suggestions are made, not only in ways of identifying early learning difficulties in young children but in suggestions about educational and therapeutic techniques.

Educational provision and techniques designed to help brain damaged children have been largely centred on the perceptual motor disorders. In the U.S., the growth of special educational facilities has been strong in the past decade: we have mentioned the early work by Strauss and Kephart (1955) at the Cove School for brain injured children, Wisconsin and we have also mentioned the educational work of Cruickshank (1961) with its emphasis on providing a distraction free environment: Marianne Frostig (1964, 1968) at the Centre for Educational Therapy, Los Angeles, has followed up her diagnostic test of visual perceptual development, with a remedial programme that is designed to train for any of the specific weaknesses denoted by her tests, such as in figure ground confusion, perceptual constancy, etc. Her work is also concerned with language development and she places great emphasis on all developmental areas, based on very comprehensive assessments. Useful recent reviews by both Cruickshank and Frostig can be found in Loring (1968). Gallacher (1960) reported on a first-rate study of ways of tutoring brain injured children: although he modestly admitted the educational gains were small, he considered that the individual one hour per day tutoring might be much more effective than group work for such children and that it might be possible to use peripatetic tutors within the ordinary school system as a result of this.

In the U.K. very little specific provision has been made, it being generally considered that most brain damaged children could, on the whole, be adequately catered for in existing remedial groups in special schools. This situation, however, is not very satisfactory and a more concentrated effort could give rise to more expertise in helping such children. We have noted the work of Tansley (1967), with its emphasis on Kephart's educational programme: a few preliminary studies of Frostig's remedial methods have emerged, such as Tyson's (1963) on a small group of cerebral palsied children, and Lansdown's (1970) and Horn's (1970) studies of small groups of non-cerebral palsied children who showed perceptual motor difficulties. On the whole such work has tended to produce slight improvements, in terms of increased scores on the Frostig perceptual tests, but not necessarily in the educational attainments so far. This kind of work needs expanding, and it is likely that some highly trained teachers would produce more favourable results. More sophisticated techniques, including the use of operant conditioning and a variety of electronic aids such as the Touch-Tutor (Thompson

1971) are showing promise and there is a need, of course, for more intensive studies of the effectiveness of various educational methods. These must be based on a much more thorough understanding of the precise nature of the learning disorders than we have at present.

(e) *Emotional instability*.—There is a rough parallel between hyperactivity, distractibility, motor inco-ordination and perceptual confusion that we have so far described, and a comparable kind of fluctuation in the child's emotional life. For example brain damaged children have been described as 'over-excitable, uninhibited, explosive, over-reactive' and minor changes of routine are seen to provoke great outbursts of rage or grief. Objective studies of these characteristics are difficult to carry out, since we still need to develop reliable techniques of measurement, but clinical observation and our case studies leave no doubt about the high 'emotionality' of certain brain damaged children. These are partly the result of their neurological condition, such as a basic weakness in controlling their feelings under certain conditions of stress, and indirectly, through the frustrations that are caused by their other difficulties, *e.g.* the confusion that arises from motor clumsiness in an otherwise bright child, and the reactions of adults to these difficulties which, in turn, impinge on the child. The admonishment to 'Look more carefully and watch what you are doing' may be a fair one for normal children but it is not necessarily fair to a brain damaged child. He may be trying to look carefully, but finds it impossible to perceive accurately, so that his mistakes may appear to the adult to be sheer carelessness or even wilful disobedience, with resulting anger on the part of the adult, and consternation on the part of the child.

This sort of situation can be considerably relieved when the parents and teachers fully understand the child's excessive emotionality may be a direct outcome of his neurological difficulties and that he is not simply being 'bloody minded' or attention seeking. An attitude of calm acceptance can also be helpful.

Birch and his co-workers have provided many useful concepts and much sound advice about the handling of children with differing 'temperaments' or deeply characteristic ways of reacting to their environment, such as we see in brain damaged children. We never observe brain damage directly, but only its consequences, such as the child's behaviour. Now the latter is rarely determined by brain damage alone: it is a product of many factors, not only his neurological condition, but his relationship with his environment and the people within it, including family reactions, community attitudes and such factors as whether his neurological impairment has led to a delayed entry to school, and to frequent hospitalizations, etc. In other words, when a child has a handicap, it is very likely that the environment that surrounds him will deviate from normal. Therefore he has to contend with two factors. Birch's work helps us to understand the ramifications of this: for example different parents react differently to children who might be, at least initially, showing the same patterns of behaviour, such as distractibility or emotional lability. In a fascinating longitudinal study (Thomas and Birch, 1968) of differences in the behaviour of very young babies, Birch shows the possibilities of rating levels of activity, rhythmiticity, adaptability, sensitivity, distractibility and general mood, resulting in rough classifications such as 'intensively reactive' or 'placid and easy' at the extremes. Given such behavioural characteristics, the question then arises: are the parents' reactions matched or mismatched, in relation to these? In other words their child rearing patterns may either be harmonious or dissonant in respect of a particular child's 'early temperament'. For example an intensively reactive child confronted by an intensely reactive adult, who meets temper tantrums with temper tantrums, is likely to have his difficulties severely aggravated.

Birch's work is still in its experimental stages but is proving useful in reminding us to consider children's behaviour as a closely linked process involving both environmental and organic factors. In work directed at helping handicapped children, the exact assessment of the role of organic factors and their influence on the child's behaviour and learning is crucial.

Language disorders: Aphasia, Central deafness and Dyslexia

So far we have concentrated on children showing perceptual motor and other impairments, whose language development has, by contrast, been relatively good. Some children show discrepancies in the other direction. Their perceptual motor skills are relatively high, whilst their language development is relatively low. Do discrepancies in this direction suggest some kind of brain damage, perhaps of a different kind? This is not so in every case. Language development is dependent on a whole host of environmental factors as well as on basic neurological and physical factors. Normal language development depends particularly on 'social imitation' and the desire to communicate through speech, both on the part of the child and the persons surrounding him: on the intactness of the child's physical and sensory state, notably his control of breathing and tongue movements, and, of course, on his general intelligence. There is a very small group of children who appear to have all the necessary environmental, physical and sensory facilities (including good hearing) for speech and language development, yet fail to develop the latter normally, for reasons which might well be linked with 'minimal cerebral dysfunctioning'.

Receptive and Expressive Aphasia:

ANN: normal birth, weight 7½ lb, healthy, walked at 13 months, used words at 12 months, phrases at 2 years, and all development reported normal until aged 3½, when she had a very feverish illness diagnosed as a form of 'measles encephalitis'. Ann was very ill and feeble for several weeks, then started to show gradual physical recovery and became alert once again and able to play with toys constructively, etc. However, her speech did not recover at this stage: she used very few words and tended instead to point and gesture: furthermore she did not appear to hear spoken instructions.

At age 3¾ audiology assessment showed puzzling features. She did not respond to spoken instructions even at a maximum loudness although she responded very quickly to gesture and was generally co-operative and helpful and sociable: she stared at faces a great deal.

Her responses to non-speech sounds such as music boxes, rattles, animal noises, etc. were erratic but occasionally quite good: response to pure tones, very poor, but after enormous encouragement she responded to conditioning tests, at about 50 decibels above threshold for most frequencies.

A moderate hearing loss was suspected but not enough to account for her developing language failure. But subsequent assessments a few weeks later proved that her hearing for pure tones and various other sounds was virtually normal. Yet there was still no sign of a return of her language skills.

She was noted in interview and at home to be a co-operative, sociable girl, responding well to gestured instructions. Normal intelligence was confirmed on non-verbal tests (Merrill-Palmer Scale I.Q. approximately 110), and the diagnosis of receptive and expressive aphasia, due to encephalitis at age 3½ was made.

Her subsequent progress confirmed this: and soon after age 5 she was admitted to a special residential school for children with speech and language difficulties. Her general development was satisfactory and she learned to read at a simple level at age 7½ years, and was soon able to follow simple written instructions, *e.g.* she was able to learn some language through visual, but not through auditory-comprehension channels and her language development remained virtually nil. She learned to identify a few animal noises and would occasionally use a word but on the whole she was unable to attach meaning to sounds.

Children with severe and definite receptive language difficulties, such as Ann, are very rare: they represent an extreme example of very selective brain damage, following a feverish illness, which had, by peculiar chance, virtually destroyed her language function, although her other abilities were almost intact. She showed none of the other behavioural and learning symptoms of brain damage, such as hyperactivity, distractibility, perceptual motor difficulties and emotional lability. Mild forms of partial aphasia are more common, but these are difficult to disentangle from all the other causes of language failure, including social, emotional and cultural deprivation, and severe subnormality. See Mittler (1970) for an excellent review of work in this field.

Central deafness is a term referring to a similar condition. The work of Taylor (1964) has shown the existence of a few children, some of whom had attended deaf schools for some years, whose language development is extremely limited and who gave every impression of not being able to hear, but when subjected to very specialized audiology techniques, including E.E.G. audiometry, proved to have normal or at least considerable hearing; the difficulties of these children are very similar to those we mentioned in connection with aphasic conditions, namely a failure to interpret the sounds that they hear.

Combinations of ordinary hearing losses, such as peripheral nerve deafness, either mild, partial or severe, with some degree of central deafness or aphasia have also occasionally been observed, and possibly account for the fact that some deaf children make very little progress in spite of long term educational help. However, such combinations are the exception rather than the rule and not much is known about their treatment prospects.

Educational approaches, partly based on work with aphasic adults, such as those who have lost their language skills following a severe head injury, are best exemplified by the work of McGinnis (1963). These are based on 'association techniques', *e.g.* initially an attempt is made to teach several dozen nouns by gradually building up individual sounds which are then synthesized to form the words: short phrases are then gradually introduced, through repetitive drill, and the complexity of the language stimulation gradually increased, taking great care not to overload the child with too much language that he simply cannot comprehend or execute.

Dyslexia

Language comes in many forms, spoken and gestured, etc. and an important form is our response to written language. Failure to read effectively has serious consequences for a child, affecting not only writing and spelling but most other school subjects, even including mathematics in that the pupil cannot handle written problems. The terms 'dyslexia' and 'word blind' are popular amongst medical experts (Critchley, 1964) but are not generally favoured by educationalists and psychologists who object to such precise labelling of certain children. It is very rare indeed to find a child whose sole problem is that he cannot read although his development is otherwise normal and he is of an age when we would expect him to read. Most children with reading difficulties have other educational difficulties as well, usually determined by many causes—emotional, cultural and neurological, and it can be misleading to regard the majority of such children as simply 'dyslexic'.

Reading failures are common amongst school-children: Morris (1966) found that at aged 8, almost 14 per cent of Kent schoolchildren were reading either not at all or extremely poorly, compared to their chronological ages. However, some of these reading difficulties could be accounted for by generally low mental age or intelligence: intensive studies by Rutter, Tizard and Whitmore (1970) in which the factors of mental age and intelligence were controlled, suggest that specific retardation, defined as reading ages more than two years below mental age, occurred in nearly 4 per cent of the children. It cannot be assumed that more than a very small fraction of this 4 per cent were dyslexic, for the majority also showed retardation in other areas, relative to their intelligence, especially in writing, spelling and mathematics. One-third of these children also showed anti-social behaviour and the authors pointed out the difficulties in determining which came first—the educational failure or the anti-social behaviour.

Clearly with reading and other educational difficulties we are concerned with a very complex situation and there are many explanations to be considered, including emotional disturbance, social and cultural deprivation, poor teaching, for as Morris points out very few junior school teachers have been trained in remedial techniques, together with subtle neurological difficulties in some cases, occurring more frequently in boys than girls, that are probably related to minimal cerebral dysfunctioning. These subtle neurological difficulties include: difficulties in motor co-ordination, visual perceptual and visual motor difficulties (very important in the early stages of learning to read), faulty cerebral dominance, such as left-handedness or mixed handedness/eyedness, and failures in language development from infancy. In research by Rutter *et al.* the evidence concerning these neurological defects was too indefinite to support the view that a specific dyslexic syndrome exists: although many of the children showed subtle neurological dysfunctions, sometimes with a family history of similar difficulties, the effects were rarely -confined to reading but affected other areas of learning and behaviour as well. The term dyslexia should therefore be used very sparingly in spite of the fact that some parents seem to find it comforting to have what passes as a definite explanation of their child's educational difficulties and who may wish to evade any idea that their child might be generally retarded or emotionally disturbed.

Educational treatment of dyslexia has been developed experimentally by the Hellerup Word Blind Institute at Copenhagen, and the I.C.A.A.s Word Blind Centre in Coram's Field, London (some of the work of which is due to be taken over by the Inner London Education Authority in the near future). Many useful remedial techniques have been developed in such centres but remedial sessions totalling 1 or 2 hours per week, outside the child's school, has not proved very effective for some cases and there is a need for more highly trained teachers in remedial education who can help to set up small classes *within* a school that serves the child's community. This ensures that all aspects of the child's learning and social, emotional life can be taken into account.

A Pilot Study of Assessment and Educational Work with Children with Minimal Cerebral Dysfunctioning

In 1969 one of the authors (Bowley 1969) completed a pilot study which exemplifies many of the features of the children we have described in this chapter, including their need for carefully devised educational and therapeutic help, which although still in its experimental stages, shows promising results in some cases, in spite of its enormous complexity.

A survey of a section of the Junior School population of a London borough was carried out in 1969*. Teachers in seven Junior Schools, representing a Junior age population of 1634, were asked to identify children showing signs of restlessness, clumsiness and poor verbal and reading ability by means of a questionnaire. A total of 24 children were selected (*i.e.* 1·46 per cent) showing this syndrome with marked reading retardation despite normal intelligence. Including the schools in the pilot study the total was 34 out of 2280 *i.e.* 1·49 per cent.

* Reported in *Dev. Med. Child Neurol.*, **11**, No. 4, 493 (1969).

These children, in the majority of cases, were then given a detailed neurological assessment and an electro-encephalogram as well as a psychological assessment. The following neurological evaluation was made of the group:

Motor—inability to hop or stand on one leg; ataxia in heel/toe walking; choreiform jerks; slowness of movement; dysarthria; physical immaturity; abnormal E.E.G. in some cases.

Dyspraxic—involving voluntary or schematic movements of limbs, face or eye, or construction in two dimensions or drawing or writing.

Perceptual—visual, tactile and possibly auditory agnosias and specific reading difficulties.

Language—developmental dysphasia and word poverty.

Psychological—restlessness and short attention span.

All of these children showed one or more of these characteristics.

The psychological assessment was planned to be a fairly comprehensive survey of the child's intellectual, perceptual and linguistic skills and disabilities, usually requiring two interviews. It included the Wechsler Performance Scale, tests of vocabulary, reading and arithmetic, the Illinois Test of Psycho-Linguistic Abilities, the Frostig Perception test and the Bender Gestalt Designs. By this means an attempt was made to explore the child's strengths and weaknesses, with a view to planning remedial measures.

The following were considered to be the factors contributing to the child's learning difficulties:

Language immaturity—slow onset of speech and growth of vocabulary; a low Language Age on the I.T.P.A. was common though verbal comprehension was good, coupled with poor auditory or visual memory and sequencing ability. This last was shown by almost all the children.

Visual-spatial disabilities—difficulty in copying shapes or recalling designs, difficulty in some figure-ground and spatial relationships tests and a tendency to reverse letters and words.

Distractibility and poor attention were very evident both during testing and teaching periods and were frequently reported from school.

As a result of this study a remedial class was set up for a small group of children showing these difficulties between the ages of

8 and 10 years and with I.Q.s above 90. A carefully structured programme was planned to meet their special needs which included perceptual training, using Frostig techniques and other devices by the occupational therapist, speech therapy, using the Language Master and other methods by the speech therapist, and remedial reading, using visual aids, practical material, drawing, reading games and carefully chosen books to suit the child's stage of progress by the teacher and psychologist. These specialists worked as a team with the group of six children and so a great deal of individual attention was ensured during the session, which took up one morning a week. The rest of the time was spent in their ordinary schools. Each child received a great deal of praise and encouragement and the atmosphere of the class was accepting, tolerant and stimulating. None of the children showed serious emotional problems but many had become discouraged and unco-operative at school and some had played truant. They were regarded by their teachers as dullards or trouble-makers, as lazy, inattentive and unresponsive. They flourished on the special treatment they received by the Centre and made quite remarkable progress in many cases.

The following are fairly typical cases which illustrate the com-plicated background and their problems of learning.

K.A. at the age of 8 had a reading age assessed at the 4½ year level. His spelling was chaotic and his writing unintelligible. He was restless, distractible and moody in school. When he was reprimanded he would often abscond from school and slip off home. His parents were rather simple, but very concerned people and K. was especially devoted to his mother. Methods of upbringing had been rather permissive. K's older brother had similar learning and behaviour problems.

Neurological assessment noted odd choreiform movements of shoulders and lips, slight ataxia of the lower limbs, dyslalic speech and the E.E.G. record was suggestive of epilepsy though he had never had any fits. Sensation was normal. Minimal abnormal neurological signs were recorded.

Psychological assessment showed a W.I.S.C. Performance I.Q. of 90, a Language Age of only 6·2 years (I.T.P.A.) with very poor results on memory and sequencing tests. Arithmetic was at about a 6 year level but he could only read some five words on the Burt Reading test. Frostig Perception test results were good, but he did badly on the Bender Gestalt copying designs test. His teacher assessed his score on the Bristol Adjustment Guide as 32, indicating quite severe maladjust-ment.

K. became a faithful member of the group. He never truanted on the day he was due to come to the Centre, but he was often moody, restless and distractible. Very short lesson periods were given at first, frequently changing the type of occupation. He did a lot of colourful drawings of which he was very proud. He enjoyed dexterity and perception games and self-corrective reading games involving matching and word discrimination. Phonics were gradually introduced and he soon got interested in the Pirate books and the Micky Mix-Up* series. He had a lively sense of humour, always enjoyed a practical joke, could tell a good story or riddle and became quite a popular member of the group. He attended 6 terms once a week and his reading age rose from a $4\frac{1}{2}$ year level to $7\frac{1}{2}$ in that time. He became really keen on reading for its own sake and improved in attentivity, motor skills and general stability. At school he won medals for swimming, became a school prefect and no longer absconded. At 10 years of age he was discharged from the Centre with flying colours. Progress has been maintained.

D.R. at $7\frac{1}{2}$ had a reading age of 5·2 years and a marked speech defect. His health history was poor. Though of normal birth weight, he was late in talking, of small stature, had an odd facial expression and slight kyphosis. His E.E.G. record showed a low convulsive threshold. His brother had had fits and also showed an abnormal E.E.G. His bone age was normal and also his skull, spine and chest X-ray. However, he had missed a great deal of early school life through colds and chest complaints. He had received a great deal of speech therapy and his speech was gradually improving.

His Stanford-Binet I.Q. was 98 and his I.T.P.A. Language Age 6·2 years. Bender-Gestalt designs and memory sequencing test results were poor, but his Frostig Perception Quotient was high. Arithmetic was about average, but his reading was more than 2 years retarded.

He had been a little over-protected at home on account of his frequent ailments, but family relationships were affectionate and caring.

He too was a child with a rather difficult temperament, moody, aggressive, lacking in self-confidence and 'work-shy'. He needed diplomatic handling. He responded to adult friendliness, and quickly showed great proficiency in perception exercises. The Language Master intrigued him and his speech continued to improve. He had a great many different interests and began to enjoy books for their story content. He made intelligent guesses from the context and worked rapidly through the Wild West Readers† and the Pirate books. His concentration was good and he was annoyed when interrupted. He became more independent, increased in self-control and after five terms attendance had gained over 2 years in reading standard. Near his 10 year birthday he was discharged so that he should have an

* *The Three Pirates.* S. K. McCullagh. Griffin Readers. Arnold; *Micky Mix-up.* D. H. Stott. Holmes, Glasgow.
† *The Wild West Readers.* C. C. Prothero. Wheaton.

uninterrupted last year in the junior school and because he had nearly caught up.

These sort of children cannot make much progress in a large class full of distractions, movements and noise. They cannot learn well by global methods and need special techniques and a carefully structured form of teaching. They usually cannot work on their own and need far more individual attention than an ordinary teacher can give them. They tend to drift into day dreaming or undisciplined behaviour, and severe maladjustment may be the end result. Our progress rate in the remedial class has been high and this intensive work has proved therapeutic in the widest sense; for general stability, attitude to work and educational achievement have greatly improved. Increased physical maturity has helped and we have found it is best to start with children at the early stage of their junior school career, at 7, 8 or 9 years of age, when time is on our side and a sense of defeat not too firmly entrenched.

Future Work with Brain Damaged Children

The next decade should show a consolidation of many of the tentative ideas we have expressed in this chapter, concerning the causes, the incidence, the learning and behaviour problems and the educational and other treatment of these children. Although our present knowledge is sketchy, the ideas we have described represent a useful addition to our knowledge of certain children's difficulties, that cannot be explained by other means. The term 'brain damage' is unsatisfactory: few writers can avoid using the term, but a more satisfactory one might be 'specific learning difficulties' as used by Francis-Williams (1970) in her excellent survey of this field. Much finer diagnostic and assessment techniques need to be developed by neurologists and psychologists and, of course, many more experiments in educational techniques need to be pursued.

Organizations and Literature for Parents

In this country, compared to the United States, there are no fully recognized national organizations that produce literature and guidance specifically for brain damaged children, it being generally felt in official quarters that their needs can be met by existing Hospital and Local Education Authorities and Schools Psychological Services. However, some advice concerning some problems can be obtained from:

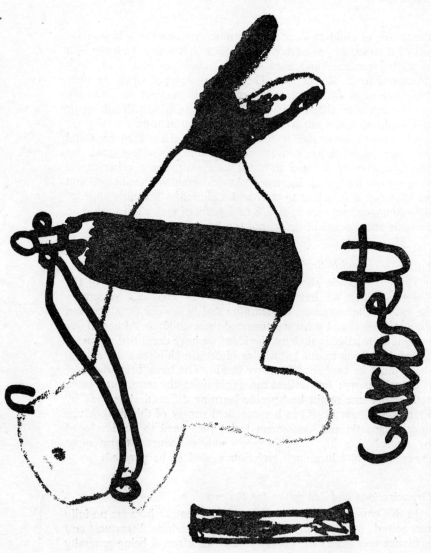

FIGS. 3–6.—Drawings by children with minimal cerebral dysfunction and reading retardation.

Fig. 4.—Girl, 9½ years.

FIG. 5.—Boy. 9 years.

Michael Wheeler

FIG. 6.—Boy, 10½ years.

The Spastics Society,
>12 Park Crescent, London, W1N 4EQ, largely concerned with children whose brain damage is accompanied by physical difficulties.

The Invalid Children's Aid Association,
>126 Buckingham Palace Road, London, S.W.1, which has been concerned with children showing language and reading difficulties.

Literature for parents is not abundant in this country, but the following is available:

A book by William Cruickshank *The Brain Injured Child in Home, School and Community* published by Syracuse University Press (1967).

A pamphlet by Helmer R. Myklebust *Learning Disorders: Psychoneurological Disturbances in Childhood* obtainable from: Rehabilitation Literature, 2023 West Ogden Avenue, Chicago, Illinois 60612.

A pamphlet by Margaret Newton *Dyslexia: A guide for Parents and Teachers* obtainable from Department of Applied Psychology, University of Aston in Birmingham, Gosta Green, Birmingham, B4 7ET.

A pamphlet by M. Golick *Learning Disability* published by the Canadian Broadcasting Co. obtainable from Dillon's University Bookshop, 1 Malet St. London W.C.1.

References

ABERCROMBIE, M. L. J. (1964a). Perceptual and Visuomotor Disorders in Cerebral Palsy. *Little Club Clin. in Dev. Med.*, No. 11. London: Spastics Society/Heinemann.

ABERCROMBIE, M. J. L. *et al.* (1964b). Visual perceptual and visuomotor impairments in physically handicapped children. *Percept. Motor Skills, Monogr.*, Suppl. 3, V, No. 18.

ABERCROMBIE, M. L. J. (1965). On drawing a diamond. Article in *Penguin Science Survey* B.

ABERCROMBIE, M. L. J. (1968). Some notes on spatial disability: movement, intelligence quotient and attentiveness. *Dev. Med. Child Neurol.*, **10**, No. 2.

BIRCH, H. G. (1964). *Brain Damage in Children. The Biological and Social Aspects.* Baltimore: Williams & Wilkins.

BIRCH, H. G. (1965). Auditory Visual Integration, Intelligence and Reading Ability in School Children. *Percept. Motor Skills, Monogr.* **20**.

BORTNER, M., editor (1968). Evaluation and education of children with brain damage. Illinois: Thomas.

BOWLEY, A. H. (1969). Reading difficulty with minor neurological dysfunctioning. *Dev. Med. Child Neurol.*, **11**, No. 4.
BRENNER, M. W. and GILLMAN, S. (1966). Visual motor ability in schoolchildren: a survey. *Dev. Med. Child Neurol.*, **8**, No. 6.
BROWN, R. I. (1965). The effects of varied environmental stimuli on the performance of subnormal children. *J. Clin. Psychol.*, **7**.
BROWN, R. I. and SEMPLE, L. (1970). Effects of unfamiliarity on the overt verbalization and perceptual motor behaviour of nursery school children. *Brit. Educ. Psychol.*, **40**, No. 3.
CLEMENTS, S. D. (1966). *Minimal Brain Dysfunction in Children.* Phase one of a three phase project, U.S. National Institute of Neurologic. Diseases and Stroke. Monogr. No. 3, U.S. Dept. of Health, Education and Welfare.
CLEMENTS, S. D. and PETERS, J. F. (1962). Minimal brain dysfunction in the school age children. *Archs. Gen. Psychiat.* **6**, 185.
CONNOLLY, K. (1968). The application of operant conditioning to the measurement and development of motor skills in children. *Dev. Med. Child Neurol.*, **10**, 697.
CRUICKSHANK, W. M. et al. (1957 rev. 1965). *Perception in Cerebral Palsy, a Study in Figure Background Relationship.* New York: Syracuse University Press.
CRUICKSHANK, W. M. et al. (1961). *A Teaching Method for Brain Injured and Hyperactive Children.* New York: Syracuse University Press.
CRUICKSHANK, W. M., editor (1966). *The Teacher of Brain Injured Children: a Discussion of the Bases for Competency.* New York: Syracuse University Press.
FIELD, J. G. (1960). Two types of tables for use with Wechsler's intelligence scales. *J. Clin. Psychol.*, **16**, 6.
FRANCIS-WILLIAMS, J. (1970). *Children with Specific Learning Difficulties.* Oxford: Pergamon Press.
FROSTIG, M. et al. (1964). *The Marianne Frostig Developmental Test of Visual Perception.* Palo Alto, California: Consulting Psychologists Press.
FROSTIG, M. (1968). Testing as a basis for educational therapy. *Assessment of the Cerebral Palsied Child for Education,* edited by James Loring. London: Spastics Society/Heinemann.
GALLACHER, J. J. (1960). *The Tutoring of Brain Injured Mentally Retarded Children.* Illinois: Thomas.
GRAHAM, F. K. et al. (1963). Brain injury in the preschool child, some developmental considerations. *Psychol. Monogr.*, **77**, No. 10.
HORN, J. and QUARMBY, D. (1970). The problems of older non-readers. *Special Education*, **59**, No. 3.
HUTT, C. et al. (1964). Arousal and childhood autism. *Nature*, **204**.
HUTT, S. J. et al. (1963). A Method of Studying Children's Behaviour. *Dev. Med. Child Neurol.*, **5**, No. 3.
HUTT, S. J. and HUTT, C. (1964). Hyperactivity in a group of epileptic (and some non-epileptic) brain damaged children. *Epilepsia*, **5**, 334.
HUTT, S. J. and HUTT, C., editors (1970). *Behaviour Studies in Psychiatry.* Oxford: Pergamon Press.
JOHNSON, D. D. and MYKLEBUST, H. R. (1967). *Learning Disabilities: Educational Principles and Practice.* New York: Grune & Stratton.
KEPHART, N. C. (1960). *The Slow Learner in the Classroom.* Columbus, Ohio: Merrill.

KEPHART, N. C. (1968). Chapter in Bortner (q.v.).

LANSDOWN, R. (1970). *A Study of the Frostig Programme for the Development of Visual Perception used in the Ordinary Primary School.* London Borough of Waltham Forest.

LORING, J., editor (1968). *The Assessment of the Cerebral Palsied Child for Education.* London: Spastics Society/Heinemann.

MCGINNIS, M. (1963). *Aphasic Children.* Washington. Alexander Graham Bell Association for the Deaf.

MITTLER, P. (1970). *The Psychological Assessment of Mental and Physical Handicaps.* London: Methuen.

MORRIS, J. M. (1966). *Standards and Progress in Reading.* Slough, Bucks.: NFER.

PIAGET, J. and INHELDER, B. (1956). *The Child's Conception of Space.* London: Routledge & Kegan Paul.

REYNELL, J. (1969). *Infant and Young Children's Language Scales, Manual and Test Material.* Slough, Bucks.: National Foundation for Educational Research.

RUTTER, M., GRAHAM, P. and YULE, W. (1970). A Neuropsychiatric Study in Childhood. *Little Club Clinics in Dev. Med.,* Nos. 35 and 36. Spastics Society/Heinemann.

RUTTER, M., TIZARD, J. and WHITMORE, K. (1970). *Education, Health and Behaviour.* London: Longman.

SCHULMAN, J. L. *et al.* (1965). *Brain Damage and Behaviour.* Springfield, Illinois: Thomas.

STOTT, D. H. (1966). A general test of motor impairment for children. *Dev. Med. Child Neurol.,* **8,** No. 5.

STRAUSS, A. A. and KEPHART, N. C. (1955). *Psychopathology and Education of the Brain-injured Child,* Vol. 2. New York: Grune & Stratton.

STRAUSS, A. A. and LEHTINEN, L. E. (1947). *Psychopathology and Education of the Brain-injured Child,* Vol. 1. New York: Grune & Stratton.

TANSLEY, A. E. (1967). *Reading and Remedial Reading.* London: Routledge & Kegan Paul.

TAYLOR, I. G. (1964). *Neurological Mechanisms of Hearing and Speech in Children.* London: Manchester University Press.

THOMAS, A., CHESS, S. and BIRCH, H. G. (1968). *Temperament and Behaviour Disorders in Children.* New York: University Press.

THOMPSON, D. A. and JOHNSON, J. D. (1971). Teaching machines for the very handicapped: the Touch-Tutor at Hawksworth Hall. *Special Education,* **60,** No. 1.

TYSON, M. (1963). Pilot study of remedial visuomotor training. *Special Education,* **52,** No. 4.

WALTON, J. N., ELLIS, E. and COURT, S. D. (1962). Clumsy children, a study of developmental apraxia and agnosia. *Brain,* **85,** 603.

WEDELL, K. (1960). The Visual Perception of Cerebral Palsied Children. *Child Psychol. Psychiat.,* **1,** 215.

WEDELL, K. (1968). Perceptual motor difficulties. *Special Education,* **57,** No. 4.

CHAPTER III

THE CHILD WITH SPINA BIFIDA

IT has been suggested that this book would be incomplete without some reference to spina bifida which has become of increasing concern to the medical, educational and social work professions. It seems appropriate to consider this after cerebral palsy as the paralysis of the lower limbs presents similar features to those of spastic children. Although serious brain damage is usually not present, the problems of education and management merit careful attention. For up-to-date information we have drawn largely on certain sources, more especially Allen Field's excellent handbook entitled *The Challenge of Spina Bifida* and the research reports by Bernadette Spain in the *Quarterly Bulletins* of the Research and Intelligence Units of the G.L.C. (1969 and 1970).

Incidence

The condition known as spina bifida (split spine) has become more common and of greater importance from the point of view of adequate educational provision in this country. Owing to improved surgical measures developed since 1958, when the Spitz Holter valve was introduced, a greater number of spina bifida children have survived and the death rate has considerably reduced in the first year of life. The incidence amongst live births has been estimated in London as 2 per thousand (Spain, 1969, 1970) similar to the incidence of cerebral palsy and much higher than congenital blindness, 0·6 per thousand. Mortality however is high, and varies according to area to some extent owing to the lack of adequate special units to treat these babies outside some large cities. The greatest number of these children die at birth or within the first year of life. In a study of 600 spina bifida children in the Greater London Council area initiated in 1967 (Spain, 1969, 1970) approximately 35 per cent had survived to over 2 years. Mortality after the age of two is relatively slight and it was estimated that at least 30 per cent would reach school age. It is further estimated that between 55 or 60 children will need education in P.H. schools each year and that 9 or 10 will require places in training centres or hospitals for the subnormal. This is only a preliminary estimate and future figures may increase or decrease, but they indicate the approximate size of the educational problem.

Description of the Condition

Spina bifida results from the fact that the protective bony arches in the baby's backbone fail to develop adequately to enclose the spinal cord at some point along the spinal track. The effect is that a swelling develops quickly after birth containing fluid (meningocele) and sometimes the spinal cord and stretched nerves attached to it (meningomyleocele). Usually the swelling is in the small of the back, but it may occur in the neck area or at the base of the skull when the condition is more serious. The result is paralysis of the lower limbs (paraplegia), skin insensitivity, and incontinence of the bowel and bladder. In some 70 per cent of the cases, the additional complication of hydrocephalus (water on the brain) occurs. This is due to the fact that the cerebro-spinal fluid cannot be fully absorbed owing to a partial block in the circulatory system. This means that internal pressure is increased and an enlarged head is the result.

Causes

The condition may be due to arrested foetal development sometime early in pregnancy at a stage when the spinal cord is being formed. It may be partly genetic in origin and partly racial and is especially noted in the Celtic people rather than Mongolians and Negroes (Laurence, 1969). Its causes may also be linked with faulty diet, the effects of pollution such as by radio-active materials or insecticides, an illness of the mother at a critical time or the proximity of the menopause. It can also be the result of a serious fall or a car accident.

Treatment

Early surgical treatment is usually essential in the great majority of cases if the baby is to survive. Usually this consists in removing the lump on the child's back and covering the area with a skin graft. This highly skilful operation should be carried out in the first 24 hours of the child's life. Later operations achieve less satisfactory results.

If hydrocephalus is a complication, surgery is undertaken at 2 or 3 weeks of age to insert a pressure valve known as the Spitz Holter just beneath the skin behind the ear connected by a plastic tube to the head's reservoir of fluid at one end and to the right receiving chamber of the heart at the other. At a given pressure the valve automatically opens and the excessive fluid is drained off and absorbed into the blood stream. If this is done early enough and if other brain damage has not occurred, there will be no damage due to compression and the child's intelligence should develop normally.

Early physiotherapy is arranged which the mother can carry out under expert guidance so that frequent long journeys to hospital with a heavily incontinent child can be avoided. The purpose of physiotherapy is to keep the child's muscles strong and in balance and to prevent contractures especially in the hips, knees and ankles. Before the crawling stage the child can start moving around by pulling with his arms, sitting on a trolley such as a 'Chailey Chariot' or a 'Surfskater'. These are easily propelled and cannot tip easily and the child can be strapped in for safety. This activity encourages exploration and provides first hand experience of size, shape, texture, position in space, colour, movement and sound. These experiences may well reduce later visuo-spatial difficulties in learning which are common among children with brain damage.

When he is on the threshold of walking the right type of caliper may be supplied with hand sticks or 'plonks', and the right gait can be taught him. Later he will manage a tricycle or kiddicar perhaps. Mobility should be given every encouragement. Walking without aids is rare among these children, but later they can learn to play football, stool ball, learn to swim, enjoy badminton or even a tug-o-war in calipers.

The valve inserted in babyhood must be periodically checked, for intra-cranial pressure, due to a faulty valve, may result in convulsions or even blindness. Early symptoms of distress are irritability, loss of appetite, sickness, headaches, drowsiness or a squint. This may mean that the valve is blocked or infected or come unstuck. The cause can readily be detected by X-ray and medical attention ensured.

Incontinence Management

The Spina-Bifida child does not achieve continence of bowel or bladder naturally as an ordinary child does between 2 and 3 years of age. He does not receive warning signals from the bladder or rectum and consequently does not know when they need emptying. If the bladder is not emptied when full it will tend to stretch, enlarge and by back pressure can compress and damage the kidneys. Waste products will circulate into vital organs and serious illness result.

Allen Field (1970) gives details about the regime necessary to control incontinence which can, if not dealt with, make the child's life a misery and prevent admission to a school. The child needs to drink a great deal of water, between 5 to 7 pints a day and this should be established as a habit. The bladder should be emptied every 2 hours and twice during the night. For males a penile urinal attachment can be used, made of soft rubber and easy to take to pieces and to clean. With the female an operation is usually necessary to insert a stoma, often called 'a red cherry', attached to a collecting bag which must be emptied every 2 hours. Very careful attention to hygiene is essential if infection is to be avoided. These routines have to be learnt by the child and managed by him as soon as he is old enough. Naturally the problems of incontinence weigh heavily on the school staff and for this reason it is difficult for even a very intelligent child with poor continence control to be accepted in a normal school. Moreover he might well become miserably self-conscious and anxious about accidents.

Skin Insensitivity

The spina bifida child has an insensitive skin particularly in the lower limbs. He does not receive normal sensory messages indicating heat, cold or pain. Consequently he is especially prone to skin hazards such as burns, pressure sores or ulcers. Specially sensitive skin areas on the buttocks and on the ankles, elbows, knees and other bony prominences can be toughened by massage with soap, then rinsing, drying and applying surgical spirit and powder. Any red areas which may develop should be treated with appropriate ointment and very careful examination of his body surface should be made twice a day. Damage can so easily be done by getting too close to a fire, leaning against a radiator, stepping into a too hot bath or friction from use of calipers. Foam rubber mattresses or cushions should be used to protect the surface of the skin from friction.

Intelligence

Spina bifida children show a wide distribution of intelligence. Those with brain damage, due to hydrocephalus, tend to be less intelligent than those without. In a study of 161 year-old spina bifida babies by means of the Ruth Griffiths Scale of Mental Development (Spain, 1969, 1970) 26 per cent were found to be reasonably normal in all aspects of development. Fifty-six per cent were found to be normal at one year with the exception of loco-motor development. Eighteen per cent of those with spinal defects were below average in most functions, and of these at least 6 per cent were graded as severely subnormal. All these very retarded children had had surgical treatment for hydrocephalus. Children with hydrocephaly tend to do least well on tests requiring good eye–hand co-ordination. This suggests that quite a high proportion of spina bifida children have good ability and educational prospects are hopeful. Moreover, unlike the typical cerebral palsied child they have good hand control and normal speech in most cases.

Education

The first stage of education for the great majority of these children may well prove to be in a nursery play-group or nursery school for normal or physically handicapped children provided the management of the incontinence is not too great a problem. All the normal free activities of a good nursery *e.g.* painting, build-ing, hammering, sand and water play, chasing, fighting, dressing up, constructive imaginative play, should be available for these children just as for normal children. Speech, bodily control and social ability all develop quicker in this sort of environment.

If at 5 years the child has reasonable mobility and control of incontinence he may well fit into a normal infant school and learn as well as any other child. If he has limited control in either sphere he will be much more suitably placed in a P.H. school where allowances are made for his special difficulties, where physiotherapy is available, where control of incontinence can be taught and where a trained nurse is at hand in emergencies. We have seen many such children in these surroundings and they stand out often as more alert and more mobile than many spastic children.

Residential schools may be a necessity owing to the lack of day schools near at hand, but this should be the exception rather than the rule especially for children under 10 years of age. It is so important for them to know a normal home life, to mix with their normal contemporaries and cope with the ordinary hazards of life rather than to grow up in a more sheltered environment with a handicapped population. There are a few excellent schools for spina bifida children only, which provide all the necessary care and treatment as well as a satisfactory education, but again this implies a certain amount of segregation and lack of contact with ordinary children. Often a school with mixed handicaps provides a richer educational environment, but it is essential that proper treatment and medical supervision be provided.

Many cases are cited of children with spina bifida succeeding with 'O' and 'A' level examinations, of reaching training colleges, technical colleges or universities and of following a satisfactory career. Their prospects are much rosier than those with severe brain damage. Moreover marriage and the procreation of children is also possible.

Children with spina bifida and brain damage, and who are subnormal, will need, just as other subnormal children, training and occupation in Special Care Centres or Training Centres or whatever new name is envisaged under the new Education Act. Some will require hospital care and treatment in hospitals for the subnormal, but these are the minority.

Conclusions

Spina bifida children need early treatment as the first essential and the first year of their lives is their most critical one. If they survive that and receive good physiotherapy and early continence training, the outlook for them is hopeful. They are not especially difficult to teach though some are very distractible and some may have eye–hand co-ordination difficulties. Usually language is well developed, vision and hearing are normal, and hand control is good. Provided brain damage has not occurred educational progress should be normal. Probably about 80 per cent are educable. They need protection from certain hazards on account of their skin insensitivity, and are intelligent enough in most instances to learn to protect themselves.

Organization

The Association for Spina Bifida and Hydrocephalus
112 City Road, London E.C.1.

References

FIELDS, A. (1970). *The Challenge of Spina Bifida*. London: Heinemann.
LAWRENCE, K. M. (1969). The recurrent risk in spina bifida. *Studies in Hydrocephalus and Spina Bifida*. London: Spastics Society/Heinemann.
SPAIN, B. *Quarterly Bulletin of the Research and Intelligence Unit*. Greater London Council, June 1969, No. 7; Sept. 1970, No. 12.

CHAPTER IV

THE DEAF CHILD

The Need for Understanding

A SERIOUS handicap, such as deafness, tends to isolate a child from normal life, unless we take steps to prevent such isolation. A handicap makes special demands on the child: he is cut off from many of the experiences and opportunities for learning that ordinary children enjoy, and has to make constant and considerable efforts to achieve things that come relatively easily to ordinary children. For example, ordinary children learn speech and language, more or less naturally and spontaneously in their early years, as a result of certain inborn abilities, coupled with an environment that includes speech stimulation, from adults and other children. Ordinary children learn language almost 'incidentally'. But for severely deaf children, it must be taught, gradually and skilfully.

A severe handicap also makes special demands of the parents: to understand exactly what the handicap means to the child, how it impinges on his life, and then to work out ways of lessening its effects and promoting the child's learning in as many directions as possible. The crucial part the parents play in their child's early years of learning cannot be too strongly emphasized and it follows that the help that experts can give must be directed as much to the parents as to the young handicapped child himself. Most of the growing numbers of doctors, teachers, psychologists, therapists, health visitors, and social workers who have specialized in helping handicapped children and their families now realize that the best form of help consists not of occasional visits to experts for treatment, but of advising parents of the best way that they can help their young child within the natural setting of his home

We must also mention that a serious handicap makes demands not only on the child and his family, but on the wider community, including the neighbours, shop-keepers, the man in the street, and so on, most of whom will have had little or no contact with seriously handicapped children. In the past the majority of blind, deaf, and spastic children tended to remain isolated in hospitals, remote boarding schools, and other institutions and this picture has been changed in recent years as we move towards less isolation and more 'integration' for the handicapped within the normal community. The general public's attitudes to the handicapped are improving, but there is much work still to be done in promoting true understanding and acceptance.

The deaf are often misunderstood because their handicap is less obvious than is the case with the blind and the spastic. Deafness fails to evoke the immediate sympathy that a more obviously dependent spastic or blind child can evoke: yet the handicap of deafness is a formidable one, when it is realized that the untrained seriously deaf child is cut off not merely from sounds, but from speech, and is therefore drastically cut off from so many kinds of social contact and so many opportunities for learning. The major efforts of the parents of young deaf children must therefore centre on fostering the child's ability to communicate. There are many ways in which a mother communicates to her child: by her facial expressions, her gestures, by touching him, by picking him up, by cuddling him, and so on: the young severely deaf child can understand these but he is almost completely cut off from the most commonly used, most precise, easily remembered, and far-reaching way that a mother communicates to her child, namely, that of speech. He cannot hear the prohibiting 'No' every time he goes near the electric fire; he cannot hear the encouraging 'Good' when he first succeeds in building a tower of bricks. He cannot hear the compromise, 'Have Teddy instead', or 'In a minute', or the reassuring 'See you in the morning'. It is not only the words that he misses, but many of the *concepts*, the ideas, the ways of thinking, that lie behind the words: for example, the *ideas* of postponing or compromising on his wishes, are difficult for the deaf child to grasp, since he is denied the use of words in having such ideas explained to him. Furthermore it is not only the words and the concepts that he misses, but the guidance, comfort and reassurance that follow from the words, and it is not surprising that he is often bewildered and frustrated.

If we can gain an understanding of the difficulties that follow from the fact that a child is deaf, we can go far in overcoming these difficulties and reducing the frustrations, and can begin to work out a positive plan for his care and training and education, so that when he is older he is both willing and able to communicate as much as possible with hearing people, and thereby take his place in the community.

Before continuing with these topics let us first consider how many deaf children there are and, briefly, the question of why they are deaf and what different kinds of deafness there are.

The Incidence, Causes, and Types of Deafness

Hearing losses can be of any degree, from very slight to very severe, and even total deafness is occasionally found. Many children's hearing losses are temporary, such as those caused by blockages and infections: these are known as conductive hearing losses, they impair the hearing of at least 5 per cent of children for short periods of time and nearly always respond quickly to medical treatment.

In this book we are largely concerned with the type of hearing loss known as a 'nerve deafness', which is not medically treatable, but can be treated through training at home and through therapy and education. There are four degrees of hearing and language impairment:

1. Mild hearing losses, sometimes described as 'hard of hearing', which interferes very little with the child's language development and requires very little specialized help, other than assuring people's *awareness* of the mild loss so that they do not confuse it with backwardness or inattentiveness.

2. Partial hearing loss, leading to difficulties in hearing an ordinary conversational voice, requiring a hearing aid in most cases, and training at home in how to make good use of the considerable hearing that remains and combine this with lip-reading, if the child is to avoid difficulties not only in hearing other people's speech, but in developing his own speech. Given ample language stimulation at home during the early years, it has been found that many such children can attend ordinary schools at age 5, with occasional supervision from a visiting teacher of the partially hearing (Ewing, 1961). Others can attend a special unit for the partially hearing attached to an ordinary school.

3. Severe hearing loss: failing to hear a conversation unless very loud and at close range, and even then frequently failing to understand what is heard because of lack of experience: requiring intensive and regular training at home as early as possible, in making some use of a hearing aid but relying a great deal on lip-reading. A few children with serious hearing losses develop enough language to attend ordinary schools, but the majority attend special units, more and more of which have the advantage of being attached to ordinary schools, so that the

child remains in contact with the ordinary community.
4. Profoundly deaf: again requiring intensive training at home as early as possible, able in some cases to hear just a few sounds through a powerful hearing aid, but nothing which sounds like speech, and relying almost entirely on lip-reading and of course requiring intensive and specialized help both at home and within a special school for very deaf children when older, where many of the children eventually develop some speech and understanding of speech. Some experts, however, are dissatisfied with the amount of language that current 'oral' methods of education are giving to very deaf children, and are advocating some return to earlier 'manual' methods of education, including the use of gesture and signs and finger spelling. We will discuss this controversy later.

Many studies have indicated that just under two in every thousand children have a sufficient loss to warrant the use of a hearing aid. In England and Wales in 1967, approximately 6500 children were attending Deaf and Partially Hearing Schools and Units (Dept. of Education and Science, 1968). The exact numbers of partially hearing children with hearing aids attending ordinary classes in ordinary schools is not accurately known but probably in excess of 6000. This total of approximately 12,500 school children known to have sufficient hearing loss to require a hearing aid, gives an incidence of 1·7 per thousand, to which must be added many hundreds of children outside the formal school system, such as children with multiple handicaps in hospitals and other units. Although the number of deaf children is large enough to give rise to the development of excellent audiology and educational services, voluntary associations and clubs, it is not large enough for the general public to have encountered personally the problems of severe deafness in children, and parents will find it necessary to explain very fully to friends and neighbours what is involved.

There are many different causes of deafness: the ear is a very complicated organ, and may be affected in a variety of ways, and so produce various types of deafness.

Some children are born deaf, either due to some inherited defect in the ear and its nerve connections to the brain, to the illness of the mother during pregnancy, or to difficulties during the birth process. A great deal has been learned about the effects on the unborn child of certain infections of the mother during pregnancy. Rubella (German measles) occurring during the early months of pregnancy, has been found, for instance, to be a cause of deafness, a cause which is now being eliminated either by ensuring that women are exposed to rubella prior to pregnancy, or by injections. Blood group incompatibility between parents is another occasional cause of deafness at birth, which is gradually being eliminated, such as by prompt exchange transfusions. Children may also lose their hearing in infancy or childhood as a result of such illnesses as meningitis, scarlet fever, and measles, and also, very occasionally, as a result of accidents.

Some deafness is caused by blockage or infection of the middle ear (which conducts the sound to the inner ear). Prompt medical treatment is often effective in improving this type of hearing loss.

The type of deafness that is our main concern in this chapter is that which is due to the damage or disease of the inner ear or nerve fibres. This is termed nerve deafness; it is different from conduction deafness in that there is no treatment known at present that can bring back hearing to a person suffering from this type of deafness. In this case, when the inner ear itself is damaged, we have no means of providing a substitute for the delicate and intricate mechanism that transmits sounds to our brain. In many cases of nerve deafness there is an uneven loss of hearing over the different parts of the musical scale. For instance, the child may be unable to hear notes of a high pitch, but hears those of low pitch fairly normally. This particular type of deafness is termed 'high tone deafness'.

It must be emphasized that it is extremely important to make every effort to discover the causes of deafness and to seek specialized medical advice about any possibilities of treatment. When medical or surgical treatment proves impossible, as is the case with 'nerve deafness' in the light of our present state of knowledge, it is still important for the parents to have as much knowledge as is available about the causes. The question 'Why is my child deaf?' is often uppermost in their minds when the deafness is first discovered, followed by concern about whether other children they may have will be affected, and whether their children's children may also be handicapped. In many cases the cause of the deafness is well known, such as rubella during the mother's early pregnancy, and carries no risk to subsequent children. At the other extreme, in a few cases, there may be a strong history of deafness in the family and the risk to further children can often be calculated. Since nearly 50 per cent of the children in Fraser's (1964) study of 2355 severely deaf children were considered to have a genetically determined type of deafness (usually due to a recessive gene in families with *no* known history of deafness) the importance of genetic counselling of parents about any risks to any future off-spring, must be emphasized. Given the facts (such as that there will be in the light of the family histories of the two parents, a one in four chance of their next child having a hearing loss) the parents can then make their own decision. In other deaf children, at least 10–20 per cent, the causes are simply unknown. In all cases a thorough medical investigation and advice to parents about possible causes is essential. The deaf child himself will want to know when he is older. A comprehensive review of recent research, particularly into the causes of deafness, has been edited by L. Fisch (1964). More general books on causes and treatment are those of Davis and Silverman (1960) and Whetnall and Fry (1971). A strong plea for a new effort to discovering methods of treating nerve deafness is to be found in Jack Ashley's article (1971)

The Detection of Hearing Losses in Young Children

At what age can we tell whether or not a child has a hearing loss? Usually before the age of 12 months. This early detection is very important and in many areas valuable screening tests are carried out by Health Visitors and other Local Authority staff, who can then refer all babies who have failed the screening tests for more thorough examinations at specialized E.N.T. and Audiology Units. Usually about half the children referred to Audiology Units turn out to have a hearing loss, and in these cases no time must be lost in advising parents who have a deaf child, giving them a clear indication of what his difficulties are and helping them to provide simple home training as soon as possible. The present-day clinical tests of hearing in a young child consist largely of skilled observations of his reactions to a wide variety of sounds, loud and soft, high and low pitched, within a quiet room and under carefully controlled conditions. For example, the baby's attention must not be too deeply engaged in any particular activity and when the sounds are made, great care must be taken to ensure that he neither sees nor feels the examiner making the sounds. The ordinary baby under about 5 months of age is rarely mature enough to turn his head towards the sound, but usually shows some kind of response, such as a slight movement of his eyes, blinking, shifting his leg or hand, or interrupting his movements. Experienced personnel can observe these muscular responses to quite gentle sounds such as rattles, squeakers, rustling paper, etc. in babies under 5 months of age, and, combining these observations with a careful consideration of the parents' observations at home (*e.g.* is the baby easily awakened by sounds), can say whether the hearing is likely to be normal or not. Great importance must always be attached to the mother's views about her baby's hearing. If she is convinced that he cannot hear, she is usually right, and her testimony has even greater weight if she has other children with whom she can compare her baby's response to sounds at home.

After 5 months of age, the ordinary baby has enough muscular control and interest in his surroundings to turn his head to locate the source of the sounds visually, and the observations become more reliable. If, for example, the baby turns briskly and accurately both left and right to most of the gentle sounds, including high pitched ones, and care has been taken not to let the baby see or feel our movements, there can be nothing seriously wrong with his hearing.

But what if the baby fails to show any signs of responding to these sounds? This does not necessarily mean that he is deaf. A small number of babies simply show little or no interest in sounds until after the age of 6 months and another group fail to respond to sounds because their development is slow in general. It is in such cases that the skilled observations of the Audiology Unit team, usually consisting of an otologist, a psychologist, a teacher of the deaf, and an audiometrician, is essential. For example, if the child who fails to respond to sounds also fails to respond to visual stimuli, such as a moving light, and to touch, such as a puff of air on his cheek, then his difficulties may be more a matter of slow general development rather than of a hearing loss in particular. The Audiology Unit team look at the child as a whole before trying to pinpoint a particular difficulty such as deafness.

The tests we have described so far are known as *distraction* tests of hearing. Soon after the age of 12 months we can also use the most important test of all—the testing of the child's speech and understanding of speech. At ages 12–18 months, many ordinary babies can say a few words and show some appreciation of their meaning, and follow simple spoken instructions such as 'Show me the ball' or 'Where's Mummy' and provided we have been careful in our testing, using a quiet voice and giving no visual or other help such as by gesturing or allowing lip reading, such tests can prove considerable hearing to be present. Failure does not necessarily denote deafness, but combined with further distraction tests of hearing and observation of his general behaviour, such as alertness to visual and tactile (sense of touch) and social stimulation, these *speech tests* can provide very valuable information about the presence of a hearing loss. A monotonous flat tone of voice is also an indication.

By the age of 2, a wide range of toys and pictures can be presented to the child, and even if he cannot name them, we can determine whether he can understand simple spoken instructions, such as can he point to the car, to the doll, to the ball, etc. Failures in such tests of the understanding of language at the age of 2 are usually significant, provided one is sure of the child's co-operation. More sophisticated speech tests after the age of 3 years include tests of understanding words which include high-frequency sounds, such as ship, foot, fish, which some children have particular difficulty in hearing compared to lower tone sounds (Reed, 1958).

By the age of about $3\frac{1}{2}$ years a further kind of testing can be applied in addition to the distraction and speech tests and this is known as a 'conditioning' test. The child is engaged in play and is taught to put a peg in a hole or a brick into a box when he sees a drum being beaten and when we are sure that he is interested and understands the game, the drum is gradually taken out of sight so that he then has to rely on his hearing. Then sounds of varying loudness and pitch are given at various short intervals of time and a fairly accurate picture of the child's hearing can be obtained by experienced observers who understand children's behaviour, the effect of hearing loss and the nature of the sound stimuli. A valuable guide and set of equipment for distraction, speech, and conditioning tests for young children is to be found in Mary Sheridan's (1958) 'Stycar' hearing tests.

By the age of 4 years the majority of children can be reliably tested with headphones, through which sounds are fed by an audiometer, of definite loudness and pitch, and provided the audiometrician can secure the child's full co-operation and attention, so that he listens carefully to sounds which can only just be heard, a very accurate chart of the child's hearing can be obtained, for both ears. The following are two examples of children's responses to an audiometer. For simplicity we have shown the responses of one ear only and will regard the hearing loss in the child's other ear as virtually the same.

The loudness of sound is measured in decibels, shown on the vertical column of the audiogram. Quiet sounds, such as rustling leaves or a whisper, measure at about 40 decibels. An ordinary conversational voice in an ordinary room at 3 or 4 feet distance is at a level of about 60–70 decibels. A loud drum beat at 3 feet is at a level of about 90 decibels. Sounds above the level of 100 decibels begin to feel unpleasant for both hearing and severely deaf children, such as the sound of a pneumatic drill at close range at about 110 decibels. A hearing loss of about 20 decibels, as shown

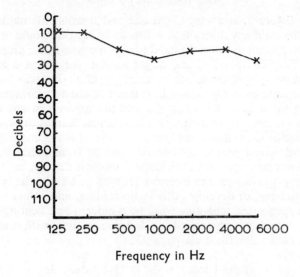

FIG. 7.—Audiogram showing mild hearing loss.

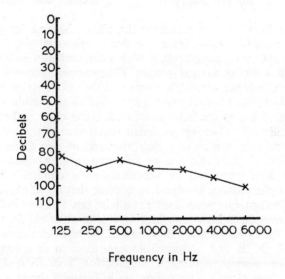

FIG. 8.—Audiogram showing severe hearing loss.

in our Figure 7, is a very slight one and it would be unlikely to cause the child any difficulties. A loss of 40 decibels would in many cases be enough to cause the child to miss a considerable proportion of ordinary conversation and might warrant the use of a hearing aid, but rarely specialized schooling. A loss of 60–70 decibels means that the child certainly cannot hear much of ordinary conversation, without the help of a hearing aid, and the supervision and expert help of a teacher of the deaf would be essential in most cases. A loss of 90 decibels, as shown in Figure 8, is a severe loss, and although the child would derive considerable benefit from a hearing aid, he will not hear speech as we know it through the aid, and would need very specialized and intensive training in making the best use of his hearing, to develop skills in lip-reading, and would usually require specialized schooling when he is older. These hearing losses can be roughly summarized as follows, in line with the four categories we described on page 93:

(a) mild loss	15–30 decibels
(b) partial loss	30–65 decibels
(c) severe loss	65–95 decibels
(d) profound loss	95 decibels and above

The audiometer also measures the child's hearing for various pitches or tones, ranging from low tones, such as middle C on the piano, at 256 cycles per second, to high notes, such as a high-pitched whistle at 4,000 cycles per second. (The recently adopted metric term for cycles per second is Herz, and the abbreviation Hz will be used in future.) Speech sounds are made up of combinations of these tones and, as we have mentioned, some children have particular difficulty in hearing particular tones, such as the high ones. This distorts the speech that they hear and in turn distorts their speech. Special adjustable hearing aids such as those which amplify only the high notes can be provided. These children's hearing losses are often detected rather late, because they appear to respond very well to ordinary sounds such as a faint tap. The first indication of what may be a high tone hearing loss in such children is the fact that their own speech omits most of the high-tone consonants, such as f, sh, th, and s. Speech appears to them as a rumble of low-pitched sounds, making it difficult for them to understand and say words clearly. The audiogram in Figure 9 shows a typical high-tone loss.

The early detection of hearing losses is of great importance and the hearing tests for young children that we have described, many of which were developed by the Ewings in Manchester (Ewing, 1957), should be given to all children who show even slight difficulties in hearing or speech. The results obtained are reliable in the majority of cases, even with babies who were formerly considered too young for hearing tests. The tests are not yet completely scientific or 'objective' but in the hands of personnel who are experienced in audiology work many accurate hearing tests can be carried out well before the baby is 12 months of age. Severe hearing loss in otherwise normal babies can usually be detected during the first few months of life.

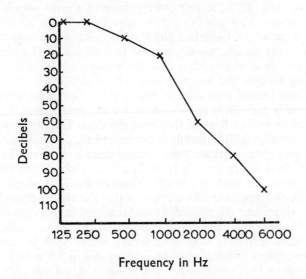

FIG. 9.—Audiogram showing severe high tone hearing loss.

Hearing Tests for the Multiply Handicapped

With the majority of young children, hearing tests can be carried out quite accurately by experienced personnel. Problems in testing arise, however, when the multiply handicapped, such as those children who are emotionally disturbed or who show autistic or hyperactive behaviour, those who show obscure language disorders, the cerebral palsied and certain rubella children who may also be blind as well as possibly deaf, and certain categories of subnormal children, who are sometimes too immature to attend to a stimulus with any reliability. In all these cases, the behaviour and language problems may or may not be aggravated by the presence of a hearing loss, and it is often difficult to be sure about the latter, in the midst of so many other handicaps. This is where the skill and experience of the audiology team is really important. Their observations on the child's responses will be based on a close study of the responses of thousands of children, with one basic question in mind—is the child at least occasionally responding in any way to the sounds the examiner is making, to the sound and nothing but to the sound, and if so, what level of intensity of sound, at what frequencies, is required. The phrase 'at least occasionally' is important. Nobody expects children, or even adults, to respond regularly to a given sound. Boredom, for one thing sets in after the novelty has worn off and with many hyperactive, disturbed children, the audiologist expects him to ignore the sounds, usually because he is preoccupied with something else. And when such a child does respond, we expect him to be using his eyes and his sense of touch, as well as any hearing he may have. Indeed with difficult multiply handicapped children we deliberately give them massive cues, for example letting them see and feel as well as hear (if they can) the drum initially, rewarding their responses with tremendous praise and encouragement, in the conditioning tests that we have already described, where the child has to place a peg in a hole or knock a brick off the table in response to our massive signals. Then gradually the signals are reduced, the props are taken away, so that the child will no longer see the drum and the examiner's gestures, and instead has to start using his hearing, first for very loud signals and then gradually to softer ones—reverting to massive signals if and when his attention wanders, then returning again to discreet signals when he is again co-operative. Frequent changes in play material and types of signals are also important to avoid habituation or boredom. Such procedures usually take several sessions during which most of the child's responses will be quite useless as far as judging his hearing is concerned: but a certain percentage of his responses, much more than could occur by chance, will, to the skilled audiologist, show unequivocal responses (or failures to respond) to sounds, of more or less known intensity and pitch. These observations, in the context of the audiologist's clinical experience are usually sufficient to detect whether a multiply handicapped child also has the burden of a hearing loss. In some cases of course his handicaps might be considerably aggravated by such a loss, for example the restless behaviour of children who have had meningitis is often aggravated by the fact that their hearing loss denies them the use of language in exploring and controlling their environment, and modifying their behaviour.

From these descriptions of audiology work with difficult children, one can see the need to develop more efficient 'objective' tests, which will be less dependent on the co-operation of the child and on the clinical intuitions of the examiner. These objective tests are based on the theory that if and when a child hears a sound, there must, somewhere within his person, be an accompanying physical, electrical or chemical change, resulting from the fact that certain nerves are being stimulated. The task then is to discover and measure these accompanying changes, whether by electrical waves in the brain (known as E.E.G. or evoked response audiometry), by exact measurement in breathing or pulse rates or skin potential (known as psychogalvanic skin response, P.G.S.R. audiometry). In E.E.G. testing the child need hardly co-operate at all, since he can be put into a light sleep. Records of electrical and muscular activities can be carried out electronically and analysed by a computer, although observers do differ at present on the interpretation of some results.

The difficulty is that these objective techniques are simply not reliable enough yet. They tell us, with the help of very elaborate equipment, a great deal about the hearing in some children, but not in others, and these others tend to be precisely those children whom we have already described as difficult to test, such as hyperactive and multiply handicapped children. Objective hearing tests on these groups of children so far tend to produce a confusing picture but work along these lines is promising and has been well-described by Jerger (1963) and Taylor (1964). The minute analysis of the characteristics of the cries of new-born babies is another experimental objective technique that may eventually prove helpful in early detection of handicaps such as deafness (Wasz-Höckert, 1968). In the next decade it is likely that a combination of several techniques, objective and subjective, will prove to be the most valuable approach in assessing the hearing of multiply handicapped children.

The Psychological Effects of Deafness

When a child is found to have a serious disability, such as deafness, the psychological consequences can be profound. The parents' first reactions on being told of their child's deafness is often one of shock and bewilderment, followed by a multitude of questions.

Some of these questions reflect very deep feelings, for example

'Why did it have to happen to my child?' or 'Why has it happened to me?' with an underlying feeling that in some mysterious way the parents feel responsible for the deafness and somehow caused it to happen. Such strong feelings of personal responsibility for the handicap are of course completely without scientific foundation— nearly all deafness is caused by factors completely outside the control of any persons.

Other questions are of a more rational level, such as 'Is it certain that he is deaf?', 'What caused the deafness?', 'Can it be cured?' or 'Will our child always be deaf?', 'Will he be able to manage ordinary school?', 'What sort of job will he do?'.

These are important questions, spelling out the ramifications of the child's handicap now and in the future, and demanding careful and factual answers and frank confession of ignorance in cases where the facts are unclear, rather than vague reassurances that 'everything will be all right'. There is no point in denying that coming to terms with severe and permanent handicaps does make special demands on the courage and skill and understanding of the parents, and calls for considerable adjustment on their part, particularly in respect of their hopes and plans for their child's future. Parents are helped by the knowledge that the handicapped child's problems are the problems of all people and that society at large has become increasingly aware of its responsibilities in recent years. In other words, the parents are not alone and there are many individuals and organizations available to help if and when they need help.

Parents are also helped by the knowledge that most of the handicapped children's difficulties are very similar to those of ordinary children, such as problems of temper tantrums, of disobedience, messy eating, so-called laziness, disappointments at school, and so on. The deaf children certainly have no monopoly on these problems and we must be careful not to assume that all their difficulties are necessarily due to their deafness. Deaf children vary as much in their behaviour as do ordinary children and on the whole they are helped or hindered to a large extent by the example that their parents set for them.

Parents are also helped to come to terms with the handicap when they realize how much they can do to minimize its effects: and this is particularly so in respect of the upbringing of deaf children compared to many other handicaps such as severe mental retardation.

Let us briefly consider the psychological effects of deafness now from the child's point of view, effects which parents must understand if they are to help overcome some of them. We can compare the start of the day for a young child of normal hearing and for a child who is severely deaf.

The young hearing child wakens from his sleep, perhaps because of a slight noise of a car or a bird. He gets out of bed, and goes to the window to look at the car. He thinks about its colour or shape and perhaps imitates the sound of its engine. He is reassured that breakfast will not be very long in coming by the sound of crockery in the kitchen and the low murmur of parents' voices. Eventually he hears the sound of mother's footsteps in the passage leading to his bedroom, and he jumps back quickly into bed, since he knows that mother does not like to see him out of bed. She smiles, they talk, she finds his dressing-gown, and he is told to find his slippers and then go to the bathroom.

For the young, severely deaf child, who has had no training, the start of the day is very different.

He is awakened not by any sound, but perhaps by light. When he is awake he does not know whether his parents are out of bed. He cannot hear footsteps (but he might feel very slight vibrations of the floor). If he is hungry he hears no comforting sounds from the kitchen, and does not know whether the time for breakfast is near or far (but he might detect a smell). Crossing to the window he sees something outside. He has no name for what he sees, and his thinking about it is limited by the fact that he has no words (since he has never heard any words) in which to express his thoughts.

Suddenly the door opens. Things happen very suddenly for the deaf child. It is his mother coming into his room: he had no warning of her approach through the sound of her footsteps. Mother smiles and he returns her smile. Her lips move, her facial expression changes, and she hurriedly crosses to the cupboard, hunts for his dressing-gown, and quickly wraps it round him. He may not understand why mother does this and may even resist it; she thinks he is cold, but he may not feel in the least cold. They cannot explain to each other. Later at the breakfast table all is silent. Lips move but no sounds emerge. Mother suddenly darts out of the room. The young deaf child does not know that the door bell is ringing. He looks at father and tries to work out whether he will go to work or stay at home that day.

Comparing these two examples, we can bring out several points about the problems of deafness for the young child, and ways of minimizing the effects of handicaps, starting with a very general point about deafness.

(a) *The lack of auditory background noises and warnings.*—
By this we mean that he does not hear those almost continual noises
of everyday life that normally hearing people take for granted and
hear only half-consciously, such as the distant noise of trains,
voices, doors closing, and the wind in the trees. These are important
psychologically. They mean for the normally hearing person that
life is going on and that they are in contact with it. These half-
heard noises add to our feeling of being alive and in touch with
other living beings. Many of these noises, such as in our example
the clink of crockery in the kitchen, are of a reassuring nature.
The world of the severely deaf is silent, and this silence induces
a sense of isolation.

The young deaf child does not get the warnings and promptings
that help the hearing child to adjust to things. He frequently misses
his cue, as in our example in which he did not hear his mother
approaching his bedroom, and was not prepared emotionally for
her arrival. His daily life is full of such surprises (since he lacks
warnings through sound) which, however pleasant they turn out
to be, are initially something of a shock.

(b) *Difficulties in participation in family life.*—The deaf child's
participation in family life is limited to some extent by the difficulty in communication. The untrained severely deaf child lacks
speech of his own and cannot understand the speech of others
through lip-reading. This means that he is missing some aspects
of the countless activities that a mother and child do together, such
as dressing, bathing, eating, going out, learning what he can and
cannot do, and later on, doing things with father and brother and
sister.

Modern studies in psychology have emphasized that the child's
personality is greatly influenced by these early activities, particularly those in which he participates with his mother during the
first few years of life. The baby at birth is a helpless creature,
dependent on his mother, not only for meeting his bodily needs,
but his needs for affection and security which at this stage can come
only from the mother. This stage of more or less complete dependence on mother slowly gives way to increasing independence after
the child begins to walk in his second year of life. His desire to
explore, and to gain some control of his surroundings and assert
himself, become stronger and stronger, and his wishes come into
conflict with his mother's wishes particularly in the second and
third years.

Provided that the child feels fundamentally loved and secure,
and has not been either rigidly over-controlled or his initiative and

efforts at mastering things sapped by the fact that everything has been done for him, his self-assertion and defiance gradually diminish. He becomes reasonably independent, within a framework of co-operation, capable of some control over his wishes for the sake of the wishes of his parents and other people around him.

This process of child development, through participation in family life, takes place quite naturally in the great majority of families. It also takes place quite naturally in the families of the majority of deaf children, but some difficulties do occur and can be avoided. The deaf child is not born with a different personality from that of hearing children: personality develops largely as a result of his early participation in family life in just the same way as for a hearing child, but with some additional difficulties. We will consider some of these difficulties in the deaf child's emotional development, in his forming of habits, and in his social, intellectual, and speech development.

(c) *The emotional development of the deaf child.*—All children need affection and security, and these needs are not so easily met in the case of the deaf child. For example, he cannot hear the voice of his mother, which reassures him when he is frightened. He often feels a little isolated and unsure of his mother's presence and her attention, since he cannot hear her footsteps close at hand. When she disappears from his sight she seems to him to disappear completely and suddenly. Since he cannot hear his mother, and is therefore cut off from this source of security, it is important that he should see her as much as possible. In the pram or cot, he should often be sat up so that he can see his mother in her daily activities. Light, too, is important to a deaf child, who depends a great deal on his vision, and he is therefore more readily frightened of the dark.

When he is older he may follow her around excessively, trying to keep her always within his sight. This cannot be overcome simply by thrusting him away. Independence does not develop in this way; it emerges slowly and naturally in children, provided they feel basically secure and are given opportunities to manage things without their mother's continual presence.

This business of managing things for themselves, of exploring the world around them, has some extra difficulties for the deaf child. His attempts at managing to drink from a cup, dressing himself, and putting his toys away, cannot be helped by spoken explanations as with a hearing child; and when he fails, as all children do when first attempting to master things for themselves, his sense of failure and possible show of temper cannot be so easily lessened by spoken reassurance or by a spoken suggestion of doing something else that is not so difficult.

He is, of course, helped by the gestures and reassuring smile of his mother, but only when he is looking at her. He cannot be both looking at mother and concentrating on a task such as trying to draw, in the same way as the hearing child can. It is important, therefore, that parents should not press upon him tasks that are too difficult. They must keep an eye on what tasks (such as buttoning his coat) he is ready and mature enough to accomplish and what tasks are obviously going to be difficult at his age. The difficult tasks must be shared between the parent and the child, or if it impossible at his age, some easier task or activity substituted for it. Too many failures and resulting tantrums would cause the child to recoil from independence and cling excessively to his mother or become anxious and withdrawn.

Parents who are 'over-demanding' in relation to their handicapped child are less common than those at the other extreme, parents who are 'over-protective'. By this we mean the mother who does everything for the child, who 'over-protects' him from any challenge or difficulty, so that his learning to manage things himself is greatly impaired. A certain amount of protection, beyond that ordinarily given to children, is, of course, inevitable in bringing up a severely handicapped child, helping him with vital matters, such as adequate feeding, avoiding traffic dangers, dangerous stairs, etc. Protection becomes over-protection when it is carried to extremes and when every difficulty and need is foreseen by the parents and quickly met by them, and little or no effort is demanded on the part of the child. A vicious circle is soon set up in which the child comes to rely excessively on his parents, has no confidence in his own ability to cope, and goes through life expecting similar over-indulgence from other people. This can be as great a handicap as the deafness. In some cases over-protective parents may be the ones who feel in some way guilty about their children's handicaps and shower attention on him as if to try to make it up to him.

Successful emotional development lies in keeping a balance between doing too little for the child and over-pressing him, and doing too much and smothering him; in developing an attitude of realistic acceptance of the child, of his assets as well as of his handicaps, a real appreciation of his needs, and an overwhelming desire to encourage him to achieve as much independence as is possible within the context of his handicap.

(d) *Habits and their development.*—At the age of 3 or 4 the child's drive towards independence becomes strong, and both hearing and

Communication at all ages with the help of hearing aids.

Stretching the limits of communication.

Getting the message—through seeing, hearing and feeling.

The mother as well as the child learns from sessions with the teacher of the deaf.

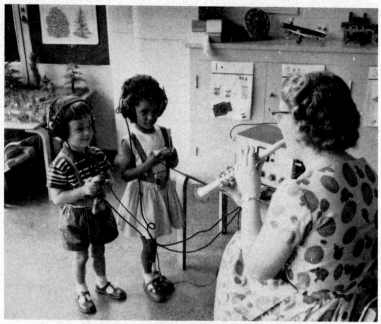

Electronic clarinet—through a powerful amplifier.

Sessions with highly amplified speech help language development.

'I can hear myself whistle.'

A modern well equipped classroom for deaf children.

Looking closely at speech.

deaf children insist on doing forbidden things as if they were seeing
how far they can go in challenging parents' rules.

The deaf child is likely to be particularly active in touching and
moving things at this stage, since touching and close looking at
things is a way in which he makes up for his lack of speech and the
fact that he cannot have things explained to him. He should, of
course, be allowed to explore things as much as possible, but must
realize that there are limits to what he is allowed to do. From his
parents' shaking their heads and from their gestures he will slowly
realize this, provided the rules that he must follow (such as not
touching the clock or turning the tap on) are applied consistently.
He must not be allowed to throw his toys one day and forbidden
the next. It is particularly difficult for him to grasp the exceptions
to the rules, *i.e.* that he may throw a ball but not his toy bricks;
patient demonstration of the difference must be made, otherwise
he will not know where he stands.

Consistent rules and routines are a very important source of
security for the deaf child, to some extent making up for his lack
of hearing the spoken word and the sounds of everyday life.
Routines are especially important in the development of habits
such as resting, eating, and toilet training. These need not present
any great difficulties. In learning to eat with a knife and fork he
will take a little longer than the hearing child, and perhaps eat
rather noisily, not being aware of the noise he is making. He can
gradually be taught to eat with his mouth closed. In toilet training
he may have more relapses after the age of 2, especially if he has
many frustrations and irritations in the day, causing a temporary
breakdown in his control of his bowels and bladder. He will be
helped by tolerance on the part of the parents, and fairly definite
routines not only for his toilet needs but for the times of various
daily activities such as meals, play, bed, etc.

(e) *Social development.*—By social development we mean the
child's capacity to form friendships and generally for getting along
with other children and adults. This development is greatly influenced by the early family life of the child, in which he first learns
to give and take and share experiences in his relationship to his
mother, and later in relation to other members of his family, and
eventually, around the age of 3, with persons outside his family
circle. With the deaf child this social development presents some
difficulty, since he can make only limited use of the speech and
understanding of speech that are so important in social relationships. Unless helped he may be solitary, preferring to cling to his
toys or to his mother instead of facing and overcoming the diffi-

culties of communicating with hearing children. Seeing other children speak and act as a result of speech in their games, he may feel left out of things and withdrawn. This is particularly so after the age of 5 when children begin to play more in groups and have to follow rules in their games.

Speech, however, is not so important in children's play between the ages of 3 and 5, as are practical activities and skills. Many deaf children benefit in their social development by attending an ordinary day nursery for part of the day and it is important that deaf children should learn to enjoy the company of hearing children. This can be helped if the attitude of adults and children in the deaf child's neighbourhood is favourable. The child's parents should explain to the neighbours as fully and frankly as possible about the deafness and what follows from it, so that they gain some understanding of his difficulties, and some appreciation of his assets. The child's first contact with hearing children will be easier if at first one companion only is invited home to play and have tea, where mother can keep a watchful eye on the situation, in the background, and can, if the companion is old enough, explain a little about the deafness, in a matter-of-fact and certainly not a pitying manner. An excellent guide to parents on these topics is that of H. R. Myklebust (1950) and the same author has published a more technical work on the *Psychology of Deafness* (1964).

(f) *Intellectual development.*—In the great majority of deaf children, there is no reason to suppose that the factors that impair their hearing have also impaired their basic intelligence. Many psychological studies (Murphy, 1957) have shown that on average the deaf children score the same intelligence quotient on tests that do not require speech or spoken instructions,* as do ordinary children. This does not mean that all deaf children are of average

---

* The following tests are commonly used by psychologists in assessing learning abilities of children with hearing losses. They involve simple gestured instructions in place of spoken instructions and consist largely of attractive puzzles, in which the children have for example to match pictures and wooden shapes, sort and classify pictures, construct patterns of coloured bricks, complete drawings that have parts missing, complete jigsaw puzzles, and arrange pictures in a correct sequence so as to tell a story: many of the following tests have been well described by Reed (1970):

For age 1½–5 years	Merrill-Palmer Scale.
3 –11	Nebraska Test of Learning Aptitude.
3½–11	Columbia Mental Maturity Scale.
4 –16	Wechsler Intelligence Scale for Children and Wechsler Pre-school and Primary Scale of Intelligence (Performance Scales).
5 –11	Raven's Coloured Progressive Matrices (1956).

intelligence; there are some very dull deaf children (approximately 15 per cent) and a small percentage of very retarded ones, who usually have other handicaps such as cerebral palsy and blindness in addition to the deafness and these are known as children with multiple handicaps; and there are some very bright deaf children, again approximately 15 per cent and a small percentage of very gifted ones, who have shown their talents in writing books and achieving high academic degrees. The spread of intelligence on tests that do not involve language is about the same amongst deaf as amongst hearing persons. Their basic reasoning powers are intact, but severe hearing losses of course reduce the extent to which the basic intelligence can be developed and expressed through language. It is possible to think without words, and as Hans Furth (1966) has shown, severely deaf children can perform many intellectual tasks that used to be considered to be largely dependent on language, such as classifying objects, discovering similarities and other concepts amongst groups of objects and pictures, and remembering a long series of numbers (when presented visually). at a level often comparable to that of hearing children, provided they are given adequate, non-verbal instructions about the tasks that the examiner wishes them to perform. However, the quick and efficient communication of thoughts, particularly in the complex and changing world of today, depends a great deal on words: new ideas, concepts, and points of view come at us from all angles and come to us, largely through the medium of words. The average child as young as 5 years has a vocabulary of at least 2000 words (Watts, 1960). Some untrained deaf children know virtually no words at this age, which means their reception, storage, classification and expression of ideas are severely reduced, they lack experience, and cannot make full use of their intelligence, compared to ordinary children.

This is why we place so much importance on language training for the deaf at the earliest possible age: not simply to teach a young deaf child to say a few words, but first and foremost to encourage him to appreciate the usefulness of language, and to develop understanding of speech. We will deal with this language training in our following section. Parents can also help the child's intellectual development by ensuring that plenty of constructive play material is available, such as wooden bricks and building materials, constructional sets, plasticine, clay, paints and large pieces of paper, sand tray, and other equipment that can be used creatively and constructively and will help to develop the child's ideas of shape and colour, distance, position and movements of objects in space, without necessarily involving language. Colour, shape, smell, taste, and the feeling of movement and texture are obviously important to a child who can hear very little. Play is, of course, important not only to foster intellectual and language development, but to express emotions, to help the child develop confidence and, when playing with other children, to learn to co-operate and share activities.

Language Development

Language has many uses. It is used as we have already mentioned, to facilitate our thoughts and this can be termed our 'inner language', a sort of talking to ourselves, as when we sit and plan tomorrow's activities; to express our thoughts and feelings to other people through speech, and to interpret the thoughts and behaviour of other people through the understanding of their speech. Language also has its written as well as its 'inner' form and its expressive and receptive spoken forms. Now nearly all language comes to us through hearing. Language develops in a child of normal hearing through the imitation of the speech that he hears around him, and by his wish to use speech to gain further contact with, and control over, his surroundings.

In the first few months of life the deaf baby's vocal cries and gurgles, which are the spontaneous, primitive foundations of speech, sound the same as those of the hearing child, but they become a little repetitive and harsh in tone towards the end of the first year. He cannot hear his own babbling vocalizations (but can feel them) and does not receive the stimulus of hearing his own sounds; many deaf children tend to become relatively silent in their second year although their speech organs are normal. It is most important that parents should try to prevent this silence. This is particularly necessary in the case of children who have become deaf after they have learned speech, and tend to become silent. The help of a teacher of the deaf is essential here to conserve their speech.

Language Training for the Severely Deaf

It must be emphasized that very few children indeed are totally deaf. Most profoundly deaf children have a residue of hearing, which means they can make some use of powerful hearing aids although they do not hear speech as we hear it. Instead they hear certain sounds, some of which may approximate blurred vowel sounds and this at least helps the child's awareness of speech, and his appreciation of some of the rhythms of speech.

A severely deaf child's understanding of speech must chiefly be fostered through lip-reading, combined with the sounds he gets through the aid. Some children are amazingly adept and eager at this and attend very well to continuous training: others make slow progress. The basic idea is that the child is taught to use his vision, combined with his residue of hearing and to some extent his sense of touch, to compensate for his hearing loss. He must be encouraged to look at his parents' lips with the aim of learning that certain movements of the lips represent, what we know of as, a word. This lip-reading first of all demands that the parents' lips be visible in a good light, roughly on a level with and within a few feet of the child's eyes, and that there should not be too many other attractions such as gestures and movements of the body to draw the child's attention away from the lips.

No child will learn anything unless he is interested in what is going on. It is vital, therefore, to link the lip-reading with the child's natural interests and activities in the home, such as feeding, playing, preparing for walks and other routines that children enjoy in co-operation with their parents.

Early training in lip-reading must not be regarded as lessons but as play. The mother must encourage her child to become interested in speech connected with his daily activities, so that he learns to appreciate that speech exists and that it has its uses, although he can hear practically nothing. For an example, let us consider the routine of preparing for a walk, the usual equipment being a coat, a hat, and a ball. We aim to associate these objects with a certain movement of our lips. We show the child the ball, saying the word rather slowly and distinctly but naturally, when we are sure he is looking at our lips. The next day we say, 'Take the ball', looking at it, picking it up, handing it to the child, repeating the word 'ball'. After several repetitions we say 'ball' when the child is some distance away from the ball, without any gestures. If the child gets the ball, all well and good, but if not, no dismay or agitation should be shown, but the word 'ball' is accompanied by gesture and movement towards it as before.

Eventually after many repetitions of the game, he will learn to respond to the movement of the lips, grasping that they mean 'ball' with no aid from gestures but still with some clues from the general situation, that of preparing for a walk.

Our further aim is that he should respond to the word 'ball' in a new situation, such as whilst playing indoors. The method can be applied constantly to other things associated with preparing for a walk, but only one or two at a time at first, and, of course, to other pleasant activities in the child's life. In this way his appreciation of speech and its value, his understanding of words, and later of phrases, will slowly grow.

This training must not be forced. It must be carried out in a spirit of play and enjoyment. Sometimes the child will be so eager and active about, say, preparing for an outing that he simply will not look at his mother's lips. Mother must in these instances be tolerant and await her opportunity to catch his interest in her lip movements. There can be no forcing the pace. The most fruitful attitude to training is to view it as a natural procedure, as indeed it is, of a mother talking to her child. He will not hear her, but will gradually learn to read her lips as they engage in pleasant everyday activities together. Rigid and formal speech training will put up a barrier between the mother and child and unsettle him in general and perhaps even cause him to dislike contact with people. One last warning about lip-reading is not to expect perfect results. Parents should try lip-reading themselves, and will realize that not every part of every word is visible : therefore some guess-work is necessary on the part of the child and considerable patience on the part of his parents. A list of useful booklets giving guidance to parents is to be found at the end of this chapter.

The severely deaf child's production of his own voice and speech is a more difficult matter than lip-reading : parents must strive to prevent the dying away of the natural spontaneous sounds of infancy (unheard by him) by showing their great pleasure at every sound he makes and letting him feel the vibrations in the throat, especially in respect of those sounds which are pleasant in tone. In general they must show him their great interest in his sounds and respond quickly to them. The process of converting these sounds into actual syllables and words is a highly skilled matter and the help of the teacher of the deaf will be essential. Most children with a severe hearing loss will need regular and intensive help from a teacher of the deaf and many excellent day schools are available for them. Their early training, however, is very much the concern of the parents and in most areas in this country a peripatetic teacher is available to give guidance and advice to the parents in their very important task of laying the foundations to the child's language development. Given these early foundations nearly all children can develop some degree of inner language, of speech, and understanding of speech. Their rates of progress vary enormously in these respects, some children making excellent progress which enables them to communicate quite well with hearing people under favourable conditions. Others develop language much more slowly even after years of training and the reasons for this are not always clear. In a few cases there may be some limitation in the child's intelligence: others appear to lack the necessary attention and drive and eagerness to communicate and are generally over-active and restless. Others may be emotionally immature and disturbed, perhaps as a result of the 'over-protective' attitudes of some parents, which we have already mentioned. A very small number of children have been shown to have considerable, and in some cases normal hearing, but to be completely unable to attach meaning to what they hear: this condition is described as 'central deafness' or 'receptive aphasia', and is extremely rare. But in many cases the reasons for the poor progress are not at all clear. Alternative means of communication, such as finger spelling or signs, may be helpful at a later age if the oral methods we have described are not fruitful after many years of experience. The oral methods are successful for many severely deaf children and we must bear in mind that even a small degree of language development is of enormous benefit in allowing at least some communication between the deaf child and the hearing world.

Manual Methods of Communication

Manual methods of communication, such as by finger spelling and systematic signs have a long history and have been in use for centuries amongst deaf adults. In the present century, with the introduction of hearing aids and new ideas amongst educationalists, manual methods have given way to the oral methods that we have described above, largely with the aim of helping the deaf to communicate more easily with the hearing world—most members of which know nothing about finger spelling and signs.

In recent years, however, some experts have been arguing the case for a partial return to manual methods. The manualists maintain that decades of oral methods in the education of the very deaf have simply not worked for the majority of children, who are alleged to leave Deaf Schools at the age of 16 with very limited language. The manualists maintain that the net result is not only very limited communication with the hearing world but little real communication between the deaf, whose oral education will have denied them any systematic training in the use of signs. It is further argued that oral methods are satisfactory only for a small proportion of bright and industrious deaf children. An excellent statement of the manualists' case is to be found in an article by Gilmour (1971): there is also some discussion of these problems in a D.E.S. report (1968).

The oralists maintain that their methods have led to miraculous results in some cases and although it is admitted that too many very deaf children leave schools with limited language, this is considered to be due to the fact that many of these children were not properly taught, early in life—that their oral education has not been concentrated enough, has not made effective use of hearing aids and that many residential Deaf Schools are too isolated from hearing people, which has left them with little incentive to develop oral means of communication. Further, the oralists maintain that the introduction of manual methods in Deaf Schools might as it were, drive out oral methods, which are known to be a slow, long-term process of learning.

There must be room for compromise on these opposing view-points. Some research, such as by Birch (1964) suggests that manual methods, if properly used as part of a wider programme of developing communication skills, may actually encourage oral skills. Perhaps a combined oral and manual approach should be instituted, at least for some very deaf children who are not responding to purely oral methods : such children could then use one or other method, depending on whether the child was communicating to a deaf or to a hearing person. We must await further studies before a definite opinion can be given on the possibilities of combining a manual with an oral approach for certain very deaf children, but it seems that more attention must be paid to the teaching of manual methods, at least for the multiply handicapped children. Experiments at Meldreth Manor School for multiply handicapped subnormal spastics, using simple standard gestures, have shown promising results, including increased attempts to use speech, amongst a small group of very deaf children (Levett, 1971).

Language Training for the Partially Hearing

The partially hearing child develops language in a very different way from the severely deaf. The latter is very dependent on seeing and feeling speech, whilst the partially deaf can use hearing to a large extent if properly fitted with and instructed in the use of a hearing aid. Modern hearing aids are small and lightweight, and are being used increasingly with very young children, even before the age of 6 months. With such very young children, however, the aid must be used only for short intervals and under expert advice. Hearing aids have some limitations. They do not always bring the child's hearing up to normal standards. They amplify not only desirable sounds such as speech, but undesirable noises such as the rustle of the child's clothing and extraneous noises such as footsteps, which may irritate the child. The speech heard through them is often distorted to some extent, particularly where the child is more deaf to the high tones; the ordinary aid tends to over-amplify the low tones for such a child, and it is a fact that very loud sounds are almost as irritating and unpleasant to the deaf child as they are to the hearing child. If we amplify the sound too much it becomes painful: if we amplify too little, the sound is too faint for the child to understand the speech. Lastly, the aid does not enable the child to locate the direction from which the sound is coming.

In view of these limitations it is essential that the aid should be regarded as one part of the programme of language training, and not as an isolated, cure-all piece of apparatus. Its introduction to the child must be accompanied by pleasant activities such as listening to music, or playing a favourite game so that the sounds he hears through the aid will soon have real meaning to him.

It will help if the aid is used sparingly at first, with the volume control fairly low, especially in noisy situations such as in a busy street, so that no loud sounds frighten the child. Gradually he will be able to tolerate louder sounds.

Parents must always try to show him the source of the sound. When he hears a dog barking they must point out to him where the dog is. In this way the sound he hears will begin to have real meaning for him, and he will be more able to tolerate loud sounds when he knows what they mean.

The only way of overcoming the difficulty that hearing aids simply do not provide anything like perfect hearing for many young partially deaf children is to encourage the child to use lip-reading in addition to the aid. This is most important, since it is the com-bination of lip-reading with a hearing aid that will provide the most effective means of communication. Some sounds, especially high tone sounds such as f, th, s, are too faint to be heard through the aid, but they are easy to lip-read. Other sounds, such as many of the vowels, cannot be seen on one's lips but fortunately, these are loudish sounds, well received through the aid. So the combination of aid with lip-reading is the best approach. There are occasions when one will want to separate the two, for some special training periods. The teacher of the deaf, for example, will show parents what is known as 'auditory training' in which the emphasis is on encouraging the child to listen very carefully so that he can discriminate between words which sound alike and during such periods of concentration on the qualities of sounds, of enhancing the child's appreciation of what he hears, visual stimulation such as lip-reading and gesture should be eliminated. But in the partially hearing child's everyday communication, both lip-reading and the sounds heard through the aid are used. Gestures and miming, however, must be used only occasionally. Parents and children are very tempted to use them. For example, the phone rings, the child does not hear it, so the parent is tempted either to point to the phone or to mime a dialling or lifting of the receiver motion with his hands, instead of gaining the child's attention to his face and clearly saying 'The telephone is ringing' so that eventually the child will learn these words after many repetitions. Too many gestures reduce the child's incentive to persist with true language training that can eventually be so much richer than mere gestures. Obviously it would be unnatural to try to eliminate all gesturing, but it should be reduced to a minimum.

When a child is first fitted with an aid, the speech that he hears through it will have little or no meaning for him, because he has most likely not heard it before. It will therefore be necessary to teach him the meaning of words, and if he has already learned to lip-read several words and phrases these will be a valuable basis upon which to build. This building-up must proceed in much the same way that we have outlined in the previous section on lip reading for the severely deaf child. The rate of progress will be greater since he will be hearing a certain amount of speech through the aid as well as seeing speech on the lips. During the part of the day when, with a very young child, the aid is not being used, he can benefit by hearing his mother's voice very close to his ear. The partially hearing child's speech production will be very much more akin to ordinary speech than the speech of the severely deaf child.

In encouraging and training the partially deaf child's voice and understanding of speech (through lip-reading combined with the hearing aid) it is essential, as we saw in the section on the severely deaf child, to utilize the everyday natural activities of the child and his mother, maintaining his interest in speech and his desire to communicate. When he begins to appreciate the value of speech and find joy in verbal contact with people, he will then truly appreciate his hearing aid. But the child's desire to communicate must first be nourished by the parents. This desire will not be encouraged by over-pressing the child to respond to speech: too much shouting through his hearing aid is likely to make him 'keep himself to himself' and prefer restful silence.

The golden rule of language training is to take every opportunity to talk naturally about everyday activities and experiences and play. The parents should concentrate on a certain number of words and phrases at a time, repeating these until they are well known. It is vital to maintain the child's lively interest and give him continuous encouragement, emphasizing his successes rather than his failures, so that his confidence in his ability to communicate is gradually strengthened. Speech and comprehension of speech are developed in a partially hearing child largely by constant exposure to speech sounds, and these must reach his ears loud enough and often enough, in situations where their reference to the child's own world can be readily appreciated.

Electronic Aids

As we have mentioned, equipment such as hearing aids must be regarded as part of a programme of language training for the young child. He must learn to make sense out of the sounds he hears. For the majority of children the Government-issued Medresco Aids are satisfactory instruments offering a considerable range of intensities and frequencies of sound, but some children need more versatile aids. For very severe hearing losses and losses affecting higher tones and for some children who have particular difficulties in tolerating loud sounds (a phenomenon known as recruitment), more expensive commercial types of aids are sometimes recommended. More varieties of the Medresco would be useful. The very small aids (known as post-aural or head worn) that fit behind the ear are helpful for mild to moderate hearing losses, but are not powerful enough for the majority of severely deaf children.

Some experts recommend the provision of two aids, or two ear pieces fed by one aid in cases where the hearing loss is virtually the same in both ears, but opinions are divided on whether these techniques really help and we must await further studies.

The loop system is a way of getting better performance from a hearing aid in certain situations. It simply consists of a length of wire arranged around a living room and connected to a radio, T.V. or tape recorder loudspeaker output, and the electrical impulses in the wire can be picked up by a special coil inserted into the hearing aid, enabling the child to hear a high quality of sound anywhere in the room without the usual interference from surrounding noises. A leaflet on this subject has been published by the National Deaf Children's Society for the guidance of parents.

Auditory training apparatus is simply a large and very efficient type of amplifier, for providing carefully adjusted intensities of sound through headphones, and is a very useful adjunct to home training sessions.

Teachers of the deaf use all the above equipment in their school and home training work, and experiments are proceeding with more advanced electronic equipment such as in the field of 'visible speech', which presents to a severely deaf child a visual pattern of the sounds that he is attempting to produce, on a type of T.V. screen, so that he can be helped to attain speech sounds that more nearly approximate the normal pattern. With advances in electronics over the past decade, we can look forward to a wider variety of aids for many types of handicapped children. For example there are experiments with 'speech machines', that can receive spoken language and transfer it into written form, so that a hearing person can communicate with a severely deaf and speechless one: the latter can type a message in return, which could be translated into a spoken form, to be heard by the other person. These are interesting experiments limited at present by the time factor—they produce slow communication compared to normal rates, but with increased computer assistance, such speech machines should eventually prove useful.

Schooling

The ordinary child goes to school for a variety of purposes, not only to acquire knowledge of school subjects, but to learn them in such a way that he develops his abilities to think for himself, to share experiences at work and play with other children, and contribute to the work and play of the group, and so learn more and more about the wider society and his possible place in it. A great deal of this learning takes place through the medium of language, both written and spoken, so we must ask to what extent can children whose hearing losses have impaired their language, participate in ordinary school life and share the life experiences of ordinary children?

The answer is an increasingly optimistic one. Many factors that we have described in this book, including the better facilities for the early detection of deafness leading to early and sustained home training, the increasing help available from visiting teachers of the deaf, and the provision of better hearing aids, have resulted in more deaf children being successfully 'integrated' with the normal school and community. An excellent description of the educational possibilities for deaf children is to be found in an article by Michael Reed (1964).

Children with a mild hearing loss, of say less than 35 decibels, are likely to have so little impairment to their language development that they can cope with normal schooling without special help other than the fact that they should usually sit near to the teacher in the classroom, and that all the staff should be aware of the mild hearing loss so that they can occasionally make slight allowances for it.

Most children with a partial hearing loss develop enough language to profit by ordinary schooling, usually with the help of a hearing aid, especially if they have had the benefits of early training at home. At least occasional supervision by a visiting teacher of the deaf is essential, and in cases where the hearing loss is marked and the child's language development is noticeably below that of the other children, weekly training with a teacher of the deaf is essential. The teacher can also give valuable advice to the other staff about ways of providing opportunities for lip-reading, using the hearing aid effectively, and ensuring that the child's difficulties are understood by all the staff and the other children.

There is much to be said for giving the majority of children with a hearing loss a trial in an ordinary school, starting at the nursery stage, so that they have experience of mixing and communicating with the hearing world.

The trend from special schooling to ordinary schooling has been strong in the past decade and carries many advantages, and even some severely deaf children have successfully managed ordinary schooling. But not all partially hearing children and certainly not all severely deaf children can cope with ordinary schooling. Their language, for several reasons, remains several years below their age level so they are under a constant sense of strain in trying to keep up with the lessons and with the social life, particularly in the later stages of the junior school career where language in all its forms becomes very important.

The answer lies in a compromise: the Partially Hearing Unit attached to an ordinary school. These units which have developed since 1945, prior to which there was little or no official distinction between the partially hearing and the deaf, provide specialized teaching and a full range of aids to a small group of children, usually less than 10, who can share many of the activities within the normal school, and if their progress is good, can eventually join the ordinary school classes for the majority of their lessons. Provided the children have been carefully selected and their ordinary school teachers carefully advised about their needs, valuable work can be accomplished in these Units. Three excellent Ministry surveys highlight the strengths and weaknesses of recent arrangements (D.E.S., 1963, 1967, 1968).

The very severely and profoundly deaf child will usually need more specialized and intensive training than the Partially Hearing Unit can provide since their very limited residues of hearing mean that they can derive only a certain amount of help from powerful hearing aids and other amplifying equipment, and their speech and understanding of speech must be developed largely through their vision and sense of touch. Progress through these means, although remarkably good in some cases, is often not rapid enough, although experiments are being made to form special units for severely deaf children, attached to ordinary schools, as described by Dale (1967). In our present state of knowledge and training techniques the majority of very deaf children still attend a special school for the deaf and this represents a certain degree of 'segregation' from the ordinary community. The effect of this segregation is less in a day school, than in a residential school and many large towns have sufficient numbers to warrant a special day school, which enables the children to remain in contact with the hearing community at least for a large part of the week. The numbers, however, are too small to permit day schooling in all parts of the country and boarding schools are necessary on these grounds. They are also necessary in some cases where the family background is very unsettled or where the child has handicaps in addition to deafness, such as cerebral palsy or visual defects, requiring very specialized teaching. The Spastics Society, for example, has two units for partially hearing children who are also cerebral palsied. Residential schooling is also available for other exceptional groups, such as deaf children and adolescents who are emotionally disturbed, those who are blind, and for very intelligent and mature pupils requiring grammar school or technical education. Schools are also available for slow learning (educationally subnormal) pupils.

Opinions vary on the age at which young children should enter boarding school. Some teachers of the deaf advocate early admission so that intensive training can be started during the early formative years in the child's life, before he has developed fixed habits of limited communication, such as simply by gesture. But most teachers realize that there are risks in separating the young child from his family and that the child may become emotionally disturbed as a result of early separation, and this could outweigh the advantages of early training. It is now becoming increasingly rare to recommend children under the age of 7 for residential schooling.

As more teachers of the deaf become available to organize more intensive home training and improve facilities within the ordinary school, it will be possible to reduce still further the number of deaf children who attend boarding schools wherein, in spite of the high standards of teaching and general skill and devotion of the staff, it is virtually impossible to overcome the disadvantages of separating children from their home and the normal community. These disadvantages become depressingly evident when the deaf child has reached the age of 16 and after many years in a very specialized school environment, is suddenly expected to find his way in the normal hearing world of which he has had so little experience. Of course some boarding school provision will always be necessary for some of the very specialized groups of children we have mentioned and whatever type of school the child attends, whether it be an ordinary school, a Partially Hearing Unit attached to an ordinary school, a special day, or a special residential school, it is essential that the parents and the school should work in close co-operation, so that they share common aims and expectations about such matters as the child's rate of progress and the means of achieving this progress. As one example of gaining closer contact between home and school, we can note the provision at one of the Spastics Society's Residential Partially Hearing Units in which facilities are offered to enable parents to come and stay at the school for certain periods. Weekly, Monday to Friday, boarding at a deaf school can also further the deaf child's contact with home and the normal community.

The Child's Future

What are our aims and expectations generally in respect of the young child with a hearing loss? What sort of adult do we hope will be fostered by the means we have briefly described in this book? We hope first and foremost that he will be socially mature, able to enjoy the company of both deaf and hearing people. In the past it had often been noted that the deaf mixed only with the deaf, leading to a kind of 'minority group' feeling that led to little contact with the life of the wider community. With the improvements in early assessment and home training, and increased education within the normal community, the partially hearing, and to some extent the severely deaf, now have a greater chance of a wider social life, not only because they are more accustomed to contact with hearing people, but because the latter are more accustomed to meeting the deaf, or are at least gaining more understanding, through the medium of books, plays and T.V., of persons who happen to have a handicap.

Of great importance in achieving social integration, is of course the ability to communicate effectively through speech and writing.

Most partially hearing children achieve these adequately, but for some severely deaf children, considerable difficulties persist into adult life. Although there are many examples, such as the studies by the Ewings (1961) which have shown the successes achieved by many severely deaf persons, adequate communication with the normal hearing world does not come easily, as several moving autobiographies have testified. Francis Warfield (1948) who is partially hearing, described for example the tensions at adolescence that arose from her marginal position, as it were, on the periphery of the normal hearing community, struggling for some time to conceal her handicap: whilst David Wright (1969) who became totally deaf at age 7, describes in very moving terms his tremendous fight to achieve his ambition, a very high one for a deaf person, namely that of becoming a writer. Most of the published success stories of this kind are the result of a combination of exceptional talent and persistence and in most cases long-term help from parents and teachers. Since most deaf children are of average rather than exceptional ability it follows that by no means all will achieve sufficient language to allow anything like normal integration within the community, and as we have mentioned, alternative means of communication, such as by 'manual' rather than 'oral' methods are necessary for these, given our present knowledge and techniques and willingness to apply them. These manual methods have the advantage of facilitating communication between deaf persons, but not between the deaf and the hearing— the latter would need someone to interpret the finger spelling. This kind of barrier to integration which all severely handicapped persons suffer in some form, has to be recognized, and whilst continuing our efforts to reduce such barriers (*e.g.* by earlier assessment and training and better electronic aids) we must, in our present situation, accept a goal of *partial* rather than full integration for some very handicapped persons. (An example of partial integration is seen in the recent formation of social clubs for both 'physically handicapped' and 'able bodied' persons, known as P.H.A.B. clubs.) Perhaps a measure of the wisdom and maturity of a community is the extent to which its members can adapt to quite deep *differences* between certain groups in its midst—whether the differences be those of colour, political outlook, intelligence or handicap—and yet retain an over-riding sense of unity and mutual respect. A pluralistic society does not expect all members to be cast in the same mould. The goal of integration in some form, is the ideal, and if the wider community can meet the deal half way, in coming to terms with the handicap, both the deaf and normally hearing persons can enjoy a fuller life.

Finally we hope that the adult will have maintained a reasonable level in his educational work, especially in reading and writing, so that the written word is always available to him and that he will be able to take up employment in one of the many hundreds of occupations that do not demand a normal degree of speech and hearing, such as many branches of engineering, photography, woodwork, chemistry, and so on.

These aims of increased integration are being increasingly realized as we gain greater understanding of the handicap, and learn how to bring parents into partnership with experts, in our endeavours to overcome the difficulties. We are also learning how to bring home to the wider public the fact that handicapped persons, like all persons who appear different from the majority, are the proper concern of us all.

Organizations and Literature

The two organizations concerned with the deaf, providing many valuable services are The National Deaf Children's Society, 31 Gloucester Place, London, W1H 4EA, and The Royal National Institute for the Deaf, 105 Gower Street, London, WC1E 6AH. These organizations provide many books and pamphlets on home training, and equipment including hearing aids, and issue on loan certain kinds of equipment such as auditory trainers. The N.D.C.S. produces a quarterly magazine entitled *Talk*; the R.N.I.D. a monthly entitled *Hearing*. Concerning schooling, a list of schools is available from the National College for Teachers of the Deaf, c/o Royal School for Deaf, Exeter, but advice on schooling for a particular child should normally be obtained from Local Authority and Hospital audiology experts and final recommendations about schooling are usually the responsibility of the Local Education Authority. General advice from a variety of experts—social workers, educationalists, E.N.T. specialists, hearing aid experts, club organizers and careers advisors can usually be obtained through the R.N.I.D. and N.D.C.S. to supplement advice that is available from local clinics, schools and Audiology Units. The authors would like to thank the N.D.C.S. for the photographs in this chapter.

Useful pamphlets for parents include the following:

A Guide for Parents of very young Deaf Children by D. H. Grossman (N.D.C.S.)

Suggestions to Parents of Deaf Children by D. M. C. Dale (N.D.C.S.)
Your Child's Hearing by Lady Irene and Sir Alexander Ewing (N.D.C.S.)
Notes on High Frequency Hearing Loss in Children by L. Fisch (Hearing Clinic, London Borough of Haringey)

Most of the following books and articles, referred to in this chapter, can be borrowed from the R.N.I.D. library.

References

ASHLEY, J. (1971). Deafness—personal viewpoints. *Hearing*, **26**, No. 4. London: R.N.I.D.
BIRCH, J. W. and STUCKLESS, E. R. (1964). *Relationship between Early Manual Communication and Later Achievement of the Deaf*. Research Project No. 1269. U.S. Department of Health, Education and Welfare.
DALE, D. M. C. (1967a). Deaf education—A new approach. *Special Education, incorp. Spast. Q.*, **56**, No. 4.
DALE, D. M. C. (1967b). *Deaf Children at Home and at School*. University of London Press.
DAVIS, H. and SILVERMAN, R. (1960). *Hearing and Deafness*. New York: Holt, Rinehart & Winston.
DEPARTMENT OF EDUCATION AND SCIENCE (1963). *Survey of Deaf Children who have been transferred from Special Units to Ordinary Schools*. London: H.M.S.O.
DEPARTMENT OF EDUCATION AND SCIENCE (1967). *Units for Partially Hearing Children*. Educational Survey 1. London: H.M.S.O.
DEPARTMENT OF EDUCATION AND SCIENCE (1968). *The Education of Deaf Children*. London: H.M.S.O.
EWING, A. W. G., editor (1957). *Educational Guidance and the Deaf Child*. Manchester University Press.
EWING, I. R. and EWING, A. W. G. (1961). *New Opportunities for Deaf Children*. University of London Press.
FISCH, L. (1964). *Research in Deafness in Children*. London: N.D.C.S./Blackwell.
FRASER, G. R. (1964). Causes of deafness in 2355 children in special schools. In *Research in Deafness in Children*, edited by L. Fisch. London: N.D.C.S./Blackwell.
FURTH, H. G. (1966). *Thinking Without Language: Psychological Implications of Deafness*. New York: The Free Press.
GILMOUR, A. J. (1971). Shades of grey. *Hearing*, **26**, No. 5. London: R.N.I.D.
JERGER, J. (1963). *Modern Developments in Audiology*. New York: Academic Press.
LEVETT, L. M. (1971). Discovering how mime can help. *Special Education, incorp. Spast. Q.*, **60**, No. 1.
MURPHY, K. (1957). Psychological testing. In *Educational Guidance and the Deaf Child*, edited by A. W. G. Ewing. Manchester University Press.

MYKLEBUST, H. R. (1950). *Your Deaf Child: A Guide for Parents.* Springfield, Illinois: Thomas.

MYKLEBUST, H. R. (1964). *Psychology of Deafness.* New York: Grune & Stratton.

REED, M. (1970). Deaf and partially hearing children. *The Psychological Assessment of Mental and Physical Handicaps,* edited by P. Mittler. London: Methuen.

REED, M. (1958). *Hearing Test Cards.* The Royal National Institute for the Deaf, 105 Gower Street, London, W.1.

REED, M. (1964). Principles of education of deaf and partially deaf children. In *Clinics in Developmental Medicine,* No. 13. *The Child Who Does Not Talk,* edited by C. Renfrew and K. Murphy. London: Spastics Society/Heinemann.

SHERIDAN, M. D. (1958). *Stycar Hearing Test.* Slough: National Foundation for Educational Research.

TAYLOR, I. G. (1964). *Neurological Mechanisms of Hearing and Speech in Children.* London: Manchester University Press.

WARFIELD, F. (1948). *Cotton in my Ears.* New York: Viking Press.

WASZ-HÖCKERT, O. *et al.* (1968). The Infant Cry, a Spectographic and Auditory Analysis. *Little Club Clin. Dev. Med.,* No. 29. London: Spastics Society/Heinemann.

WATTS, A. F. (1960). *Language and Mental Development of Children.* London: Harrap.

WHETNALL, E. and FRY, D. B. (rev. 1971). *The Deaf Child.* London: Heinemann.

WRIGHT, D. (1969). *Deafness, a Personal Account.* London: Penguin.

CHAPTER V

THE BLIND CHILD

THIS chapter is based primarily on observations made by one of
the authors when consultant psychologist to the Royal National
Institute for the Blind.

Incidence

Fortunately the number of blind children in England and Wales
is not very great. In January 1969 the number of blind children
between the ages of 2 and 16 years, who were educable and attending nursery or special schools was 1,020. This does not include
children on waiting lists for admission to schools. The incidence of
blind children in England and Wales at the same date was 1·58 per
10,000 of the school population. The number varies from year to
year to some extent because the causes of blindness vary. A hundred
years ago blindness due to smallpox, 'inflammation' and 'fever'
was comparatively common, but these conditions rarely occur
nowadays as a cause of blindness in this country on account of
vaccination against smallpox and the high standard of nursing.
There was a considerable decrease in the number of blind children
between 1923 and 1943, but between 1946 and 1953 a marked
increase occurred due to a condition known as retrolental fibroplasia which I will explain shortly.

The children whom I knew best were those who were being
educated in the Sunshine Home Nursery Schools of the Royal
National Institute for the Blind, some 250 children in any one
year. Part of my work consisted in visiting these schools to assess
the progress and development of the children and advise on their
care and education. Some of the children spend 5 or 6 years in
these nursery schools, and by seeing them regularly in familiar
surroundings one comes to know them well. There is very great
interest in watching their development and their ways of learning.

Causation

I do not intend to discuss the causes of blindness to any extent,
as this matter is dealt with fully in medical literature. The majority

of the children with whom I came in contact are born blind or with very little vision. Among the commoner causes of their conditions are optic atrophy, congenital cataract, hydrocephalus, microphthalmos, buphthalmos and a post-natal condition known as glioma; but the most important cause of blindness in babies, especially between 1949 and 1953, has been retrolental fibroplasia.

The exact cause of retrolental fibroplasia is still obscure. It occurs in premature infants of low birth weight who have had to be reared in oxygen tents. It has been suggested that in high and prolonged concentrations of oxygen the immature tissues of the eye suffer changes which ultimately result in permanent scarring of the retina. In a clinical study of 283 blind children under five years of age seen between October 1951 and December 1953 it was found that 151, or 53·3 per cent, were suffering from this condition (Potter, 1954). In the majority of such cases the babies are born 1 or 2 months prematurely, and their birth weight is often below 3 lb. Convulsions tend to occur, and in a number of cases the mother is reported to have suffered from toxaemia. Twins are fairly common. Retrolental fibroplasia children tend to be rather frail, small in stature and sometimes difficult to rear. Their physical development, in the early stages of growth, is likely to be slower than many blind children.

It is difficult to assess the mental ability of such children when they are very young because it may well be that intellectual ability is influenced by poor physical development. In studying over a hundred children suffering from retrolental fibroplasia and giving intelligence tests where applicable, I found that their intelligence level covered the whole range of ability from well above average to well below average, but that rather a higher proportion than normal fall into the lower group. It seems evident that in some cases the eye is not the only part of the nervous system affected, but damage may also have been done to those centres in the brain concerned with movement of the limbs, hearing, speech and mental ability. Until more of these children have been followed through it is too soon to judge whether retardation, both mental and physical, may not be made up. It is encouraging to note than in a total of 177 blind children suffering from retrolental fibroplasia, seen between 1946 and 1951, Potter considered over 50 per cent to be normal or above normal in intelligence, about a quarter somewhat retarded, and less than a quarter mentally defective.

Among the illnesses after birth which may cause blindness, tuberculous meningitis is important. In such cases the child's general physical development may be seriously impaired, but often a good recovery takes place. It is encouraging to find how well some of these children progress if given good nursing and educational care, despite the additional handicap of partial or total blindness which may have occurred. The child may have to learn to walk and talk again, and to go through all the stages of development which were arrested by the onset of the illness.

It is important to remember that the child, who *becomes* blind and is not born blind, has certain definite advantages on account of his visual memory, his recollection of a seen world, but this memory will fade as time passes. The partially sighted child can avoid obstacles and grasp objects more accurately than the blind child, but partial sight especially if it is variable, can lead to great confusion in perception and errors in judgment which cause certain problems in learning the three R's. I will discuss the special difficulties of the partially sighted child later.

Assessment of Mental Ability

In order to decide whether a blind child was likely to benefit from education in a Sunshine Home Nursery School it was necessary to make some assessment of his mental ability. This is an important and a difficult decision to make, and I had found that a number of factors had to be taken into consideration.

The cause of blindness must be carefully noted. Experience has shown that certain conditions such as optic atrophy or microphathalmos are more commonly associated with brain damage than certain others, *e.g.* glioma or cataract.

The fact that the baby may have been premature will almost inevitably retard physical growth in the first year of life, and this in turn may limit the opportunities which encourage mental growth, although in time the child may recover lost ground.

Children with eye defects may have to spend considerable periods in hospital, and it is important to have this information. The baby may have spent the first two weeks of his life in an oxygen tent and many subsequent weeks in hospital. Many blind children have to be examined periodically in hospital under an anaesthetic or attend for some form of treatment, such as needling for cataract. The important process of building a relationship, of becoming attached to one person, usually, of course, the mother, who feeds and fondles, dresses and washes the baby may be delayed or interrupted by hospital care. Normally the mother provides the incentives for mental growth through her interest in and her encouragement of her baby. The security of her affection and care provides the child with the basic quality of good mental health and enables him to learn and to develop normally. Some children are more disturbed than others by separation from their mothers and by minor operations. Some children seem to interpret their admission to hospital as dismissal and rejection from home, and operations as a form of punishment. This is more likely to be the case if family relationships are not very happy or stable, or if the child's hospital experience coincides with the mother's illness or even the arrival of a new baby in the family who may be thought of as a rival for the mother's love. The disadvantages of this situation can be minimized if, on discharge from hospital, the child receives an extra share of mothering and rather special care and attention in his own home. His apparent retardation may disappear when he has built up a secure relationship with one adult who is important to him.

If a blind child is handicapped in movement on account of some degree of spasticity his opportunities to explore and to increase his experience of the world around him will be limited. Similarly, if he has lived too passive and too sheltered an existence in pram or cot or play pen he will have had little chance to use initiative, to try to solve his own problems or to take minor risks, and his knowledge of everyday life will be mainly second-hand, not based on his own first-hand experience. If he has suffered from neglect and lack of encouragement he will appear more backward than he really is. All these possibilities will have to be considered when attempting to estimate the child's level of mental development.

Intelligence tests, standardized on blind children, are available and provide a useful measuring rod if cautiously interpreted. In addition to these tests I have found it useful to base my assessment on incidental observations of the child in a familiar environment while playing with other children, for instance, and on reports and records of parents and teachers who are with the child a great deal. It is wise to make re-assessments from time to time. In some cases it is evident that the child is too backward to benefit from specialized education, but in a number of cases it is impossible to be certain until the child has been given a prolonged trial in one of the residential nursery schools for the blind, and this is arranged in doubtful cases. Children, who are not educable in the usual sense, may yet benefit from social training, but usually they cannot be accommodated in the Sunshine Home Nursery Schools.

It must be emphasized that many blind children are of good intelligence, capable of learning Braille and many other skills, and of earning their living later on, either in the sheltered workshops for the blind or in open industries or professions. They differ in capacity and in special abilities just as sighted children, but in addition they usually develop special sensitivity of touch and hearing which makes up for their loss of sight to a considerable extent.

The Early Care of the Blind Baby

A very experienced teacher of young blind children bases her educational methods on the principle: 'Treat him first as a child and only second as a blind child'. There is a world of truth in this simple statement.

Parents constantly reiterate, 'I don't know what to do for the best; I am sure this is a job for the experts', and some advisers misguidedly concur and recommend early admission to a nursery. The blind baby, just as any other baby, needs his own mother more than anyone else in the world to care for him during his first years of life. It is best to try to forget that he is different from any other child, but talk and sing and frolic with him, just as much and *even more* than with a sighted baby. His needs are primarily the same; affection, security and consistency of care. From the very beginning he needs to be made to feel that he is one of the family, and that the whole family unites in sharing the special opportunity and the special interest that his upbringing entails. He needs a few special things over and above all the usual considerations that any well cared for baby would receive. He needs rather more *demonstration of affection* by petting and cuddling because he cannot see the affectionate expression in her face, although the tone of her voice will be an important indication of his mother's feelings for him. He needs more *talking to,* and to hear more conversation and explanation about the objects and events in his world because his experience is so restricted by lack of visual information. He needs more *encouragement to be active,* more incentive to sit up, to crawl, to stand and to walk, because ordinary visual incentives do not exist for him, and because, since he cannot judge accurately the position of obstacles, he is fearful to adventure and explore on his own as a sighted child would do.

Parents of blind children often ask for advice on general management and care. The Royal National Institute for the Blind has drawn up a number of simple pamphlets on such subjects as feeding, toilet training, playthings and other aspects of care. Meetings for parents have been arranged from time to time so that they may discuss their problems, exchange knowledge and gain information. These have proved very popular.

A Parents' Unit has been set up attached to one of the Sunshine Home Nursery Schools. This is a cottage in the grounds of the school where the parents and the child can stay for a week or so.

The parents have the opportunity of seeing how the children in the nursery school are handled, and are given advice and guidance in the handling of their own child. This is a great help for parents.

Feeding.—Many parents find particular difficulty in regard to the whole question of feeding. In general, feeding the blind baby should follow the same methods as those used for a sighted child. Breast feeding is best both for physical and psychological reasons. The physical contact with the mother is of special value to the blind baby, who cannot see her face but is aware of her feelings towards him by the tone of her voice and the touch of her hands and body. It is an experience of very real significance to the small child, and blind babies seem to resent weaning even more than sighted babies. Weaning needs to be gradual, from about the sixth month, and the baby needs to be accustomed to different tastes such as orange juice, meat juice, and later sieved vegetables and cereals quite early. The usual routine should be followed, and as soon as the teeth begin to erupt, the child should be given something to bite, such as a rusk or biscuit. Blind babies seem more reluctant to accept solids than other babies. Possibly this is because they are more fearful of new experiences and tend to be more dependent and reluctant to leave babyhood behind. Frequently children come to the Sunshine Home Nursery Schools who at the age of 3 are still not eating solids and are not fully weaned from a bottle. It increases the child's difficulties in adjustment to a new environment if the process of weaning has to coincide with his first experience of separation from his own home. The mother is the best person to wean the child, and this should happen before he is 3 years of age.

Blind children may well take longer over the messy stage of learning to feed themselves than ordinary children. A spoon is difficult to manipulate if one cannot see the food on the plate and the easiest and most natural way to pick up the food is by the fingers. This latter method helps a child to find out about the food he is eating in the most effective way; and, what is more, the food does not get cold or unpalatable while he chases it vainly round his plate. The next stage is to put a spoon into his hand, and help him to find the food on his plate, which should have a turned-up rim like a puppy's plate, and guide the spoon to his mouth. It is a short step from this stage to independence in feeding matters. Three-year-olds can be quite skilful at feeding themselves if they are encouraged to do so, although they are naturally inclined to be untidy during the process. Sometimes a spoon in each hand will help to discourage finger feeding. It is, of course, most important to avoid giving blind children food that is too hot, or containing bones or other unpalatable substances, though as they get older they learn to take the pips out of oranges or grapes most competently if carefully guided. It is a delight to watch young blind children in the nursery schools eating ice cream or jelly, their skill almost equal to their enjoyment!

Toilet Training.—The process of toilet training may need to be rather more gradual than in the case of sighted children, but it is a mistake to prolong the wearing of napkins when it is clear that the child can indicate his needs. It is best to delay definite training until the child is nearly a year old. By then he has gained more control over his muscles and he can usually express his wants vocally. He should have been able to establish a good relationship with the adult responsible for him by then, and will co-operate in order to win her approval if he is given gentle encouragement. He needs plenty of praise for successful efforts and only mild disapproval when accidents occur. It is unwise to keep him sitting too long on his pot. If he feels frightened about using it, he may feel safer if he is held in a comfortable position on his pot on his mother's lap. Usually by the time he is two years old he will be fairly reliable, but if he is unwell, over-tired, over-excited or especially disturbed by anything he is likely to relapse. It is wisest to establish weaning, and some degree of independence in regard to feeding, before taking any definite steps in regard to toilet training. Obstinacy and difficulty in regard to feeding often occur if toilet training is started too early and with too much pressure on the child. Usually a small child will be able to relieve some of the tension which may centre round this issue by playing with sand and water.

Bathing and Dressing.—Young blind children show great delight in playing with water, and bath-time provides a good opportunity for this. They become more relaxed muscularly; they enjoy vigorous play with boats and rubber toys, and it is a pity to rush and scurry through bathing when this can provide an outlet for energy and an occasion for experiment and discovery concerning the properties of water!

When washing a blind child it is helpful to talk to him about the objects he is feeling—the soap, face-cloth, nail-brush, rubber duck or any toy in which he is interested. Similarly, when dressing or undressing one naturally talks about the garments he is handling so that he comes to associate their texture and shape with their names. He likes to be told the colour of his clothes, and of other people's, and frequently asks about this as he gets older. If he is born blind he can have no conception of colour. His interest may be due to the fact that he hears sighted people talk about colour constantly, and feels this is something important and which he must know about also.

Gradually the child learns to wash, undress and dress himself, but these skills will naturally be difficult for him to acquire. Five and six-year-old blind children are usually fairly competent, but may still need help with buckling sandals or tying laces. They will enjoy their independence in these matters if given proper encouragement.

Development of Speech.—The speech of a blind child will develop just as fast as that of a sighted child if he is given sufficient encouragement and if the adults around him take time and trouble to talk to him. Blind children ask a great many questions and enjoy using words a great deal. Sometimes they seem to talk just for the sake of talking, using words which they do not fully understand and concerning objects or events of which they have had no first-hand experience. This is known as 'verbalism'. In order to avoid this it is important to give the young blind child *as many and as varied experiences of everyday conditions as is possible.* One needs to talk about the objects he handles and the sounds he hears in terms that he can understand. 'Look! these are your new shoes I bought when I was out shopping. They are made of soft leather, and they have one button to do up which you will soon be able to manage yourself.' In the matter of sound, one might say: 'Yes, I can hear the milkman, too. His milk bottles make quite a clatter, and I can hear his van coming along the road.' One has to interpret the environment to the blind child constantly and help him to make his own observations and his own discoveries. A good game to play out of doors is to sit still and count all the different sounds you can hear—a distant train, a tractor ploughing, a cock crowing, a boy whistling, the wind in the fir wood and so on.

It is well to remember how a blind child learns about his environment, and it is important to give plenty of opportunity to listen and to touch. In a vocabulary test his definitions show the way he comes to know about objects. An 'orange' is 'something you eat, has pips in it'; a 'puddle', 'to splash in'; a 'tap', 'you knock quietly like this'; an 'envelope', 'a square bag to put a letter in'; 'straw' 'to suck juice through'; 'scorch', to burn something when you're ironing'; and a 'hat' was once defined as 'a cylindrical object which fits exactly on your head'!

The golden rules are to tell the child about everything around him with reference to the real objects, to talk a great deal to him, to answer his questions fully, though sometimes turning them back to him with the request, 'You tell *me* this time', and above all to encourage him to make his own discoveries and report his own findings. If he can tell you about 'a lovely baby lamb at the farm, with thick curly hair and a very wet nose who keeps bleating and tries to suck my finger' you will know that this is from first-hand experience.

Blind children, just as other children, love to hear stories told or read to them, and will listen attentively usually much longer than sighted children. It is important to choose stories carefully. Stories that depend for effect on sound imagery such as those in the *Listen with Mother* series are most appreciated. It is not much good reading a story which is profusely illustrated, which contains allusions to incidents and objects outside the blind child's experience and which need tedious and long verbal explanations to make them intelligible.

Play and Play Material.—The toys that a blind baby needs and will enjoy are not greatly different from those for a sighted child. They should be strong, 'bangable', suckable, washable and capable of withstanding tough baby-handling! Up to about 6 months of age the baby needs little more than a cuddly toy, a rattle with bells and a rubber toy that squeaks, but after six months he will appreciate a wider variety. He needs especially toys that will make noise, and he will be just as happy with the kitchen utensils—spoons, colanders, saucepan lids, empty tins (with no sharp edges, of course), as with the most expensive musical box or musical teddy-bear. When he begins to show signs of locomotion he needs toys which encourage movement and effort. A rubber ball with a bell inside, a pull-along toy with a bell attached interest him and help to give him the right direction when he is beginning to crawl or learning to walk. Blind children are hesitant about movement and timid about learning to walk because of the many unknown and unseen hazards they may encounter. They may need a good deal of patient encouragement and persuasion to try to get about on their own, and the baby's mother is the best person to give him the necessary confidence. Toddlers get a great deal of fun from pushing about an empty perambulator or a sturdy horse on wheels. They need toys which are heavy enough to resist them and which will give them sufficient support in the early stages of learning to walk.

Blind children, just as all children, show great delight in water play. They will spend a great deal of time at the kitchen sink if allowed to turn the taps on and off, and make their own discoveries with toys which let the water through—funnels, sieves, rubber piping, old colanders, tin teapots and so on. They need a rubber apron and wellingtons to safeguard their clothes, of course. Sand is always an excellent play-fellow. If the seaside is not near at hand, a sand tray or pit in the garden is a good investment. Earth, water and clay are all natural and valuable materials for a child to use in his play activities, but for the younger child who still takes objects to his mouth to investigate their properties more fully, dough made from flour, water and salt is a good substitute.

Blind children develop great sensitivity of touch, but in the process of acquiring this they need to explore a great deal with their fingers. It is to be expected that very delicate, fragile materials easily become damaged, and it is a waste of money to present a blind 3-year-old with a beautiful doll's house with elaborate fittings unable to stand up to explorations by eager fingers. Mechanical toys are of little real value to a blind child, except sometimes to urge him to movement, and last a very short time. Small cars and miniature wheel toys are enjoyed. Miniature animals are not of much interest because they have so little connection with the live animal. Their texture and their size are different, and they do not make the same noise. One has only to compare a painted wooden cow, whose colours the blind child cannot see, with the real cow in the field on the other side of the hedge to appreciate how little relationship exists between the two! Nevertheless, in order that the blind child does not feel greatly different from other children, it is probably best to give him much the same type of play material and let him put it to the use he prefers. He will enjoy fitting toys interlocking bricks. He likes to have dolls and teddy-bears, but does not play with them a great deal, although he may insist on taking one or several of his favourites to bed with him especially if away from his own home. Although partially sighted children will feed, wash, dress and push their dolls about in perambulators, blind children usually prefer other children for family play, and will push empty perambulators about quite contentedly because they can get no pleasure from seeing a doll dressed up in pretty clothes.

An important principle in the choice of play material, as in the case of ordinary children, is to make use of the natural material around you. Acorns, chestnuts, pebbles, sticks, different kinds of leaves and fruits, grasses, moss, shells and seaweed are of intrinsic interest to every small child. It is, of course, necessary to explain about poisonous fruits and toadstools, but children will learn this kind of thing very quickly. Continuously to forbid a blind child to touch for fear of getting dirty is tantamount to saying 'don't learn', 'don't grow'. Flowers grown indoors from bulbs fascinate blind children, but they are handled so frequently to measure their growth that their chance of survival is not very great!

Blind children tend to be rather passive and inactive because movement is obviously more hazardous and requires more effort for them. They, therefore, need more stimulation than sighted children and like to be played with. This does not mean that they need to be nursed a great deal or pushed in a swing or rocked on a horse or amused by gramophone or radio all the time. A blind child will enjoy a game of ball. He may like you to help him push his horse or pull his truck, or jump or climb or dig. When he has become familiar with his own house and garden he will be able to find his own way about and will not need to have his hand held all the time. If you call to him or clap your hands he will discover that it is quite safe and good fun to crawl or toddle across the grass out of doors. Later he will be running about freely and able to avoid obstacles with comparative ease. Of course, it is necessary to safeguard the child from obvious dangers such as steep stairs, open windows, unguarded fires, and open doors can cause unpleasant bumps if care is not taken.

Blind children usually learn to play with other children rather later than sighted children, but by about 4 years of age they will enjoy imaginative play. There are certain difficulties in regard to play companionship. Sighted children tend to treat the blind child too greatly as a baby, or as a passive partner, or ignore him altogether because he cannot keep up with the pace of their games. Herein lies one sound argument for letting a blind child attend nursery school where there are children with a similar handicap and similar problems to solve.

Family Attitudes

The attitude of the family to the young blind child is a matter of great importance. It requires a great deal of courage to accept the fact that their baby is blind, and a considerable degree of maturity to plan realistically and constructively to provide the best possible care for him. Many parents find it very hard to face this issue and their distress in regard to the baby's disability deserves all the sympathy and understanding that relatives, friends and professional workers can give them.

It seems that there are two usual attitudes of parents to blindness in their children. The first arise out of their natural distress and their natural but misguided desire to shield the blind child from any kind of harm. The child is smothered with mother love. He is protected from any kind of experience which might prove difficult for him. He is constantly sheltered from the hard, cold world and hedged round with reiterated admonitions—not to touch lest he hurt himself, lest he damage something. His every wish is anticipated and he receives very little encouragement to fend for himself. He is not encouraged to learn to crawl or to walk and may be kept amused by devoted and docile relatives, by wireless and record-player. He thus lives a very passive and indulgent kind of life. Both dangerous and interesting objects are kept well out of reach, and he is gently but firmly discouraged from experiments in self-help or from tentative efforts to find out about his environment for himself. At 3 years of age he appears at first sight to be mentally defective. Usually he cannot walk, and he talks very little because his environment has been so restricted. Usually he is afraid of strangers and strange places, and is very reluctant to leave his mother's side. Often such a child is still bottle fed and is adamant in refusing to accept solid foods. He is seldom toilet trained. He is unwilling to explore a new environment or to handle new toys.

Such a degree of over-protection can thus only retard the development of a blind child and is certainly mistaken kindness. A normal blind child, unless handicapped by illness or long periods in hospital, will walk alone in a room with which he is familiar and enjoy climbing up and down stairs by about eighteen months of age. By about 2 years he may well have acquired both bowel and bladder control if given patient and reasonable training. By 3 years often he can feed himself with a spoon if given a plate with a turned-up rim so that the food cannot slip off. Before he is 5 he can learn to ride a kiddy-car and even a tricycle. By the time he is 6 he can tell his left from his right hand, which is, of course, useful in giving him directions to find the toys he is looking for. To watch children in a Sunshine Home Nursery School climbing, scrambling, rolling down grassy slopes, steering prams or tricycles with unerring skill, and swinging high and fearlessly on an open swing is an education itself, and has proved so for many an over-devoted mother.

The second family attitude, which is not so common, fortunately, occurs in some cases when the mother has had special problems to meet in the bringing up of the family—economic stringency, marital difficulties, or constant ill health, for instance. The birth of a blind baby just tips the balance, and the mother feels unequal to the situation. She feels unable to show affection to the child, turns away from him and rejects him emotionally. She handles the child with distaste, and tends to ignore him as much as possible. She is likely to apply to her local authority for the child to be cared for away from home as soon as possible. Such a child suffers just as any other child who has never had real affection in babyhood. He may become a very emotionally disturbed child indeed. Lacking basic security and maternal love, and receiving none of the normal incentives from his own mother to grow and develop, he is likely to withdraw into himself and become remote and unresponsive to people generally. In such an instance both mother and child need help. The wisest decision, if the problems at home cannot be solved, is for the blind child to be placed in a Sunshine Home Nursery School. Sometimes when this is done and close contact maintained with the parents a new relationship can gradually be built up between them and the child. Relieved of the strain of caring for the child primarily themselves, they may be able to accept responsibility during holiday times, and the child be able to make affectionate relationships with the staff of the school, which to some extent make up for the rather limited love he receives in his own home. Sometimes a good holiday foster home can be found if family circumstances remain too difficult.

In general the best place for the *young* blind child is his own home. Accepted and cherished by his whole family, he is made to feel that he belongs there, and that he, too, has a contribution to make towards family happiness. He needs to be loved, encouraged, and sometimes scolded by his own parents, just as any ordinary child, until such time as he appears ready to benefit from the companionship of similarly handicapped children and from more specialized education. This may be any time *after* he is $3\frac{1}{2}$ or 4 years of age if he is emotionally well developed. Sometimes it is wisest to wait until after 4 years of age, and sometimes instead of attending a Sunshine Home Nursery School, even though he can remain there until he is 7 or later, the best plan may be for him to attend a primary school for blind children at 5, the compulsory age for school attendance.

The decision about the *early* admittance of a blind child to a Sunshine Home Nursery School is always a difficult one. There are, of course, the exceptional cases when, owing to the death or illness of the mother, and when there are no relatives who can assume responsibility for the blind baby, his acceptance is the best and most satisfactory arrangement. Sometimes housing conditions are very difficult and even dangerous for a small blind child, and the mother, overburdened by the care of a large family, cannot give the necessary care and attention to his welfare. Sometimes the reverse situation exists. The rest of the family are somewhat neglected because of the mother's natural absorption in the care of the young blind child, and it may result in the greatest happiness for the greatest number if the blind child goes early to the residential school. This is not the ideal solution for children under 3 years of age, for such young children may well feel displaced in their mother's affections, and intensely jealous of the brothers and sisters who remain at home, but it may be the only practical one. The whole position has to be considered very carefully before such a decision is made.

Many parents of blind children make the decision to apply for admission of their children to the Sunshine Home Nursery Schools because they realize as the children grow up that these schools 'contribute to the care and training of the blind child something which the family cannot'. It is evident that the excellent all-round education offered by these schools can supplement and enlarge upon all that a rich family life has contributed to personality growth in the first few years (Brown, 1954).

Residential Care

Owing to the geographical distribution and the small number of blind children in this country, it is inevitable that the Sunshine Home Nursery Schools are residential. The advantages and disadvantages of residential care for young children must be considered realistically.

Some well-intentioned people constantly urge parents to send their blind children to these nursery schools in babyhood so that they can receive specialist care from a very early age. Unless the baby is ill, when he may require expert nursing care in a hospital, by far the best arrangement is for him to remain at home and receive his full quota of mothering just as any other small child. The parents may need advice from those experienced in the care of young blind children and may gain a great deal of help by visiting a Sunshine Home Nursery School and discussing their problems with the staff. They may benefit from a short stay at the Parents' Unit to which I have already referred.

Between 3 and 4 years of age the blind child, who has built up good secure relationships at home and is developing normally will benefit, as I have said, from the company of children similarly handicapped, and from the right kind of stimulating environment where achievements suited to his age and capacity are expected of him. It is almost inevitable that a certain amount of tension will surround a handicapped child in his own home. Parents and relatives find it very difficult to refrain from showing anxious concern about his movements and his tentative attempts at initiative and independence. The atmosphere in these nursery schools is free from this tension and anxious concern, and it is much more possible for the child to learn to explore and to meet some of his own problems effectively. The readiness with which the child can adapt to this new environment will depend on the quality of family relationships. If he feels secure and well-loved by his family, especially his mother, he will be the more able to enjoy relationships both with adults and children outside his own home, and feel safe and able to learn in a new environment. At 2 years of age he has seldom reached this stage. After 3 a good adjustment is much more probable. But a great deal will depend on the child's early experiences, the disturbance caused by periods in hospital or by family upheavals, for instance, and it is rash indeed to generalize when each child and each family situation is so different.

In recent years a great deal of publicity has been given to the possible harmful effect on the child's mental and physical growth by early separation from the mother, and evidence has been collected to support this view (Bowlby, 1951). Anyone who has had experience of the work of a Child Guidance Clinic will know that this viewpoint must be taken seriously. Everything possible must be done to make the transition from home to the nursery school gradual and easy. The parents can prepare the child carefully by talking about the fun and the companionship he will have at school, and by visiting the school with him beforehand. The mother should go with him and if possible stay the first night or even longer to help settle him in. Telephone calls at a definite time can be arranged so that the child can hear his mother's voice and talk to her himself. Letters and small presents provide an important link with home. Parents are encouraged to visit and sometimes have the child home for week-ends if it is feasible. Half-term holidays and the usual school holidays are spent at home unless family circumstances are very difficult. Usually one member of staff is made primarily responsible for a new child, and this helps him to settle in more easily and become accustomed to the rest of the staff and children. With skilful planning it is possible for a young child to feel accepted and appreciated as part of a small community, usually consisting of about twenty-five children and a high ratio of staff to children. His needs will be well understood, and he will receive much individual attention from a sympathetic and fully trained staff. At the same time his loyalty and affection for the members of his family can be preserved by frequent contacts and by the manner in which the staff keep alive memories of home and link home life with school life. When it is clear that separation from home is very disturbing for a child, a return home is arranged if it is at all possible.

DONALD was only 18 months old when he was admitted to a Sunshine Home Nursery School. The reason for his early admittance was the mother's poor health and very unsatisfactory housing conditions. Donald was very upset by this parting from his mother. He cried constantly for over 24 hours, repeatedly calling for his mother. He refused food and would not sleep until exhausted by crying. It seemed impossible to comfort him by petting, nursing or by any possible kindness. Contact was made with the authorities and the position explained to them. It transpired that recently the family had been re-housed and that the mother's health had greatly improved. Contact was made with the family, and they were asked if they could now have Donald home. The answer was an emphatic 'yes'. By eight o'clock the same evening the father, mother, older sister and two friendly neighbours arrived in force, and a grand family re-union took place. The mother confessed that, like Donald, she had been unable to eat, sleep, or keep from crying since he had left. Everybody was revived with cups of tea, and Donald, sleepy but happy, returned home. Since then friendly contact has been maintained between the home and the school, and when he is older, perhaps at 4 years of age, he may be re-admitted and settle in happily.

PEGGY was 3 when she came to a Sunshine Home Nursery School. Her mother had had a nervous breakdown and could not take the responsibility of caring for a blind child any longer. Peggy was very fretful and cried a great deal. She clung to an old fur cape of her mother's which she had brought with her and carried wherever she went. Unfortunately, soon after she had begun to feel more at home she had to attend hospital for an examination of her eyes under an anaesthetic. This experience upset her again, and it was decided to ask the mother to come and stay at the nursery for a few days and discuss the possibility of a return home. This seemed to reassure Peggy a great deal and she agreed to her mother's departure without too much disturbance. One nurse was made primarily responsible for her care, feeding, bathing, toileting and so on. The old fur cape remained her constant companion. She returned home in the summer holidays, and when I saw her again in the autumn she was taking full part in the children's activities. The fur cape was allowed to remain on her cot, a comforter at bedtime, but not needed at other times.

JEAN, aged 4 years 3 months when she came to the residential nursery, seemed to be quite at home almost at once. She was a very intelligent and attractive little girl from a sensible home where she had been encouraged to be independent from the start. She was very self-possessed, very sociable, and enlisted the other children in her imaginative play with great skill. She showed great delight in all the activities provided in this new environment and lost no time in exploring and exploiting them. She was visited, or went home at week-ends. Clearly she had gained a great deal from this experience of living in a community where her special needs were well understood.

In a study undertaken by Lewis (1954) of five hundred children, who had been 'taken into care' and who were seen by her in a reception centre, it is made clear that early separation from their mothers did not *invariably* result in emotional disturbance in the children. A small percentage showed no disturbance at all. It was found that many of these children had been able to find other persons to stand in their mother's stead. It is important not to exaggerate the possible ill-effects of early separation, but it is equally important to be aware of them and to make arrangements that as much individual 'mothering' as possible is assured to the child who leaves home before he is 5 years of age. The older, the more independent and mature the child, the happier his home and the greater the care with which he has been prepared for leaving it, the easier is his adjustment to a small community such as the residential nursery. Thirty children is about the maximum for such a nursery group, in my opinion, and a ratio of about one member of staff to two children if emotional problems due to separation from the parents are to be minimized. No one would deny that the adjustment to nursery school life may be difficult for the child, but one hopes this is not achieved at too great a cost. The achievement of a good adjustment to this new environment, which is so specially adapted to his needs, may well prove an enriching experience which may increase his self-confidence and develop his personality more fully.

The children who come to the Sunshine Home Nursery Schools may stay until seven years of age, and in some cases until nine years of age, if their development is rather slow. The nursery school serves to accustom the child to school life in the easiest and pleasantest way possible and makes the transition from home to school more gradual. The atmosphere is informal and homely, and these schools are now recognized as playing a valuable part in the child's early training and adjustment. They serve, too, as a bridge to the somewhat more formal training and education provided in the primary schools later. In the ensuing pages the educational methods used in the Sunshine Home Nursery Schools are outlined.

Educational Methods

Introductory.—Gradually we are coming to realize that, although the blind child is deprived of one of the five senses, he is yet able to build up a vivid picture of the world around him. He learns about the objects in his world by 'finger sight', by touch, and by sound, by smell and by taste. He becomes an excellent listener, and by training his hearing becomes especially acute. He can often tell who is approaching by the sound of the person's tread. He can tell what he is having for dinner by sniffing in the direction of the kitchen. It is on these terms and through this media that we must educate him, rather than constantly bewail the obvious limitations imposed upon him by his lack of sight. If he is born blind, he can have no real appreciation of what he is missing. We must recognize that he appears to gain very vivid impressions indeed of every- thing going on around him, although they must be very different from ours, and often rather distorted and incomprehensible. But there is a great deal that he can enjoy—sometimes even more so than the less perceptive sighted child. He delights in the rustle of his feet in dry leaves, the splash he can make in a muddy pool, the feel of the gloss on the horse chestnut, the woolly lining of a bean pod, the sleekness of the cat's fur, the texture of velvet or of taffeta. He can become just as excited as any other child about the crackle of a bonfire, the explosion of fireworks, the breaking of ice, the tune of a musical box or the call of the cuckoo. He likes to sniff the scent of new mown hay, of garden mint, of toilet soap or frying onions. In some schools gardens have been specially designed to include a wide range of aromatic herbs, shrubs and flowers. The children love to handle and smell these, and gradually come to know their names.

Herein lies the moral. It is essential to allow blind children to handle things. To prevent them is to restrict growth and know- ledge. They need, of course, to learn to avoid obvious dangers— contact with very hot or sharp objects, for instance, but they quickly learn reasonable caution. I have seen blind children using, under supervision of course, scissors, hammers, saws and even garden shears.

It is the task of the adult to interpret the world to the blind child where his own sensations fail him. It is best to avoid a 'hothouse language' omitting all mention of colour or other visual data because the child does not like to feel so different from ordinary children that a special language has to be used for him, but it is wisest to accentuate the part he can understand best—texture, sound, size and smell. Blind children are usually curious about colours, although they cannot, if born blind, have any visual appreciation of them; and it seems best to use colours in describing an object so that they can learn to associate them with the right objects, *e.g.* a red pillar box, blue sky and so on.

Probably somewhere about 6 years of age, the blind child comes to realize that he is different from other people—that he can only 'see' the things that he can touch, while other people can know about distant things more clearly, and 'can read books without having to learn Braille,' as an intelligent child of 6 expressed it. At first it appears that a blind child thinks this superior knowledge about distant objects and reading without Braille is the prerogative of adults. It is only later that he discovers that he will not acquire this ability as he becomes adult, and that certain experiences, certain skills, and especially freedom of movement in unfamiliar environments will be denied him. This realization seems to come at adolescence, more particularly when the problem of occupation has to be solved. It is then that he has to come to terms with the situation and learn to make an adequate adjustment to the demands of a sighted, competitive world. It is then that he will need our constructive sympathy and skilled help, but *not* our pity and sentiment. If his early education has been wisely planned and given him a good first-hand experience of the world around him, he will have learnt to compensate for his handicap, sometimes to a remarkable degree, and in some ways at least be able to compete with sighted persons.

The educational methods appropriate for the blind child between the ages of 2 and 7 follow much the same line as those used for the sighted child of the same age except that the three Rs are taught by different methods and certain activities such as painting, scissor craft, for instance, are not really applicable to blind children. Certain aspects of their education need special emphasis, however.

Confidence in Movement.—One of the first things to teach little blind children is to move with confidence. It is important that they do not get the habit of shuffling or groping, but learn to get about on their own with reasonable caution. As soon as they come to know their environment, which is remarkably quickly, they can achieve this if they are not constantly led by the hand, but are given encouragement to explore and to adapt physically to their environment. Naturally fires, high windows, steep steps have to be guarded, but the sighted adult is continually amazed at the skill the blind child shows in avoiding obstacles. I have seen children of 4 and 5 run up and down stairs, steer tricycles, motor cars and perambulators around the garden, swing on high swings, climb up camouflage nets and jungle gyms, jump and splash in a paddling pool and dance to music quite freely. Of course, they meet with occasional bumps, but they become very adept at avoiding collision. They appear to develop an acute sense, possibly of hearing, which makes them quickly aware of an obstacle within range. Some children have a better sense of direction than others, but in a school to which they are accustomed it is quite unnecessary to lead them by the hand. In a strange environment, in a busy street, or when out for a country walk, of course, they need guidance, and in such cases it is necessary to have sufficient staff to help them or for a partially sighted child to take the hand of a totally blind child, which he will readily do.

It is important that blind children are given opportunity to explore and to use their muscles with energy. If left to themselves they naturally tend to be passive and sedentary, for they know then they are safe. They need more incentive in babyhood, as I have said, to sit up, to roll, to crawl and to walk. They continue as they grow older to need incentive to move freely, to lose their fear of open spaces, and incidentally to find out from first hand experience about the world around them. Ball games, rythmic space out of doors and indoors can help towards this end. Physical activity, such as wall-bars, climbing frames, swings, ladders, shutes, barrels for rolling, water in which to play, and plenty of free open space out of doors and indoors can help towards this end. Physical exercise, of course, improves general health, and by means of it digestive troubles and cramped muscles can be avoided. One's aim is to help the blind child to keep his head up, his shoulders back and to walk and run easily but carefully, and this without nagging. It is far better to say, 'Oh, I can't see your pretty face if you keep your head down', than, 'I keep telling you, don't poke your head down like that all the time.'

Self-Help.—In ordinary nurseries and nursery schools one normally tries to teach a little child to help himself in all the ways that he will enjoy and of which he is capable. Dressing, undressing, feeding, washing and toiletting are among the skills which threes and fours and sometimes twos acquire without much difficulty. All these skills are much more difficult for a blind child, and many mothers take the easiest way round by continuing to spoon feed, both literally and figuratively, long after it is really necessary. It is characteristic of many blind children that they tend to lack initiative and drive to become independent, because presumably it is pleasanter and easier to be waited on. Some children admitted to the Sunshine Home Nursery Schools are, even as late as 4 years of age, unwilling to walk, showing a distinct preference to be carried, have never tried to feed themselves and refuse most solids, continue to wear napkins and have never attempted to dress themselves.

It is even more important to help a blind child to help himself than a sighted child: for only by this means will he learn self-respect and pride in achievement, which will help him to overcome his sense of inferiority and difference from other children which may develop later. But such training requires infinite patience and time, the last named being often in short supply in the ordinary family home. In the nursery a child is urged to pick up what he has dropped, to go and find his ball for himself when it rolls away from him, to take off his own coat and pull on his own wellingtons, to use his spoon to discover the choice morsels on his plate, or even his fingers if he cannot yet manage a spoon. Gradually the child finds delight in this sort of achievement. He no longer has to wait on the whim or the time of the adult. There are, of course, occasions if the child is tired or perhaps not very well when he reverts to a more babyish stage, and it does not follow that, because a child has on one occasion fastened his shoe buttons, he can or will do so on all occasions. Sometimes I think in nursery schools we demand too high a standard from little children who, had they remained at home, would not have expected to be so competent and independent. There is clearly a happy mean.

Feeding yourself when you cannot see what is on your plate takes time, and one does not want the child to tire of an unequal struggle and leave food grown cold and unappetising. Naturally, one helps by holding the child's hand and by scooping up the food for him with his spoon when he is in difficulties. Also, to tell him what he is eating and what is to follow is encouraging. He will want to finger his food longer than a sighted child and the messy stage lasts longer, but somewhere between 3 and 4 he will have acquired a good deal of proficiency. I have often taken small blind children out to cafes and noted the speed and the skill with which they demolish ice cream using a spoon in a dish! To the casual observer it would hardly be noticeable that they could not see.

Toilet training, just as with sighted children, needs, as I have said, to be gradual and gentle. Regular times for potting help a great deal, and potting time at the nursery is always quite a merry affair and a sociable one. There is a very different atmosphere to that resulting from the anxious concern of a mother who is impatient with the messy stage of child care and has very high standards of cleanliness out of step with the natural development of the little child. It is a mistake to leave a small child sitting on his pot too long. Rather let him sit on his pot on your lap, and if, after a try, he is unwilling to oblige, it is wisest to leave well alone and be prepared for results in the inappropriate place and often at an inopportune time! Threes and fours usually manage to keep themselves both clean and dry, certainly in the day and often at night, if given normal encouragement and little censure for occasional mistakes. It will help a great deal if the toilet is easily accessible, and if the fittings are of the appropriate size.

Water play is one of the special delights of the blind child, and bath time is to be enjoyed and not hurried over. Again it is quite a social occasion in the residential nursery, and much conversation and cheerful song goes on. The children enjoy helping to wash themselves, although this is primarily a job for the adult. Washing face and hands and cleaning teeth can be achieved quite competently by threes and fours, however, although the process may be rather drawn out for the sheer fun of turning taps on and off.

Few children enjoy tidying up after their play, and blind children find putting toys away in the right place often very difficult. It is always easier to pull things out than to stack them neatly away. Lockers for individual treasures help, and cupboards should have plenty of room with things kept in the same place so that the child knows just where they go. But a good deal of adult help will be needed here. A blind child can learn to hang up his coat if his peg is within reach, and put away bricks in a box if the box is in the accustomed place.

Gradually as muscles develop and experience increases the blind child learns to do more and more for himself, and his joy and pride in his independence, if wisely fostered, grow enormously.

Social Adjustment.—In addition to being rather dependent the young blind child is notably rather egocentric. This is especially marked if he has been brought up by a devoted family who give in to his every whim, and if he has learnt only to take and never to give. Naturally blind children cannot be so aware of social responses as sighted children, because they cannot see the expression of the faces around them and cannot respond to the smiles they do not see. They judge a great deal by tone of voice, but this is sometimes deceptive. There is a danger of blind children becoming too wrapt up in themselves, and of becoming too withdrawn from the world around them. They become immersed in their own fantasies, remote from reality and fail to make social contacts.

Many of the mannerisms commonly noted in the blind—rocking, head banging, finger-waving, head-shaking and various forms of masturbation—are related to this fact. This child's interest turns inwards; he seeks to gain satisfaction from himself, from his own bodily sensations and his own imaginings.

If developed in the right way, however, a blind child comes gradually to respond to adults in a friendly natural way, enjoying appreciation and attention. But usually by 3 years of age he has not learnt to play freely with other children as ordinary children do. It is always a good sign when such a child is willing to take the hand of another child or can combine in a ring in a musical game. The characteristic behaviour of blind children of 3 years of age is to play beside other children, and although they make occasional contacts and responses, they are usually immersed in their own activities and more willing to tell adults about them than children. But by 4 years old much more effective contact is made. Free imaginative play is evident, and blind children, just as sighted children, come to appreciate the company of other children in enriching their play and furthering their purposes. They will combine to help each other push a truck; they will join a tea-party game; they will accept the role of 'mother' or 'baby' in family games. This marks an important step forward. They rapidly learn give and take; they accept leadership or assume it. They are protective or aggressive by turns. They gain support from other children against the demands of adults, and they reduce their sense of dependence. Older children can be remarkably helpful with smaller blind children, and generosity is commonly witnessed in the matter of sharing of sweets or small gifts in the nursery school.

Learning to live in a community is one of the things that a blind child can learn readily in the special nursery school environment. He meets children equally handicapped, with the same problems to solve and the same limitations. He can compete equally with them. He is not always left behind or ignored; nor does he need to be helped and sheltered as commonly happens if he remains in a sighted community. Until he has learnt to find his feet in such a community he cannot play his full part in an ordinary community, although it is important that he maintains contact with ordinary children. This contact with the sighted world involves always certain difficulties in adjustment, and from an early age it is important to help the child to come to terms with them.

Two-year-olds then are not really ready for group living and are better cared for in their own homes if at all possible. Threes may not gain a great deal but are less likely to be bewildered than twos. Fours certainly can gain a good deal and, provided family contacts are maintained, can enjoy life in a residential nursery to the full.

Outside Contacts.—We find that the first thing to do in the residential nursery school with blind children is to make them feel secure and familiar in their immediate surroundings. They need the same adults to care for them day by day, and they need time to become accustomed to the geography of the house and garden. They learn to move freely and find their own way about slowly. When they have achieved this, usually somewhere about 3½ or 4 years of age, they will enjoy adventuring further afield. Here is the teacher's opportunity. Gradually one can widen their horizons and increase their experience of the ordinary everyday occurrences in the world around them. One begins in a small way by making sure to be on the spot when the coalman or the dustman or the laundry man calls. These events lead to many questions and stimulate interest. Then short excursions to collect sticks or conkers or bluebells or blackberries can be arranged as the need arises. When the children become older and more confident, more ambitious projects can be arranged. I know groups of blind children of 5 or 6 and 7 who frequently visit the neighbouring farm, or the level crossing, others who go regularly to spend pocket money at the village shop, or to the post office to get stamps. Trips have been arranged by bus or trains to a zoo, to a fair, to a lighthouse, to a cattle market and to children's concerts. Christmas parties at home and 'abroad' mean contact with other children, and many invitations are received from private families to tea from time to time.

The object of such 'educational' journeys is, of course, to familiarize the blind child with the ordinary happenings in the world around him and teach him poise and confidence in a less sheltered environment than his own home or school. Great care must be taken not to provide too many and too stimulating experiences. Blind children become frightened and bewildered by too much noise in a strange environment. But adjustment to the sighted world has to be made if the child is to function as a useful citizen and not remain dependent and sheltered all his life. In his early school days the process can begin. Blind children enjoy participating in the doings of children in the community. They can attend Sunday School or church services. Children from the ordinary schools can be invited to play with them. I have often joined in picnics, snow fights, bonfire celebrations, or Christmas parties with blind children and young visitors. There is no doubt that such occasions help in this process of adjustment, in their general social education as well as in providing them with fascinating new experiences.

Manual Dexterity.—The blind child learns through his fingers; they serve him in place of eyes. It is therefore important he should develop sensitivity and dexterity with his hands. If he is to be able to read, he will have to learn Braille, and this involves skilled use of his fingers. He needs experience of shape, size, texture and volume, and a good deal of 'sense training material' is now on the market, or can be home-made which will suit his need. He will enjoy simple peg boards, nests of boxes or cups, a pyramid of rings decreasing in size, screw toys, boards with insets of different shapes, buttons he can sort, or pieces of material that he can match. There are certain constructional toys and various fitting toys which are useful, but with ordinary bricks he does not achieve a great deal unless he has just a little vision. He has learned to concentrate for quite long periods on this type of activity, and in the nursery school he is encouraged to settle down to some such occupation for a short time to help him to develop the habit of concentrated work.

He will spend a lot of time experimenting with water, and he can be given a great variety of different utensils, colanders, tins, funnels, rubber tubing, teapots, which will encourage experimentation. Similarly, he will enjoy sand, clay, plasticine or dough, but he is far less constructive with these materials than sighted children because he cannot see the results. He loves to handle such material and he will fill buckets with sand, roll plasticine into shapes, and cut out dough into the shape of animals. He is often interested in mechanical things and, just as any other inquisitive child, will enjoy taking a bicycle bell or an alarm clock to pieces even though he may not be able to put it together again.

He will also enjoy doing small jobs in the house and garden which involve manual skill—washing clothes, polishing shoes, shelling peas or beans, gathering pine cones for the fire, and countless other simple occupations. He is increasing his skill and his experience, and at the same time feels he is playing his part and is not merely a by-stander.

If all goes well and the child becomes dexterous with his fingers and shows capacity for concentration, learning to read and to write Braille can begin soon after 6 years of age. It is best to postpone this until the child shows real interest and a desire to learn, because it is an abstract form of learning, more difficult than ordinary reading and writing, and some children will learn it later than others. There is a great deal else which can fill the child's day when he is young, and a premature start in Braille is likely to result in poor interest and application.

Creative Activities.—It is not easy for blind children to make something which is satisfying to themselves and to the eyes of adults. Nor is it easy for them to find many outlets for their imagination or for the expression of emotional conflict. Painting serves no useful purpose unless the child has some perception of light or colour, when he may enjoy covering a whole sheet of paper with some bright colour. He cannot reproduce shapes or designs which he has never been able to see; nor can he enjoy the results of his labours with a paint-brush. He may enjoy finger painting just for the feel of it, but his results will be largely accidental.

Modelling can provide satisfaction and good emotional outlet, but I have found with children under 5 years of age that the activity is more experimental and manipulative than creative. They enjoy squeezing, pummelling, rolling and cutting clay or plasticine or dough or glitter wax, but they do not usually achieve recognizable results until somewhat later. Children of 6 and 7 do produce quite well-defined objects, such as 'sausages', 'eggs', 'worms', 'pancakes', 'plates', 'boats' and even 'aeroplanes', given some assistance as regards technique by the adult.

Sand and water play is a healthy outlet for blind children just as for ordinary children. The experimental and manipulative period lasts a long time with the blind child. But the experimenting leads to discoveries if the child is given a good assortment of utensils for this play. Strong feelings of destructiveness, aggression and hostility can be ventilated by this means in a harmless and satisfying way. Emotions centering around the whole process of toilet training can also be expressed.

From this stage the partially-sighted child may progress to making simple shapes with sand and water. From destructive play develops constructive effort, and it is clear that the handling of the material gives great satisfaction as well as the actual creative achievement which will usually bring him adult approval also.

Free imaginative play in which a group of children may take part will, of course, provide excellent opportunity for the expressing of feeling, the development of ideas and social co-operation. This, as I have said, seems to occur rather later with blind children than with sighted children, but by 5 years of age it is a common feature. One group of children whom I know well devised a fascinating game concerning the Royal Family at Coronation time, and the small 'Queen' could be heard admonishing 'Prince Charles' and 'Princess Anne' for some misdemeanour in no uncertain terms!

'Mother and baby', 'teacher and pupil', travelling, shopping, hospitals, birthday party and Father Christmas play are also common. A great part of the play is verbal, language being an easier means of expression than practical activity to the blind child. The character of the child's play is often revealing. Blind children who are emotionally disturbed sometimes play in a rather stereotyped or solitary way, curling up in a corner by themselves, climbing into a large doll's pram or cot pretending to be a baby again. It is an improvement when they will accept another child as 'mother' and co-operate at least in a passive way. Some children play in a rather bizarre manner, pretending to be a record-player or a radio announcing programmes and reproducing melodies. This is a representation of their environment for both record-player and radio form an important part of the blind child's experience particularly at home. It often indicates a lack of contact with the social group, and is a passive interest and not a constructive one, especially if it absorbs a great deal of the child's time. Passive occupation should be discouraged so far as possible. Dramatic work with children between four and seven years can be very effective, but I will discuss this more fully in a further section.

When a blind child can play vigorously, imaginatively and socially, this is, as in all children, recognized to be a sign of good mental health.

Musical and Rhythmic Activity.—Blind children learn very early to be good listeners, and, because of their close attention, learn usually very quickly to reproduce a melody. Children as young as 3 or 4 can often play simple tunes on the piano correctly, usually extemporizing with the left hand. They learn quickly by ear, and often sing well in tune. There is a danger here of encouraging too much passive listening—a simple way of keeping them still, quiet and safe. Periods of quiet listening should be followed by active movement. Blind children can take part very effectively in *Music and Movement* programmes on the radio. They learn to march, run, walk, prance and dance. They respond best to music with a definite rhythm and emphasis. They enjoy using percussion band instruments, and can achieve quite a high standard with these. Even the smallest 3-year-old if given bells or tap sticks will begin to beat out the rhythm.

It is important that these children should be given the best as regards their musical education. For some it may become their means of livelihood. It is best if they are taught by a teacher who is a good musician and who is not dependent on gramophone or radio. They need to hear classical music as well as good popular and traditional melodies. Six and seven-year-olds will enjoy attending a public concert and listen usually with concentrated attention, especially if they are given some information about the different instruments. They will also enjoy community singing or carol singing, and will quickly learn to take parts. When they go on to the primary and secondary schools they may be able to learn an instrument, but unless they can learn to read music in Braille and are not dependent on playing by ear only, they cannot get very far.

A music period usually forms part of the programme for every day at the nursery school stage. Importance is attached to the child's ability to listen with interest and respond with action.

Development of Language.—Provided the young blind child is given sufficient encouragement, a good pattern of speech and adequate experience of the world around him, there is no reason why his speech should not develop normally, and indeed the blind child's vocabulary is often more advanced than that of the ordinary child. It is so important for him to use language to communicate, to hold the attention of the adult, and to understand what is going on around him that language develops more rapidly, usually, than loco-motion. This will not be the case if he is not talked to sufficiently, if explanations are not given concerning the objects he touches and the sounds he hears. Going for a walk with a blind child I always find to be very strenuous intellectually! He certainly asks even more questions than a sighted child, and all the time one finds one has to interpret the environment to him. 'That's a heavy lorry going by, and there's the bus coming up the hill. It is stopping to let off passengers. What a big puddle you are coming to! What a good thing you have on your wellingtons. We are nearly at the letter box. Now we can cross—that fast car has just gone by. One step up on the pavement, and now you can reach up to the letter box. Yes, it will be cleared early tomorrow morning', is a fair sample of a five minutes' walk on a wet day.

In the nursery school the teacher continues to build up language experience as the mother should have done at home. The child will listen tirelessly to stories even though he cannot enjoy picture books. But once again passive listening for too long a time is unwise, and children will enjoy dramatizing a story they have heard. I have seen some excellent renderings of Mr. Bear Squash You Flat, The Tale of the Turnip, The King's Breakfast, The Good Samaritan (the man who passed by on the other side riding rapidly up the road to Jericho on a motor bicycle!) and the Christmas Story. Dramatic work is slow even though it can be spontaneous and effective. The children cannot tell how they appear to other people, and have to be shown how to stand and to move and what actions to make. They learn by heart very easily, again presumably because they listen so well, and they can be taught poems and jingles readily.

The choice of story or poem is important. It is especially important when the child is young to relate his vocabulary to things experienced. He cannot understand words descriptive of visual imagery. Care should be taken to choose matter which includes good sound imagery, some of which the child can imitate. Stories and poems about animals are particularly valuable in this connection, of course. Tales of trains, fire engines, aeroplanes and the *Listen with Mother* stories are much appreciated. How things sound, feel to the touch, smell and taste is what matters to him. It is not difficult to go through an anthology of poems and pick out those that satisfy these requirements. Later on his repertory can be increased, but in order to avoid 'verbalism', using words without real significance, his early vocabulary should be related to his sensory experience.

In this original poem composed by Malcolm, who is aged 5 years 8 months, it is made abundantly clear that his language is related to sensory experience:

> Snow, snow, cold, cold snow,
> When the sun shines away you go.
> Where do you go?
> Well I don't know—
> Snow, snow, cold, cold snow.

Early Number Experience.—The early stages of teaching number to blind children are similar in most respects as those taught to sighted children. Learning is mainly incidental. Counting, sorting, sharing and adding are all part of everyday experience. The number of candles on the birthday cake, the number of toffees left in the tin, or pennies in the money box, the number of spoons needed at the dinner table are all important matters for speculation and discovery. At first all that is necessary is to follow the clues laid by the child and supply the correct information when needed or better still the adequate opportunities for finding out. Always the first steps in number should be related to known and interesting experience. Addition of money is far more real to a child when he has paid his own fare on a bus, bought buns for tea, ices for a picnic or stamps for his letter.

The most natural activity at first is to count, and every normal child begins quite early to count the buttons on his coat, the conkers

Physical activity helps to increase self-confidence and develop muscular skill.

[*To face page* 156

Domestic play.

Learning through manipulation.

Gaining first-hand experience.

Blind children readily make
friends with animals.　　　Constructive play.

Social play.

Learning through manipulation.

in his pocket, the steps on the stairway. He is interested in how many and also 'how much more have I than you!' Very soon too he will be intimately concerned in the weighty problem of 'how many shall I have left when I have eaten one more or given one to Betty?' Counting for fun, counting of sticks, shells, pebbles and so on, need hardly be formalized.

Number games can be introduced with 5 and 6-year-olds, either as singing games about ducks on a pond, green bottles on a wall, or catching fish in a pond, or as simple board games with dice or such as the fish-pond game. Braille numbers can be introduced as the child seems ready, so that he comes to associate the name of the number, its quantity and its Braille configuration.

Blind children usually show great proficiency in mental arithmetic. It saves so much time if, instead of trying to write the numbers, they can do the sum in their heads, and they become very quick at this in some cases. It can only take them so far, and sooner or later they will have to learn to use the Taylor Frame and the Braille notification. At first they will enjoy playing with it, making rows of soldiers facing one way so that they learn the dexterity necessary for using it. Usually it is not until after they are 7 that they are taught to set down their sums with this apparatus.

The approach then is through everyday experience, which should provide the child with good opportunities for learning about size, quantity, volume and so on. A classroom shop, with opportunity to weigh and measure and count and calculate, will be enjoyed, but visits to real toy-shops, post offices and tea-shops will make the experience even more real. An intelligent child, who is naturally observant, cannot avoid acquiring number experience. It remains for the teacher to make this articulate and to build on it when more formal work becomes appropriate. Given sufficient experience of concrete material there is no reason why a blind child should be less advanced than a sighted child. Though he may be slower in setting down his sums, he can often do it more quickly mentally. When he comes, at the Grammar School, to the intricacies of geometry and algebra, the situation becomes much more difficult for him as he cannot visualize the problems, but even so, the highly intelligent blind child can achieve this.

The Beginning of Braille.—I have left discussion of the teaching of Braille until last because this is the place it should assume in the education of children under 7 years of age. The learning of Braille is largely an abstract and formal process, and for many blind children under 7 it is quite inappropriate. It requires close concentration, a certain manual skill and an ability to analyse and synthesize sounds. It is first necessary to learn to associate the sound of the letter with the touch pattern of dots; usually the letters are taught in a sequence which is easiest to memorize and the least complicated. The child can then begin to build very simple phonic words and relate them to known objects. This gives him a very small working vocabulary. From this stage he can go on to learn another group of letters of the alphabet and so build another set of words. This process is similar in many respects to the phonic method of teaching reading, but without visual aids.

It is usually said that Braille readiness, just as reading readiness, can be put approximately at a mental age of 6. This means that quite a number of the slower-learning 6-year-olds or the backward 7-year-olds are not ready for Braille reading. It is a mistake to press this upon them prematurely, for they quickly become bored and uninterested, and their time is much better employed in more practical pursuits. An interest can be stimulated by displaying Braille name cards and labelling objects in the room. Simple matching games, sorting Braille letters into appropriate boxes, collecting objects which begin with the same sound, or thinking of as many things as possible that begin with a certain letter such as 'B' or 'S' or words that rhyme, can be useful if too much time is not given to this activity.

The intelligent 6-year-old who has a good experience and a good general vocabulary will learn his letters fairly quickly, and will very much enjoy his first book, if it is home-made and concerns the things in which he is interested. These books can be written for him with a Braille writer as he becomes ready. This is much the best way, and preferable to using one of the Braille primers which can follow later.

The teaching of Braille in its early stages is mainly an individual matter, group work other than word games being of little real value. Children show such individual variations in ability and in pace of learning, that at first it is best taught individually. Nor is it wise to spend a long time on this activity, because it does require a high degree of concentration, and it is important to avoid mental fatigue or loss of interest. However, blind children do experience a real sense of achievement when they have mastered the rudiments, and it is a great stimulus to them if their parents also learn Braille and write to them in Braille. Instead of letters from home having always to be read to them by a sighted adult, they find they can gradually read them themselves.

Writing Braille is usually left until the child has learnt to read to some extent. It is a more complicated skill than ordinary writing because the dots have to be pricked out with a tool and then the paper reversed so that the raised dots on the reverse side commence on the left-hand.

The golden rule is to hurry slowly, and study each child, to judge his state of readiness and degree of manual skill. Especially is it important to relate the words he is learning in Braille to objects or events of which he has real knowledge. His formal work should be always based on first-hand experience and related to the world around him.

The Partially Sighted Child

The child who has partial vision has considerable advantages over the blind child. He can move with greater confidence and is less likely to come into collision with obstacles. He can learn manipulative skills more easily and become more independent and self-reliant earlier. On the other hand, there are certain difficulties. His visual experience may be confusing and sometimes disturbing. He tends to peer at objects and seems to gain only a vague impression which is sometimes rather frightening to him. Sometimes he seems more apprehensive than the totally blind child, being aware of shapes which he cannot interpret. Often he is so taken up with peering at things, trying to decipher their meaning, that his concentration is poor when learning by touch. He is handicapped in learning Braille because he does not concentrate sufficiently on learning with his fingers. A blind child often learns Braille quicker than a partially sighted child.

In some cases the child's sight is variable—ranging from clarity to obscurity. He may have a good deal of peripheral but no central vision. He is likely to make errors in judgment and feel frustrated and troubled by the variable impressions he receives of the world. Learning to read and write may be rather complicated for him. He may be able to read only very large print, and learning to read by Braille may prove an irritating and rather complex process for him. He needs patient and skilled teaching. He may, however, enjoy drawing and painting, which is not possible for the blind child.

There is a further consideration to be borne in mind. Many partially sighted children have had to spend frequent periods in hospital. They become accustomed to this, but some children especially when they are very young, are disturbed by this type of experience. Treatment in hospital may result in improved vision, but in order to achieve this the child may have had to be examined under an anaesthetic, undergo a minor operation and endure a period with his eyes protected from light. All of this may be something of an ordeal to a very young child, who cannot understand fully what is happening or why he has to be away from his family and familiar surroundings. He needs careful preparation for such hospital experience and wise, considerate handling afterwards.

Further Education

The next stage of the child's education will take place in the normal primary school for the blind or the partially sighted. The majority of blind children, of course, commence attendance at these schools at the age of 5 when education becomes compulsory. The nursery school does, however, serve as a valuable preliminary stage to the more formal learning of the primary school, and if the child is attending a Sunshine Home Nursery School, he usually remains there, as I have said, until he is 6 or 7 years of age. The decision about transfer is based on an estimate of the child's ability to profit from education at this next stage. Sometimes the child seems both intellectually and emotionally ready as early as 5 years, sometimes at 7 years. The slow-learning child, who will need special school education at Condover Hall, the school for the blind child with additional handicaps, is not transferred until 9 years of age. The nursery school child, when he moves on to the primary school, should have acquired a rich experience of community life, a variety of skills, a useful fund of general knowledge and a fair degree of independence as well as the first steps in number and Braille in many cases. He may thus be at an advantage compared to the 5-year-old, who has lived rather a sheltered and often a solitary life at home.

Some of the primary schools have admission or reception classes, similar to ordinary infant schools, where formal work is not seriously attempted and where conditions approximate to the older age groups in the Sunshine Nursery Schools. This makes adjustment very much easier for the young blind child.

Owing to the small number of blind children in this country and the necessity to regionalize the schools, all the primary schools for the blind and many of those for partially sighted children are residential. I think there is no doubt that many children benefit from the community life of the boarding school and the out-of-school activities that can be provided for him as well as, in some cases where home circumstances are very difficult, freedom from the stress and strain or the anxious concern of home. But I think it is important to bear in mind that our aim is to teach the blind independence, self-respect and the capacity to hold their own in the ordinary community, rather than live a sheltered existence and grow up possibly with a rather keen sense of difference and inferiority. As day schools for the blind appear to be impracticible, it seems essential to me that firm links are kept with home life, by rather frequent week-end visits, by parents' visits to the school, by holidays at home, by letters, and, in so far as it is possible, with the ordinary community life of sighted persons. The child who is blind needs special education to suit his special needs, but he needs also to feel that he has a part to play in his own family and is an accepted member of the community in which his family lives.

My concern in this section is primarily with the young blind child, and I am not in a position to be able to describe the educational methods employed with older children. But parents should rest assured that their blind children will receive a good all-round education in all the usual subjects and in a variety of handicrafts and physical activities, and in addition will acquire sufficient skill in Braille to read, write and calculate. Senior departments of these schools cater for the secondary stage of education as well as a few secondary modern schools, technical schools, and two grammar schools.

From ages 16 to 20, training departments provide technical training in the traditional crafts for the blind, notably in basket and brush making, and in machine knitting. Thence it is possible for a blind person to work in the workshops for the blind, as a home worker in his own home, or in open employment.

From the grammar schools a boy or girl may take the necessary qualifying examinations, which admit to a university, a training college for teachers, a commercial training centre or to the School for Physiotherapy organized under the auspices of the Royal National Institute for the Blind, or to some other recognized training course. There are, therefore, various alternatives open to a blind person who has reached a high standard of education which promise interesting careers. Some blind persons become skilled physiotherapists, some follow the legal profession, some obtain posts in the social services, or as teachers, often teachers of music, and a large number become shorthand typists or telephonists, sometimes obtaining both interesting and responsible posts.

Placement Officers assist blind persons in finding suitable employment and generally advise on matters of vocational guidance. A Pilot Centre for young blind people, who have left school, has been set up by the Royal National Institute for the Blind with the approval and assistance of the Ministry of Labour. The purpose of this centre is to assess the abilities of the students, to provide further education as needed, to improve social adjustment, to investigate wider opportunities for training and employment, and generally to assist the young person to prepare for, and to obtain the most suitable employment. The last war provided a great impetus to employment of the blind in open industry, and every effort is now being made to increase the number of openings in factories. By this means the blind person can contribute in an effective way to the good of the community, and retain his self-respect by proving that he can hold his own in the open market with sighted individuals, though usually at a slightly lower income level.

The less intelligent child, as I have said, can remain at one of the special Sunshine Nursery Schools until he is 9-years-old, and then transfer to Condover Hall School, the school for children with other handicaps in addition to blindness. Here, despite his dual disability, sometimes complicated by a motor handicap due to cerebral palsy, he is taught a number of simple skills, increased self-help, the rudiments of simple handicrafts, music, physical training, a good deal of general knowledge and Braille if within his capacity. He learns to live satisfactorily in a community, to care for himself and his possessions, to undertake simple shopping, to find his own way about outside the school to some extent, and in general to become a self-respecting member of the community, though he may never prove to be wholly self-supporting. An experimental deaf-blind unit for children from eighteen months upwards is also in operation. Ways of helping these children to learn to communicate with the outside world, to talk, to play, to read, are gradually being worked out. Much research remains to be done in this field.

Parents may feel confident, therefore, that the educational needs of their blind children, whether complicated by additional disabilities or not, will be met as fully as possible.

The Hampstead Child Therapy Clinic has organized a study group on the early development of blind children and to this end has formed a day nursery school. This has been in existence since 1957 and regular visits of parents are arranged for purposes of observation and support. The study group has published a number of reports of their findings.

It is an encouraging sign to find that in some areas of London one or two blind children are accepted in nursery groups for other handicapped children attending daily or part-time.

A number of pamphlets concerning the care of young blind children can be obtained from the Royal National Institute for the Blind, 224 Great Portland Street, London, W.1. The following list refers to studies mentioned in this chapter, with the addition of other books of particular interest.

References

BOWLBY, J. (1951). *Maternal Care and Mental Health*. World Health Organization Monograph. Geneva.

BROWN, M. S. (1954). Sunshine Home Residential Nursery Schools for the Blind. *Brit. J. Phys. Med.*, **17**, 248.

BURLINGHAM, D. (1961). Some notes on the development of the blind. *Published in the Psychoanalytic Study of the Child*, **16**.

CHEVIGNY, H. (1947). *My Eyes have a Cold Nose*. London: Joseph.

DEPARTMENT OF EDUCATION AND SCIENCE (1968). *Blind and Partially Sighted Children*. Education Survey No. 4. London: H.M.S.O.

KELLER, H. (1903. Revised 1947). *The Story of my Life*. London: Hodder & Stoughton.

LANGAN, I. W. (1945). *Adaptation for the Blind of 1937. Revision of the Stanford Binet tests*. Burden Mental Research Department, Stoke Park Colony, Bristol.

LEWIS, H. (1954). *Deprived Children*. Oxford University Press.

LUNT, L. (1965). *If you make a Noise I Can't See*. Gollancz.

MAXFIELD, K. E. and BUCHHOLZ, S. (1957). *A Social Maturity Scale for Blind Pre-School Children*. New York: American Foundation for the Blind.

MONK, P. (1952). *Though Land be out of Sight*. London: Royal National Institute for the Blind.

POTTER, C. T. (1954). The problems of blind children and the responsibilities of the paediatrician. *Proc. R. Soc. Med.*, **47**, 715.

RITCHIE, J. M. (1930). *Concerning the Blind*. Edinburgh: Oliver & Boyd.

WILLIAMS, M. (1956). *Williams Intelligence Test for Children with Defective Vision*. University of Birmingham Institute of Education.

WILLS, D. M. (1965). Some observations on blind nursery school children's understanding of their world. *Psychoanal. Study of the Child*, **20**.

WILLS, D. M. (1968). Problems of play and mastery in the blind child. *Brit. J. M. Psychol.*, **41**.

WILLS, D. M. (1970). Vulnerable periods in the early development of blind children. *Psychoanal. Study of the Child*, **25**.

CHAPTER VI

THE AUTISTIC CHILD

Diagnosis

AT the present time there is an increasing interest and concern in a group of children described as non-communicating children, more especially those diagnosed as autistic. The diagnosis of autism in childhood is fraught with difficulties. The main problem is to differentiate autistic children from those who fail to learn normally or develop mature, social, and emotional relationships because of mental retardation, brain damage, or some degree of hearing loss. In an attempt to clarify diagnosis and describe the schizophrenic syndrome, or childhood autism, a diagnostic criterion known as the 'Nine Points' was formulated by a committee under the chairmanship of Dr. Mildred Creak (1961). This was based on the observations of a group of people who had had opportunity to study a number of such children, sometimes over a considerable period of time.

The 'Nine Points' can be summarized as follows:

1. Withdrawal from contact and marked inability to make adequate personal relationships.
2. Apparent unawareness of his own personal identity.
3. Preoccupation with objects, often inanimate objects, and failure to use them in an appropriate way.
4. Marked resistance to change in his environment.
5. Perceptual difficulties which interfere with normal learning.
6. Acute and apparently illogical anxiety.
7. Failure to develop speech.
8. Mannerisms and bizarre movements.
9. General retardation with 'islands' of normal or exceptional intellectual ability or skill.

The purpose of drawing up these diagnostic criteria was to help to recognize children with a particular syndrome, and they have proved of considerable value. They have since been modified to some extent notably by O'Gorman (1967) who discusses these criteria on the basis of his extensive experience of such children at Smith Hospital.

From experience as a psychologist working with a team of specialists at the Belmont Hospital Children's Units during the past eight years, it has gradually become easier to make a differential diagnosis. We have learnt, in some measure, to distinguish five main diagnostic groups, although overlapping occurs, and many children show features of more than one group. The five groups are as follows:

1. Children who show retardation in mental growth generally and who can, with a fair degree of confidence, be classed as severely or educationally subnormal children.
2. Children whose degree of hearing loss has impaired the growth of language and acquirement of speech and has interfered with educational achievements.
3. Children who are failing to talk or learn normally because of some cerebral dysfunction and may be described as aphasic or with minimal cerebral palsy.
4. Children who are emotionally disturbed as a result of distorted family relationships or deprivation in their environment and are developing abnormally.
5. Children who are failing to communicate, who withdraw from social contacts and are showing a number of the 'Nine Points' listed above, who may be described as 'autistic'.

The last group of children are characterized by their unusual behaviour. They make very limited contact with their environment and do not show normal curiosity. They are usually solitary, and appear dreamy and preoccupied. They make little effective contact with adults, but use them to serve their own purposes, by taking their hands to reach for what they want, to open cupboards or put their coats on, or to get a cuddle or something to eat. Sometimes they will push another child away from an adult, snatch his toy or attack him aggressively.

Most of them use no speech at all and respond in a passive, automatic way to routine. Some use gestures, or an occasional word or an expressive sound to convey meaning. They frequently show both visual and auditory avoidance, not looking at people, nor listening to adult requests or to conversation directed to them. Yet they often seem to absorb more than one would expect.

They accept an ordered routine and resent changes, often

unwilling to go out for walks or on excursions to the shops, or even to play outside. They seem to need the familiar environment and familiar sequence of events to give them a sense of safety. They seem desperately to be seeking an ordered world or a reality which they can control. Many observers have noted their obsessive mannerisms, their need to place toys and objects in straight lines, or to trace the patterns of the carpet or the wallpaper. They often cling to inanimate objects, a collection of treasures carried around with them, from which they refuse to be parted and panic if they are lost.

Autistic children do not play as ordinary children do. They wander aimlessly in playroom or garden. They pick things up, examine them briefly, and then relinquish them. Sometimes they are very destructive. They will tear paper, bite or suck dough or plasticine, bang or throw bricks about. They will splash water, let sand trickle through their fingers or toes. They will spread paint on paper but seldom draw or paint any clear object. They will spend long periods in active physical play, bouncing on a trampoline, swinging on a swing or rocker, sliding down a slide. They seldom show any really constructive or imaginative play and it is rare indeed for them to play with another child. The play of the autistic children between the ages of 4 and 8 years, which we have observed at the Belmont Hospital Children's Units, may be described as usually immature, stereotyped, asocial and bizarre.

A considerable amount of experimental work has been carried out at the Maudsley Hospital in the Social Psychiatry Research Unit on the characteristics of autistic children. Hermelin and O'Connor (1963, 1965) found that autistic children of low intelligence, whom they studied, responded positively to adults and showed greater mobility especially in regard to arm and hand movements than their control group. They also found evidence of visual imperception and verbal imperception in psychotic children between 7 and 14 years of age. Studies were also made of sensory dominance and responses to sensory and verbal stimuli. Autistic children responded better to light and sound stimuli than to verbal. Observation of these children has shown that their particular difficulty is in communication, in verbal comprehension and in executive speech.

Incidence

Owing to the difficulty of accurate diagnosis of this condition, it is not easy to estimate the incidence. Lotter (1966) states that only four or five out of every 10,000 children will develop psychosis. Now that diagnostic criteria have been more clearly formulated it should prove easier to make a more accurate estimate. In the past many autistic children may well have been cared for in hospitals for mentally retarded children or in training centres and classified erroneously as subnormal. It seems that in some cases children fundamentally normal may pass through an autistic phase as a result of some traumatic experience and later regain normality. In more recent years centres for the study and the assessment of autistic children have been gradually established and our knowledge of the number of such children in the community should become more exact.

In a careful survey in Middlesex (Wing *et al.*, 1967), it was estimated in 1964 that 4·5 per 10,000 had autistic symptoms in early childhood. Boys were more common than girls, the ratio being 2·75 : 1. It was found that more autistic children had suffered from birth complications in delivery than their siblings, and one-half had marked delay in motor milestones. Parents were more likely to be above average in intelligence, educational attainment and occupational level.

Causal Factors

There is considerable difference of opinion in regard to the causal factors producing this tragic illness. O'Gorman (1967) gives a very useful account of the present views on the aetiology of the autistic syndrome. It seems probable that organic and emotional factors are closely interwoven. Some psychiatrists emphasize the organic and some the emotional causes. Organic diseases affecting the nervous system, such as phenylketonuria, or brain damage due to anoxia, endocrine-metabolic disturbance, or delay in maturation of the nervous system, have all been postulated as predisposing factors to the illness which may be provoked by an acute physical illness or emotional crisis acting upon such a general predisposition.

Emotional explanations tend to focus on the impairment at an early stage of the emotional relationship between mother and child and the inadequacy of parents to fulfil their role. Unhappy marital relationships may disturb the natural tie between mother and child. Physical defects which render suckling difficult or any circumstances which interfere with a normal satisfying breast feeding or bottle feeding may disturb the natural mother/baby relationship. If this first, all-important relationship is never adequately established, the tendency to withdraw from human contacts and from the environment may well be exaggerated.

In considering the case histories of the many children presenting autistic symptoms seen during the past 8 years, it is possible to denote certain facts concerning the child's early development and early environment which tend to recur.

1. Mental instability in the family history is sometimes noted.
2. Abnormal obstetric histories, convulsions or 'fits' of some type with fever, acute infections such as measles or scarlet fever occurring before 2 years of age, encephalitis or an undiagnosed illness with a high temperature are often recorded, especially in early childhood.
3. An apparently normal early development interrupted by some event, such as illness of the mother or an operation of a minor type, requiring a period in hospital for the child, or a change of guardianship for the child in unfamiliar surroundings, or the birth of a younger sibling are frequently reported.
4. A disturbed marital pattern, such as desertion of one parent, or divorce or separation and re-marriage occurring, especially before the child is 3, is fairly common.
5. A distorted mother/child relationship seems in some instances to be due to difficulty in rearing the child because of his frailty, difficulty in feeding, constant crying, slowness to develop or his failure to respond normally to sounds or language. Or he may be generally passive and unresponsive. The mother does not seem able to show normal warmth of affection for the child. She tends to ignore or withdraw from the child, and the child tends to retreat into himself and begins to lose touch with people and the external environment. He seems to have no incentive to learn and if, as commonly happens, this occurs at a period of high cerebral sensitivity, at the crucial period of learning a particular skill, such as speech, some serious harm may have been done which makes the subsequent learning of such a skill extremely difficult or impossible. The withdrawal seems to be a two-way process, some element of rejection on the part of the mother and some failure to make contact on the part of the child.

Recent studies reported by Corinne Hutt, S. J. Hutt, D. Lee and C. Ounsted (1964, 1970) suggest that autistic children exhibit a physiological disorder which is one of chronic hyper-arousal of certain lower brain structures. This persistent state of arousal would account for the autistic child's need to remain aloof, and withdraw from the company of other children, to seek solitude or the protection of an adult. The stereotypes, the repetitive mannerisms such as rocking, tapping, finger twirling or wrist flicking which are so characteristic of autistic children, tend to occur on increase of stimulation, an unexpected change in routine or a novel experience. It is suggested that these mannerisms are displacement activities, a kind of safety-device which serves to reduce and regulate the level of arousal. The nervous system of the autistic appears to be highly sensitive and some means of discharging tension has to be found. It is noted that electrical activity in the brain of the autistic does not follow the normal pattern of rather slow, regular rhythms of between medium and high voltage. In contrast it consists predominantly of generalized low voltage, irregular activity, without any established rhythms. It follows that children in this state of over-arousal will be especially disturbed by excessive stimulation, states of excitement or tension in their environment and too many people. They will tend to seek comfort from close physical contact or tactile stimulation similar to an over-aroused animal. This theory would appear to go some way to explain some of the bizarre behaviour of the autistic which has hitherto appeared puzzling. Further research on these lines may help to clarify some of the perceptual and learning problems of these children.

It is clear that the aetiology is extremely complex and there appear to be many different factors operating, some that might have been prevented, some that are irremediable.

There appear to be organic factors that predispose a child to become autistic: the degree of autism and its outcome in later years is undoubtedly influenced by parents' reactions and their handling of the child.

Care, Management and Training at the Belmont Hospital Children's Units

It is, of course, very important to obtain a detailed history of the child's development and behaviour, his home environment and his family relationships. The onset of his symptoms need to be carefully noted and any association with illness or family crisis recorded. When the child had been accepted and admitted to the Children's Unit for observation and assessment, a number of routine tests are carried out. These included blood tests, urine tests, skull X-ray, electroencephalograms, sometimes chromosome studies, as well as hearing tests and psychological tests. Records and regular reports were made of the child's response to routine and to teaching, and a social maturity score was obtained on the Vineland Scale (Doll, 1947) after the child had been at the unit for some time. Drug therapy might be carried out if indicated.

A simple framework of routine was worked out for sleep, meals, play, teaching periods, and walks or shopping excursions. The atmosphere was a very informal homely one as the group consisted of six children only, cared for by two housemothers at a time in a villa type of house in the hospital grounds. The visiting staff included the psychiatrist in charge, a house physician, a psychologist, a speech therapist, and one full-time and one part-time teacher. There was also a night nurse and domestic help. In addition to this assessment unit there was a second unit apart from the hospital in an ordinary house in the town to which children were transferred when they had made sufficient progress to respond to teaching in a comparatively stable group and when all the necessary assessments and diagnostic techniques had been carried out. In some cases diagnosis and recommendations concerning placement were made without this transfer. Those who were placed in the second unit remain until they were considered ready for transfer to a suitable school, *e.g.* a school for the deaf, a school for educationally subnormal, for maladjusted children, for aphasic or for maladjusted, non-communicating children, such as the Edith Edwards School.

Contacts with parents were, of course, firmly and constantly encouraged. Half-term and all holidays were spent at home whenever possible, and parents were urged to write and visit regularly whenever possible. Family photographs were asked for, and the child urged to talk about his family. But it was evident that in many cases both parents and children gained from this severance of close contact, at least for a time. Relief was needed from the tension and pressure in the home. In the new environment the staff were more objective than a mother can ever be, yet patient, affectionate, and very understanding. The atmosphere was relaxed, friendly, tolerant, and yet controlling. The child was prevented from anti-social acts of a violent nature, from damaging or destroying furniture or clothes, from harming other children, or from managing or manipulating adults. He was given a great deal of outlet in play and physical activity for the release of energy or aggression, and a great deal of personal attention and petting if he would accept it. He was also encouraged to be independent in everyday routine, dressing, washing, feeding, and using the toilet, etc. but this came only slowly.

Social and Emotional Development

Autistic children tend to be solitary and withdrawn. Their faces show little expression, sometimes as if they were wearing a mask.

They may show very little overt expression of emotion, yet occasionally show violent rage, prolonged tantrums if thwarted, or panic with fear in an unfamiliar situation or for no apparent reason at all. In the acute stage of the illness they retreat from all contact with people. Such children may creep into bed with their clothes on and hide themselves under the bedclothes, or curl up on the floor and cover themselves with a rug. The world seems to them unpleasant, perhaps incomprehensible and uncontrollable and threatening. They seek to return to a state of warmth and comfort, a passive effortless existence which is reminiscent of the pre-natal existence.

Gradually they begin to show some fleeting interest in the adult who spends most time with them and may fix their interest on her dress, her ornaments, her hair, and occasionally her face. They may show some pleasure when fondled or picked up. They may then become more demanding of exclusive adult attention and more discriminating in their relationships, one grown-up being the favoured one. This is a marked step forward, but the adult may then become the recipient of strong ambivalent feeling, and violent swings from affection to hostility may occur. Sibling jealousy may be shown towards the other children who have claims on the loved adult. Thus, from total aloofness or mere toleration of the presence of the other children, they progress to expression of hostility and rivalry. These outbursts have, of course, to be controlled but they are a sign of returning mental health and normal emotional development. It is now possible for the child to show feeling openly. He no longer lives behind his own particular iron curtain. He may begin to play co-operatively as well as aggressively for short periods and to be aware of the feelings of both adults and children. He may show more capacity to tolerate delay or frustration and to share adult attention. Moreover, he will begin to take a more alert interest in the world around him, to show curiosity, to make points of contact, to attempt to communicate more effectively, and to begin to learn even in a group situation. At this stage the autistic child is beginning to get well.

Problems of Learning

In the course of making periodic assessments of the intelligence of young autistic children between the ages of 3 and 7 years, and from observing them in their small teaching groups, certain difficulties of learning become apparent.

It is evident that many of them remain at the sensori-motor stage of learning described by Piaget and Woodward for a much longer period than is normal. Children of 5 and 6 years can, if they can be persuaded to co-operate sufficiently, match colours, discriminate shape and size, complete simple jigsaws, and construct simple tri-dimensional models. Thus it may be possible to obtain a fairly satisfactory test result on the Merrill-Palmer Scale.* Often when the child is seen first as an out-patient, the assessment is inconclusive because no effective working relationship can be made with the child. When the child is fairly well settled in the Children's Unit, familiar with the environment and the routine, slightly more responsive to the staff, and perhaps relieved in some cases from the strain, the pressure or the emotional involvement of the home atmosphere, an adequate relationship can be made with him by the teacher or the psychologist. Then the result on a non-verbal intelligence test can give some indication of mental potential.

As the weeks go by the child will begin to enjoy short periods of concentrated activity in a one-to-one relationship with an adult. He will match pictures, sort shapes and colours, make coloured patterns, grade sizes, and place counters on number cards. He will tear and sometimes cut paper to make pictures when assisted. He will use bricks sometimes to suck or throw, sometimes to make regimented lines and later to construct models, often only in imitation. There is a stage when he cannot copy a pictorial model, but often after a period of classroom attendance it is found that he can construct the Nebraska Block Patterns from a drawing.

Language is usually non-existent. Communication, if any, is at first by gesture or expressive sounds or by jargon. Verbal comprehension develops slowly and first toys and then pictures can be identified when named. After succeeding on the Griffiths 2-year verbal comprehension test one can note the response to Reed's Hearing Test and later still to the English Picture Vocabulary Test though most of these children can only identify common objects on this test. They can distinguish difference and similarity but have great difficulty in understanding symbols, and cannot relate the pattern of letters forming a word to a picture though they will match words. On the Skemp Paired Associates Test, when the child has to associate a symbol with a picture in order to solve the problem, very poor results are obtained. This is surely linked to language retardation and indicates reading unreadiness. Many of the children seem unable to make effective links between auditory

* References to many of the tests mentioned in this section have been made in other chapters and we will not repeat them here. Further information on tests can be found in the test catalogue obtainable from The National Foundation for Educational Research, Windsor, Berks.

and visual stimuli, but with repeated training we find they will learn to name objects and simple pictures of objects and make the appropriate sounds for a train or a car for instance.

Sometimes drawing as well as gesture is used as a means of communication or of recording impressions. At first most of these children will scribble aimlessly or spread paint over the whole paper, but later they begin to copy shapes and to represent men, houses, cars, trains pictorially, sometimes with great attention to detail. A child with severe hearing loss, no speech, and some autistic features would cover the blackboard in the playroom and schoolroom with endless drawings of cars of many varieties, motor cycles, tractors, steam engines, with great attention to detail. This stage seems to represent some contact with the environment and the capacity to construct percepts, but the understanding of concepts, due to their very limited language ability, is rare indeed. The understanding of number concepts is extremely limited and the use of concrete aids continues for a long time. In a few instances it has been possible to obtain a score on the Nebraska Pictorial Association and Analogies tests. This would suggest the beginning of conceptual understanding, the recognition of a common factor, e.g. that all the pictures must be 'things you wear' or 'things to eat' or 'things that go in the air' or the understanding of the analogy that as a shoe goes on a foot so must the hat go on the head in a pictorial sequence. This requires not only an adequate degree of intelligence, but also some conception of language as a vehicle of thought. Until speech has been acquired, formal or abstract learning or the capacity to use symbols will be virtually impossible. The aim of teaching is to help the child to understand the real environment, to learn about the nature and the functions of things, to develop manual skills, and progress from the concrete and immediate sensory experiences to the more abstract and more remote. Intelligence tests are one means of measuring how far the autistic child has progressed along this route. For example, when the language age obtained on the Illinois Test of Psycho-Linguistic Abilities matches up to the mental age obtained on a performance scale and to the social age found on the Vineland Social Maturity Scale, one would judge that the autistic child has made considerable progress. But exact criteria of progress are difficult to obtain.

Operant Conditioning

A teaching technique known as operant conditioning has been used with some success with autistic children in America. A combination of speech therapy techniques and operant conditioning methods has been tried out at the Belmont Hospital Children's Units with a number of the non-communicating children. The first stage is to teach a complete repertoire of sounds, both vowel and consonant. In the therapy room all extraneous sounds are excluded and the child sits comfortably in a small cubicle in a darkened room facing a screen on which slides are projected. The therapist sits beside the child. The sounds to be learnt are magnified on a tape recorder and heard through earphones by the child. They are linked with visual clues, *e.g.* blowing at your finger for the sound P. If the child makes the correct sound he is immediately rewarded by a sweet or a sip of orange squash as well as a smile and words of approval. If he makes the incorrect sound this is followed by a frown and a 'no'. The aim is one of positive reinforcement for successful achievement and negative reinforcement for unsuccessful. Tactual cues, by having the child feel the adult's lips or throat, can be helpful too.

The next stage is to teach the child single words for familiar objects, parts of his body and names of familiar relatives and staff. The picture of the object or person is projected on the screen in front of the child at the same time as he hears the word through his earphones. He is rewarded if he repeats the word correctly. From single words the child should progress to saying simple phrases, *e.g.* 'cup and saucer', 'in the garden', 'up and down', and later to short sentences.

The rest of the staff are kept informed of the vocabulary the child has built up and are asked to use the same words frequently in the course of the day as the correct occasion arises, and expect the child gradually to do the same. Too much pressure is, of course, avoided and if the child shows resistance or anxiety in connection with the therapy sessions, which usually last about 45 minutes two or three times a week, they are discontinued.

This technique is based on the theory that the child has missed learning speech at the period of high cerebral sensitivity and has to learn from the earliest babyhood stages. It seems probable also that some of these children suffer from some perceptual defect which makes it especially difficult for them to link visual, auditory, and tactual experiences, to codify them, and to associate words with objects. They appear to have great difficulty in understanding symbols. It seems basically an organic condition in which, as Lorna Wing has said, the maturation of the parts of the brain dealing with sensory information is delayed or prevented. The physical environment around the child may be unintelligible, unorganized, and seemingly chaotic to him. He cannot organize his sensory input to make sense. Hence his clinging to familiar objects which he has learnt to understand, his confusion in strange situations, and his tantrums due to frustration. Teaching techniques which aim to reinforce and build up links between visual, auditory, tactual and kinaesthetic experiences are of great value.

Methods of Teaching

Carefully planned teaching methods have been successful in many instances in helping autistic children to make contacts with people, and with the real world, to develop speech, to improve perception and gradually to gain some understanding of concepts, of symbols and of abstract ideas. There has been a gradual increase in specialized schools working out their own particular methods with small groups of autistic children. It is important to eliminate children who are solely deaf or of low intelligence as the special methods devised are not appropriate to such children.

Psychological and neurological workers have studied the factors which seem to underlie linguistic development, *e.g.* visual and auditory perception and memory, and the child's ability to deal with sequencing and symbols. Now autistic children are characterized by their inability to select from visual and auditory, tactile, kinaesthetic and olfactory stimuli which constantly impinge on them. They are highly distractible and assailed on all sides by such stimuli. Nor can many of them link visual and auditory and tactile stimuli together into a percept, and cannot attach a name to what they see, hear and feel. Others are so withdrawn and apparently so engrossed by their own state of feeling that they shut out all external stimuli and fail to register sense impression or remember what is said to them. The brain seems to be dysfunctioning and the nervous system is not reacting normally.

A course of re-training and rehabilitation is necessary. Joan Taylor, a trained teacher of the deaf, describes her teaching methods used at Belmont Children's Unit in an article in *Child Education* (Taylor, 1969). She introduces the child to simple games consisting of matching, sorting, fitting and arranging coloured shapes. This is an activity usually enjoyed and enables the child to make some sort of order, some sort of pattern, and to reinforce his awareness of shape, size and colour. By these means a good working relationship is established and then the child can engage in a series of sense training games which help to improve visual memory (hiding and finding objects) to match what he feels with a similar object presented visually which reinforces tactile and visual sensations, to grade sizes, to repeat a pattern and produce a sequence of different shaped beads or tiles or blocks, to deal with two concepts at once *e.g.* to sort all the red and the square shapes into one pile and all the blue and round shapes into another. Attempts are also made to break into the child's obsessions and tendency to persever-ate, by unhitching his attention from one task, forgetting it and tackling the next task. He is taught to attend and ignore distractions by helping him to focus attention on the immediate task, handing him the material and reminding him of each step. Gradually he can be taught to work for short periods on his own, but for a long time these children need virtually individual teaching. Number symbols can be introduced linked with concrete objects arranged in a pattern and counting introduced, using fingers, toes, eyes, ears and then bricks, shells, conkers, pennies, etc. The understanding of the number symbol comes very slowly. Patterns of letters can be built up to make words linked with pictures and the letters can be copied under a picture of an object he has drawn, sounded to him and spoken as a name. Photographs or drawings of himself can be named and labelled. Very slowly the letter and word symbol becomes associated with the picture. But all this, which comes naturally to an intelligent child of six, has to be slowly built up in the child's mind and repeated again and again.

All of these simple techniques appear to help the child organize his sense data, to reinforce links between sensory experiences, to reduce the muddle in his mind and find the world less puzzling and frustrating to him. He is beginning to communicate by drawing, speaking and word naming and writing. He is making contact with people and objects in his environment.

Case Studies

The following case studies are of six children at the Children's Unit, Belmont Hospital for assessment, training, teaching and therapy. An account is also included of the teaching methods used by the teacher of the deaf in an attempt to develop their language ability, enlarge their vocabulary, comprehend elementary number concepts, express their ideas in some media and facilitate manual skills.

1. L.K. at $5\frac{1}{2}$ years is unresponsive to sounds, being profoundly congenitally deaf, his mother having contracted rubella during preg-nancy. Has been diagnosed as autistic, being withdrawn and functioning at a very simple primitive level. On performance intelligence tests he gains a I.Q. of 95, but his Vineland Social Age is 2 years 4 months.

He makes very inadequate relationships with adults and almost no contact with children. His play interests are messy play with sand, water, and paint, and he is rather destructive. He will enjoy physical, active repetitive play for long periods, such as bouncing up and down on the trampoline. He occassionally makes expressive sounds but has no means of effective communication and is to all intents and purposes mute.

The following are some of his teacher's notes on his activities in the classroom:

'Fetched size and colour pegs—handled them, but did not play. He took the red and white pattern blocks, built and stacked them. Made an 8-point star with small mosaic diamond shapes. Drew 4 or 5 lines on the blackboard carefully with red chalk. Played with plasticine, thumping it, sticking things in and looking at the holes.'
'Watched me playing with coloured sticks, making patterns and building a tower. He took them from me, went to the blackboard, drew 4 blue chalk lines, then red lines between and then filled it in with yellow. Went back to play with the sticks.' (This was the first attempt at representational drawing.)
'Handled beads, didn't thread them. Put them in and out of the sorting tray. I set up red and white pattern blocks. He watched, hopped about, shook and waved his hands, then touched one end to make them fall. Drew on the board with red chalk firmly and deliberately. Much scribble with many different colours and little else.'

2. G.K. at 8 years 4 months is profoundly deaf so far as it has been possible to obtain a response to hearing tests. She also suffers from frequent petit-mal attacks and her electroencephalogram suggests brain damage. She is mute and very withdrawn. She makes limited contacts with people, but shows pleasure in pretty clothes and adornments. Her mental age, so far as it could be assessed, appears between $6\frac{1}{2}$ and $7\frac{1}{2}$, indicating an I.Q. in the neighbourhood of 80. She frequently withdraws from all contact and stares into space. She accepts a routine passively and shows little emotional response, except occasional outbursts of annoyance when frustrated. Her educational achievements for a child of 8 years old are meagre indeed, as her teacher's reports show.
'She did a scribble pattern on a piece of paper and pasted it on the blackboard. She took a sheet of paper and the box of brown cardboard shapes and covered the paper with traced shapes and pasted it on the blackboard. In the playroom she sets out cups and saucers, puts the Wendy House in order. Has the doll sitting in the pram. Does not play. Does not bath, dress, undress, or feed the doll. Does not have tea-parties or cook. Has been seen to make up her face, take handbag and basket, go out of Wendy House, walk round and return home.'
'She made a bedroom scene with pictures of a window, curtains, a bed, a fire, mother, father, herself, a rug, and some furniture. She then

added further cut-outs to it, wrist watches, two or three more people making nonsense of it.'

'She made a seaside picture by pasting cut-out figures—at first in bathing suits and then some of them fully clothed—on to a background of sea and sand. She put the doll figures of mother, father, herself, and her brother in the front. She took doll, (? her brother) and threw it across the room. When it was picked up and put on the shelf, she snatched it again and tried to break it.'

The child's autism seems closely linked with her deafness and inability to communicate. She has a good relationship with her mother and spends weekends often at home which seem to be helpful. Her learning capacity appears very limited, and she still has no speech. She is a very lovely little girl and enjoys being petted and will now seek demonstrative affection from adults.

3. K.J. is, at 6½ years, an introverted, negativistic boy who shows obsessional preoccupation in hoarding objects. He dislikes change and shows excessive grief and fear reactions. He has been diagnosed as aphasic, being defective in expressive language, though of normal hearing and with an I.Q. of 106 on the Nebraska Scale. He was a placid, over-good baby, breast fed for one month and showed some difficulty in feeding later. His mother is described as anxious and over-protective and his father as tense and anxious. He seemed much disturbed at 3-years when on a caravan holiday, perhaps upset by change in environment. He makes dependent contacts with adults and likes to stay beside them. He appears to have defective visual memory and to have difficulty in linking tactual and visual sense impressions. He does use a little speech and shows capacity to understand symbols, though verbal comprehension is below average on testing. He is beginning to enjoy constructive play, to draw and to respond to teaching.

His teacher records:

'Continues to work well with me—very little by himself—more relaxed —vocalizing—pretend talking—a few clear words. Made a paper cat for him. He tore up jug and saucer and put them under the cat, indicating that the cat had eaten them. He then cut off the cat's tail and legs and made it eat those and finally its head.

'Drew his family and a caravan while I was drawing his family at the seaside. Today drew roads on a large sheet of paper. Said the space was a field full of nettles and thistles which stung you. Put the tractor in the field—another space he called a car park and filled it with cars. I made plasticine men, boys, cats, which K. destroyed by running over with cars and tractor. He repaired one cat. I said "Shall I make a cat?" He said "No, wow, wow". So I made a dog with a collar. He made the lead and fixed it to the dog's tail—pretended the dog was walking and said "toogle, oogle, oogle". He took scissors and cut off the dog's legs.

He "clipped" the dog. I said "Are you cutting its hair?" He said "Yes—lom", meaning long. I made another dog. He made it eat and walk, took off its collar and lead and made a new one. Made holes all over the dog."

This report shows the beginning of communication by drawing, expressing his own ideas and developing those of the teacher and showing a good deal of healthy aggression by this means. He shows a good deal of imagination and general knowledge. Speech consists of sounds, single words, short phrases. He is clearly making progress.

4. L.T. now 6 years old, was an 8-lb baby at birth, seemed alert, walked before 12 months and understood simple commands before 2 years. He disliked being petted and tended to shun contact. He used no speech between 2 and 5 years and thereafter used dysarthric speech or pointed or took the adult's hand to obtain what he wanted. He was disobedient and negativistic, frequently seeking to do forbidden acts and showed violent but short-lived tantrums when frustrated in any way. He insists on routine, and indulges in obsessional rituals. He refuses to play with other children and prefers to be in the garden or playroom on his own, or with an adult at hand. He is hyper-active and hypotonic. Vision and hearing are normal, as is his intelligence on performance tests (I.Q. 107). His Social Maturity age is, however, assessed on the Vineland as $2\frac{1}{2}$ years. He is beginning to show interest in educational achievements, especially in number, linking this with his obsessional preoccupations in pattern and sequences. Verbal comprehension and vocabulary are slowly developing. Autistic traits are lessening.

The progress report of his teacher is fairly encouraging.

'This afternoon for the first time he occupied himself for 35 minutes—looking round—finding things to do and doing them. Put all the cars straight in the garage. Rolled large beads through holes in a wooden bridge. Matched pictures. Took all screws off stick and put them back on. Fitted shapes into board except triangle which he threw across the room. Vocalized, pretend speech as he played, using car and train noises and an occasional shriek.'

Three months later:

'Found my box of "family at home". Named the people as he took them out: L. Daddy, Mummy, Baby (his family) and gave himself a cup of tea from a miniature teapot. I invited him into the classroom at the new unit and he accompanied me, a little nearer to the classroom each time and then retreated to the swing. At the fourth invitation he came into the classroom, took a box of cars and lined them up on a chair. Put them back in the box, carried them into the sitting-room, lined them up on a ledge, took them out into the garden and lined them up on the rabbit hutch. (No doubt he was retreating to obsessional play as a safeguard in the new situation where he as yet felt insecure.) 'He pointed to a picture I had drawn last week of his sore knee, and showed that it was better now. Showed interest in my jig-saw—naming things in it. Brought me a picture of a fire and wanted me to burn my fingers in it. This is one of our jokes. He will stand with his fingers on a picture of a fire until I show great concern and say "Oh don't do that, you'll burn your fingers".

'Lined up the doll's house furniture. Said "table". Found a chair and said "red chair". Found some fitting cups—lined them up too. Asked me to name the things he had lined up—dressing-table, stool, etc. and said the names of some himself.

'Wandered about not settling to anything. All the other children were busy. I said he must find something to do. He did a simple jig-saw. I gave him the 100 board with cubes. He did this after some insistence, made each ten a different colour, counted them. Started throwing things, not violently, tipping things out and lining them up. I stopped him. He lay down on the floor, banging his head, thumping and shouting. I ignored him until he was quiet, then insisted that he should sit at a table and do an easy jig-saw. He did this and calmed down. I sent him out to play.

5. A.C. at 5 years is a very likeable, friendly child but very distractible and brain damage is suspected. He came from a disturbed home background, with marital friction and his mother re-married following a divorce. He was found to be of average intelligence, but immature socially, hyper-active and difficult to teach on account of his limited attention span. He tended to cling to possessions and was disturbed if parted from a bag full of treasures which he carried around with him. His speech developed fast, from single words and phrases to sentences and the use of pronouns. After a period of assessment he was transferred to a school for maladjusted children where he made good progress.

6. M.A. was found to be of high intelligence. At 4 years 8 months he gained an I.Q. of 140 on the Merrill Palmer Performance Scale and at 5 years a Learning Age of $6\frac{1}{2}$ years on the Nebraska Scale. There was some instability in the family history and some difficulty in early family relationships. He had five changes of care before 12 months of age and was adopted at 9 months. The relationship with the adoptive mother was not a warm or affectionate one and speech did not develop at all.

In the Children's Unit he showed good constructional ability and readiness to learn with practical material. His most effective means of communication was by elaborate and colourful drawings, depicting cars, trains, roads, people, houses, in great detail. Verbal comprehension and identification of toys and pictures when named improved. Speech slowly improved and a simple vocabulary was built up. He is beginning to make more effective use of his good intelligence, and his autism and lack of communication are gradually reducing. He is thought to be aphasic. His hearing is normal.

Some extracts from his teacher's records are interesting:

'C. had been a week at the seaside and decided to make a seaside scene in the sand tray. M. drew pictures of a house, a boy, a car and a caravan as his contribution to add to the scene. This is the first time he has voluntarily joined in a common interest and contributed something to general endeavour.'

'C. found Mrs. G.'s name and said she was ill. We talked about this and I wrote up for C. what he was telling me. M. drew spontaneously Mrs. G. in bed, the door, the floor, a mat beside the door. This is the first time he has shown that he is aware of talk between me and other children.'

'He found some long narrow strips of paper and they seemed to symbolize roads to him. He put these end to end with one as a side road branching off and ran his lorry along it.... He can use plasticine quite well, and usually makes a railway line and a signal and a train on the line.... He murmurs with pretend speech as he plays.'

'He saw a picture of a house with a woman and a boy waving at the window. He made a long babble pointing out of the window, perhaps showing that it reminded him of his mother with him at home.'

'With five other children M. was very happily busy all the morning, constructing a complete scene on the sand tray—a long trough into which he poured water, a bridge made of large blocks with a lorry on, sheds, animals and a block road with cars on it—a combination of zoo and the seaside. He guarded his creation and marched round the room for a few minutes, keeping his eye on it.'

It is evident that M. is gradually learning to represent his environment by means of play activity, especially by drawing and creative play, and speech is slowly developing as an accompaniment to action. Social adjustment is improving; he is beginning to enjoy joint activities.

Conclusions

Childhood autism is still a condition of which the causes and the most satisfactory methods of treating are somewhat obscure. But detailed knowledge and careful observations of autistic children have increased in recent years. Successful teaching methods have been reported, and accounts of autistic children who have got well and have been able to learn and attend ordinary schools have been published in the scientific journals.

Mittler *et al.* (1965), in a follow-up study of children discharged from Smith Hospital, found that about one-third could take their place within the normal educational system. These results are somewhat encouraging.

Very careful diagnostic investigations are necessary, as early as possible. The condition can be detected by the informed observer as early as two or three years of age. Specialist advice should immediately be sought. Well staffed centres associated with children's hospitals are gradually increasing up and down the country. The National Society for Autistic Children has been extremely active and has done a great deal to publicize the problems and the needs of autistic children.

Organizations and Literature

The National Society for Autistic Children, 100 Wise Lane, Mill Hill, London N.W.7, The National Society for Mentally Handicapped Children, 5 Bulstrode St., London, W.1, and the National Association for Mental Health, 49 Queen Anne St., London, W.1 are all concerned to some extent with the problems presented by autistic children, especially the first named. Books, pamphlets, general guidance, and advice about placement or schooling can be obtained from them.

References

CREAK, M. (1961). The schizophrenic syndrome in childhood. Progress report of a working party. *Brit. Med. J.*, **2**, 889.

HUTT, S. J. and HUTT, C., editors (1970). *Behaviour Studies in Psychiatry*. Oxford: Pergamon Press.

HUTT, C., HUTT, S. J., LEE, D. and OUNSTED, C. (1964). Arousal and childhood autism. *Nature*, **204**, 908.

LOTTER, V. (1966). Epidemiology of autistic conditions in young children—1. Prevalence. *Soc. Psychiat.*, 1.124.

MINSKI, L. and SHEPPERD, M. J. (1970). *Non-Communicating Children*, London: Butterworths.

MITTLER, P. *et al.* (1965). Report of a follow-up study. *J. Ment. Defic. Res.*, **10**, 73.

O'CONNOR, N. and HERMELIN, B. (1963). Measures of distance and motility in psychotic children and severely subnormal controls. *Brit. J. Soc. clin. Psychol.*, **2**, 29.

O'CONNOR, N. and HERMELIN, B. (1965a). Sensory Dominance. *Archs. Gen. Psychiat.*, **12**, 99.

O'CONNOR, N. and HERMELIN, B. (1965b). Visual imperception in psychotic children. *Brit. J. Psychol.*, **56**, No. 4, 455.

O'GORMAN, G. (1967). *The Nature of Childhood Autism*. London: Butterworth.

TAYLOR, JOAN E. (1969). Working with non-communicative children. *Child Education Quarterly*, **46,** No. 12.

WING, L. (1964). *Autistic Children.* London: National Association for Mental Health.

WING, J. K., O'CONNOR, N. and LOTTER, V. (1967). Autistic conditions in early childhood. *Brit. Med. J.,* **3,** 389.

WING, J. K., editor (1967). *Early Childhood Autism.* Oxford: Pergamon Press.

Fig. 10.—Self-portrait by G. K. (8 years).

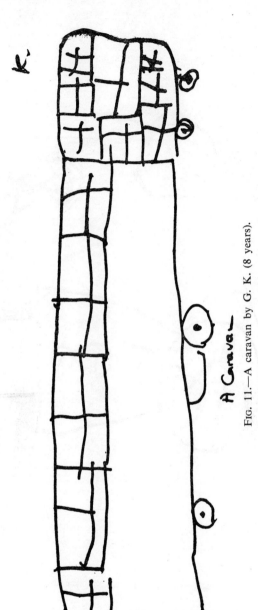

Fig. 11.—A caravan by G. K. (8 years).

Fig. 12.—A. and his mother by M. A. (4½ years).

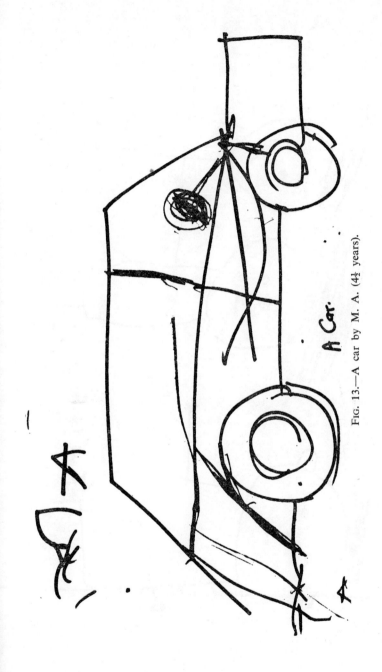

Fig. 13.—A car by M. A. (4½ years).

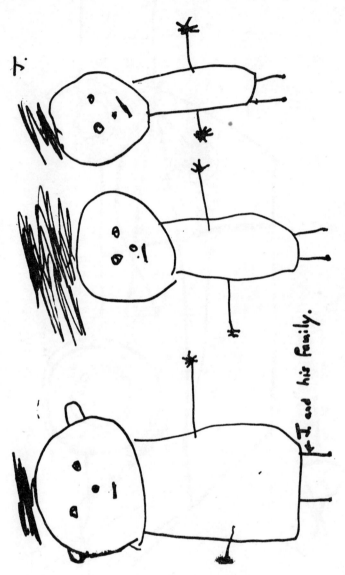

FIG. 14.—K. J. and his family by K. J. (6½ years).

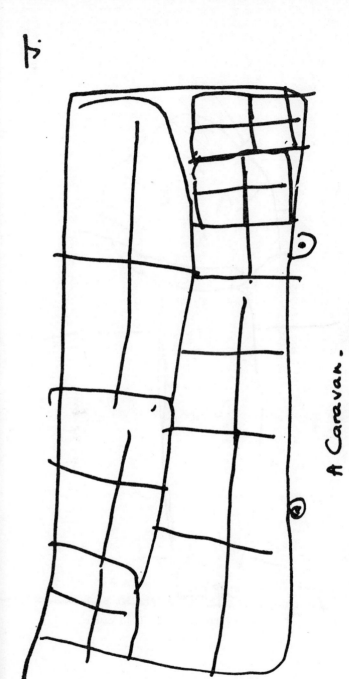

FIG. 15.—A caravan by K. J. (6¼ years).

T.   Self Portrait.

FIG. 16.—Self-portrait by L. T. (6 years).

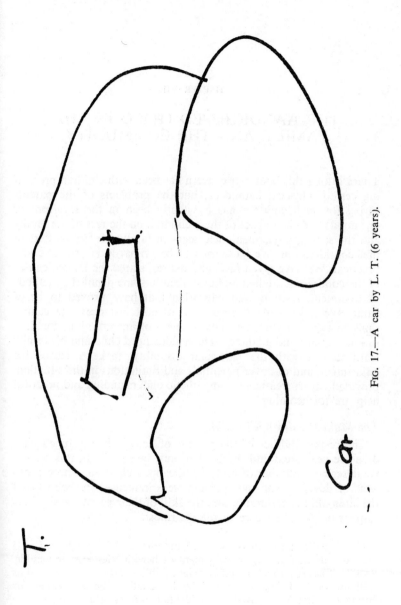

Fig. 17.—A car by L. T. (6 years).

CHAPTER VII

THE HANDICAPPED CHILD IN THE FAMILY AND THE COMMUNITY

THROUGHOUT this book our concern has been with children presenting certain physical handicaps, but the problems of the parents
caring for such children has constantly been in the forefront of
our minds and the impact of these children on the rest of the family
and the special adjustments necessary in family life are matters of
first consideration. We have tried to be primarily informative and
practical. We have given facts and figures, stated the known causes
of the conditions, studied and described in some detail the methods
of treatment, training and education that have proved to be of
value. We have made it clear that in most instances one cannot
think in terms of cure, but only in terms of amelioration, compensation, support and guidance. The handicapped child and his family
learn to live with the particular disability, make a reasonable
adjustment, and discover potentials and limitations in the situation,
provided expert treatment, sympathetic understanding and practical
help are forthcoming.

The Multi-Handicapped Child

The responsibilities of the parents of heavily handicapped children are very great and the burden must be shared. In this section
we describe a number of multi-handicapped children, whose problems of development and learning were immense, and who taxed
the strength, the endurance and the skill of their parents and others
responsible for their care to the uttermost.

1. Iris, a West Indian baby of 15 months, had been adopted at 3
months old when a proper assessment of her abilities was impossible.
Born by Caesarean section, birth weight 6 lb 3 oz, she was described as
a floppy baby; being abandoned by her mother she was cared for
during her first 3 months in a residential nursery. Her mother, who
was only 14-years-old, had an ineducable brother. Iris was subsequently
diagnosed as epileptic with rigid quadriparesis. Between 7 and 9 months
she went through a type of autistic phase, when she was very with-

drawn, non-communicative and passive. After this period she seemed to improve, babbled, turned to sounds, held toys, took them to her mouth, banged them, and by 11 months could roll over. Epilepsy was controlled by medication, though occasional minor fits occurred with head shaking and tremors.

At 15 months she was a rather silent child but could say a few words. She did not explore with her hands, but occasionally took objects to her mouth. She could sit supported, roll a little, but was very hypotonic and did not hold her head steadily. She gazed at the light and responded to sounds, turning to look and listen on either side. Assessment was, of course, very difficult. The picture was complicated by minimal cerebral palsy, epilepsy, and some autistic features. Her general development level was assessed at 4–5 months suggesting quite severe mental retardation. However, normal learning had been interfered with by her dual handicap and abnormal rearing pattern with interruptions for hospital treatment. She was certainly functioning at a very low level, but in view of the history it would be unwise to pronounce severe subnormality.

The adoptive parents were patient, kindly, and intelligent people, well aware of the situation yet determined to carry on. Having accepted responsibility they sought to obtain all possible treatment and training available for her. The mother certainly showed affection for this small curly headed, coffee coloured baby who was beginning to respond to petting and good maternal care. Two older boys in the family also played and petted the child. Perhaps it was easier for the parents in that she was not their own child and they did not feel any stigma on account of her handicap. Physiotherapy was arranged, a treatment plan outlined and later admission promised to a Special Care Centre.

2. Martin, had a normal birth and weighed 7 lb 8 oz. Unfortunately he had a disfiguring port wine stain, known as Sturge Weber's Syndrome, on the right side of his face and at 5 months had a severe epileptic fit lasting 2 days and was later diagnosed as a right hemiplegic with right hemianopia. Some calcification of the skull was noted, fits continued to occur about once a week and he had recurrent otitis. When seen at 4 years 1 month he was walking with support, could say some 12 words, could recognize people and pictures and showed a sense of humour. His intelligence was assessed at I.Q. 45–55. He could build a tower with bricks, fit peg boards and nested boxes correctly, complete simple formboards and play ball. He was eager to investigate everything.

The parents were sensible middle class people, the mother a teacher. The mother, however, was deeply distressed and showed clear signs of rejection. She found it hard to accept so handicapped and disfigured a child. The father gave excellent support and did not want the boy to be sent away from home. He was given excellent care in a day Special Care Unit. But the fits were difficult to control and the prognosis was not very hopeful. By 6 years of age the possibility of long term residential placement was being seriously considered.

3. Donald was a very intelligent athetoid but unable to speak. His early rearing had been difficult because he slept poorly and had difficulty in swallowing and chewing, so feeding was a long and arduous business. The mother found him a real problem. She became worn out with broken nights and Donald's tempers and demanding behaviour.

Day attendance at a Spastic Centre was arranged. He was, at first, tearful and unresponsive to treatment and showed much distress when left in the nursery school by his mother. The long journey to the Centre proved fatiguing and impracticable, so at $3\frac{1}{2}$ years Donald became a weekly boarder in the hostel attached to the Centre. He was at first clearly distressed at this weekly separation from his family, but for so young a child achieved quite a remarkable adjustment. In some ways he was almost too accepting and compliant, but he did co-operate in treatment and responded well to nursery school education. His intelligence was assessed as well above the average and his comprehension was excellent though he still had very little speech. Hearing and vision were judged normal, but spastic involvement of the facial muscles prevented clear speech.

At 6 years 3 months he gained a social age on the Vineland Scale of 6·9 years. He was popular, friendly and showed good interest in school work. He was taught to use the P.O.S.S.U.M typewriter, quickly grasped the code and the most appropriate hand movement was selected by means of which he could operate the lever. His behaviour had greatly improved and the tantrums seldom occurred. He became far more acceptable at home and the stress and tension there was greatly reduced. A younger sibling, of whom he showed some jealousy, added to the mother's responsibilities but she seemed more able to carry these. In due course Donald graduated to a school for Physically Handicapped Children, again as a weekly boarder. He continued to make good progress intellectually, though no great physical improvement was achieved.

This boy had made a good adjustment despite his very frustrating handicap, and the bitterness, resentment and rejection of the parents has been replaced by affection and acceptance. They clearly could not carry the burden alone.

Family and Community Care

There are many people who try to help the mother who gives birth to a child with a handicap—the nurse, the doctor, the health visitor, the social worker, the psychologist, the psychiatrist and more especially the husband, the relatives, friends and neighbours. But it does not help such a mother to be told glibly 'not to worry, it could be worse'; or bluntly 'better forget about him. Why not put him in a home and adopt a baby'; or unrealistically 'You never can tell. See another specialist. His blindness (or spasticity) might be curable; miracles do happen.'

Probably all mothers, sometime during their pregnancy, have presentiments and fears about the baby they are carrying, that all might not go well. The arrival of a baby who is recognized as abnormal, who does not move his limbs, or look or listen, or who has an unsightly birthmark, who is premature, whose delivery may have been prolonged or difficult, who is a blue baby or severely jaundiced is usually a very great shock to the mother. This is not always recognized, but clearly she needs immediate support, sympathy and help. Feelings of anguish, guilt, inadequacy or depression may well nigh overwhelm her. She may blame herself, her husband or the hospital or all three. She may turn away from the child, unable to face the fact of his disablement, and sometimes unable to feed him. She may cling to her husband for support, or she may turn against him, regarding him as responsible, and a happy marriage may end in separation or divorce.

More usually, fortunately, a disabled baby calls forth natural maternal solicitude. His urgent needs are recognized from the start. It is especially hard for the mother if the baby has to spend the first few weeks in an oxygen tent, or if he is unable to suckle because of his physical disability. It is damaging to the early close relationship of mother and child, if she cannot feed and fondle him in these early weeks of his life. But many mothers seem able to overcome this difficulty and begin to build up a close emotional tie to their baby. This close involvement of mother and child may mean that at least temporarily the husband and other children take second place in her affections. It is unfortunate if this attachment remains so close that the rest of the family feel excluded. It is from this situation that acute feelings of hostility and jealousy may arise among the siblings. The handicapped child, in their view, always seems to take first place. Special allowances have to be made for him, special treats foregone and it may not be so easy to entertain friends or go on holidays as before. Naturally enough the new arrival may be bitterly resented.

Clearly good counselling is imperative from the start. Fortunately nowadays early diagnosis is usually possible, though this is not always so, as in the case of Iris, the adopted baby already quoted. By 6 months the situation should be recognized and the truth told to the mother as soon as the doctor feels she is able to face it. The best methods of care and treatment can be worked out, and the parents may find relief in feeling they can help right from the beginning. Many mothers can carry out the correct physiotherapy if allowed to participate and given guidance from the therapist. Mothers of deaf children are the best teachers of lip reading to their babies, as it is on the mother's face that the baby most naturally focusses his eyes during feeding. He will naturally study the movements of her face and learn to interpret expression and lip movements. The Royal National Institute for the Deaf provides much helpful guidance to mothers of deaf children. Blind children come to respond to their mothers' voices and touch in babyhood and learn to interpret sound and tactile experience from a very early age. The sharing of the care of a handicapped child with those experienced in the field can be of tremendous help to parents. Parents' Units as organized both for the deaf and for the blind, where mother and child can stay for a period and be given as much practical help as is appropriate to the child's age and disability, are of real therapeutic value. Visits can be repeated when the child gets older and new problems arise. Similarly a period at a Cerebral Palsy Centre for assessment, where a number of specialists can see the child and advise on care, handling, toys, clothes, appliances and education, is very rewarding. Parents often return at 6 monthly intervals for further help, especially when facilities in their own area are very limited.

On the whole it is rare for the parents to want to place a young handicapped child in residential care, however disabled he may be. One mother, who had a severely retarded quadriplegic speechless child, with epilepsy, had organized life so that adequate care was given to the child and to her husband, and holidays arranged for herself and her husband from time to time while the child spent a week or so in hospital. When asked if she had any special problems she replied no, she could think of none!

A handicapped child can become just one of the family, accepted, loved, teased, helped, scolded and included in as many family affairs as practicable. He may call out much tender solicitude, and sometimes, of course, is overprotected by granny, mother, big sister and baby brother! But if this pitfall is foreseen, and the need for independence and self-help emphasized from the first contact with the mother it can be avoided. In one study of parental attitudes made at the Cheyne Centre the psychologist and the social worker assessed 68 per cent of 80 parents, to be realistic and constructive in their attitude, only 4 per cent to be over-protective and 8 per cent to be rejective. This study was made after the child had been attending the Centre for some months and parent counselling had had time to take effect.

Certainly the family can enjoy a handicapped child in their midst, but it is sometimes more difficult to judge how such a child feels himself. Sometimes he is very demanding and dominating and seeks to monopolize the attention of adults constantly, feeling the need for limelight and compensation. Often he must feel keen frustration. 'They run off and leave me, they know I can't keep up'; 'I never get a chance of kicking the ball or scoring a goal myself'. 'Oh how I wish I could be a ballet dancer', or 'learn to drive a car', or 'be a pilot' or 'ride a horse'—such remarks reveal inner feelings. Tantrums or fits of depression are common. Retreat and withdrawal are a means of defence. Over-compensation by phantasy, fictitious stories or over-ambitious plans for a career are typical of the adolescent facing the immense problems of growing up with a handicap. But all along the road, such children can be helped by the family and by the community. School achievements with the help of specially designed aids, Braille, the Possum typewriter, the loop system linked with a hearing aid, mean a great deal to the intelligent blind, spastic or deaf child. Adventure playgrounds and holiday clubs for handicapped children build up confidence and improve social adjustment. Vocational Guidance Centres for the disabled, sheltered workshops and special facilities in industry for handicapped adults offer employment prospects. Constructive care in Special Care Centres and adult centres give occupation and stimulus. And there are also very many voluntary organizations which are active in providing special help and in collecting money. But is this enough?

The Future for Children with a Handicap in our Society

'Just because I can't speak properly they think I am stupid'—the bitterness with which this sort of remark is made by intelligent adolescents with C.P. is a sign of the crippling effect of prejudice. Such prejudice is sometimes more crippling than the physical handicap itself. One of the most fundamental aspects of handicap is the psychological one of its effects on human relationships. Very few people feel at ease in the presence of a handicapped person: the origins of the feelings of uneasiness are very complex but seem to reflect on the whole a failure to regard the person with a handicap as a person. He is labelled instead in terms of the handicap: in other words the handicap is assumed to extend to all aspects of his personality and to affect all aspects of his behaviour. His worth as a person, his capacities for ordinary thought, feelings and activities are assumed to be very reduced or lacking and consequently he is regarded as an 'outsider' as far as the main stream of social life is concerned. We will not try to pass over the fact that a small percentage of disabled are so severely handicapped both mentally and physically that they more or less remain 'infantilized' throughout their lives, in spite of early treatment and education. The degree to which they can form relationships amongst themselves and with other people is extremely limited and some kind of 'segregated' placement, should the parents wish, is probably the kindest alternative—far kinder than euthanasia. Injustice arises when the majority are treated in such a way.

Most societies in the past (and some in the present) have tended to exclude or segregate the handicapped, brutally in some eras, more humanely in Victorian times, when most persons with obvious handicaps, who happened to survive appalling social conditions, were tucked away in large institutions, usually in healthy rural areas, out of sight of most people. In recent decades attitudes to persons with handicaps have improved. This is due to a whole combination of factors, e.g. the educational effects of voluntary society work, such as the Spastics Society, in disseminating information, pioneering proper services and research, and increased state and Local Authority concern with welfare, as part of the general trend. This is more specifically expressed in recent legislation such as the Morris Act (Chronically Sick and Disabled Persons Act 1970) which establishes the rights of the handicapped to certain facilities such as housing and access to buildings, home help and other provision, and the Seebohm Report (leading to the Local Authorities' Social Services Act 1970) providing a unified social service able to give comprehensive support to all kinds of persons in need, at various ages, replacing the fragmented piecemeal services of the past that often presented a family with ten different departments to deal with. General trends in social attitudes, towards greater tolerance of individual and group differences, although regarded as 'over-permissive' by some, have also helped towards increasing social acceptance of the handicapped.

Persons with a handicap are no longer a neglected group and in this book we have been able to describe the growing facilities that are promoting earlier and more comprehensive assessment, treatment and education. Older disabled people and most of those born before 1940 were denied such facilities and the severity of the handicaps that many of them now possess is a result of this neglect. Our next task is to explore the extent to which early recognition and help can improve the quality of life of the handicapped and help to break down the barriers erected by previous generations to exclude and segregate them. A great deal of research is urgently needed, to examine the effectiveness of the facilities provided and to find out the best ways of promoting progress.

As we have noted, conditions as complex as these call for a large team of professional workers—in education, medicine, psychology, social work, physiotherapy, speech and occupational therapy, vocational guidance and community work, and one very important lesson has been the realization that the most important members of the team are the parents. Without their unconditional love and understanding, encouragement and guidance, the child's chance of reaching his maximum possible degree of integration within the normal community is seriously diminished. It is essential that professional workers should give a great deal of thought to the kinds of help that parents and children need and to realize that much of this help is best channelled through the parents: and that as the child becomes older, his self-help and independence must be encouraged. Care must be taken not to undermine parents' confidence in themselves as parents, such as by overwhelming them with advice and allowing no scope for their own ideas. As the child becomes older, he gains confidence in himself, in his abilities to explore the limits to which he can become independent and to appreciate situations where he cannot be so, and then to accept help. Professional workers have to learn to eschew paternalistic attitudes. Skilled and well trained professionals are aware of this danger and are therefore in a position to contribute a great deal of help—in making objective assessments and reasonable predictions based on hard won experience, and within the framework of this, making available the best methods of treatment, training, education, therapy, counselling and vocational and other services. Professional workers are learning to work together in clinics, centres, classrooms and in the wider community. They bring much needed expertise to bear: they also bring much needed emotional support to parents and children in times of crisis.

Professional workers, alongside the parents, have another important part to play: that of helping to educate the public about the nature and consequences of handicap. Integration of the handicapped, complete or partial, within the normal community depends basically on the attitudes of the public. The services, the clinics, centres and schools, the local and central government facilities and statutes are vital in promoting the welfare of the handicapped—but they are no substitute for considerable thought and action concerning the general public's deeper feelings and attitudes about handicap.

Professional workers and parents are in a position to dispel fear and ignorance, by encouraging contact with the normal community as far as possible, by pressing for more research and critical evaluation of what is going on. As Arnold Toynbee has said, 'The essence of human living is the fact that there are challenges to which we can respond.' In this field the challenges are clear.

INDEX

201